THE
ORIENTAL INSTITUTE
2002–2003 ANNUAL REPORT

Cover and title page illustration: Striding Lion. Molded and glazed brick. Neo-Babylonian period, ca. 604–562 B.C. Babylon, Iraq. OIM A7481

The pages that divide the sections of this year's report feature photographs from the Mesopotamian collection of the Oriental Institute Museum.

Editor: Gil J. Stein

Production Editor: Rebecca Laharia

Printed by United Graphics Incorporated, Mattoon, Illinois

The Oriental Institute, Chicago

CONTENTS

INTRODUCTION

Overleaf. Land-Sale Document (Kudurru). Baked clay. Early Dynastic Period (ca. 2500 B.C.). Bismaya (ancient Adab), Iraq. Excavated by the University of Chicago, 1903/04. OIM A1118

INTRODUCTION

Gil J. Stein

The 2002/2003 academic year has been a time of major change and progress for the Oriental Institute. At the same time, we saw the end of an era with the loss of the legendary archaeologists Robert and Linda Braidwood and of loyal friends such as Eleanor Swift, George Joseph, and William Boone.

I am delighted to announce the opening of the Edgar and Deborah Jannotta Mesopotamian Gallery, some of whose masterpieces are illustrated on the cover and chapter dividers of this *Annual Report*. With over 5,400 square feet of exhibit space and more than 1,300 artifacts on display, this is the largest of our galleries. Museum Director Karen Wilson and her colleagues on the Mesopotamian Gallery reinstallation committee can justifiably take great pride in having designed and constructed a superb setting to exhibit the Oriental Institute's world class collection of archaeological and textual materials from the earliest known urban society. We all owe Karen, McGuire Gibson, Dianne Hanau-Strain, Laura D'Alessandro, Markus Dohner, Carole Krucoff, Clemens Reichel, Jonathan Tenney, Tony Wilkinson, and the entire staff of the museum our heartfelt thanks for the tremendous effort they put into making this gallery a reality.

The installation is truly a group effort. Many members of the Oriental Institute faculty — notably Robert Biggs, John A. Brinkman, and Christopher Woods — provided advice on, read, and edited the labels and text panels, ensuring their accuracy and reliability. Finally, it is a pleasure to acknowledge the generous financial support of numerous individuals, foundations, and corporations such as Exelon Corporation, without whom the gallery could not have been completed.

Although the opening of the Jannotta Gallery is the most visible development in the building, it is important to emphasize that throughout the year, the Oriental Institute's main mission of research has continued unabated. We have ongoing projects in the field from Egypt across to Iran, and other research continuing here in Hyde Park.

We are fortunate to welcome two new promising young scholars to the faculty of the Oriental Institute and the Department of Near Eastern Languages and Civilizations. Stephen Harvey specializes in the archaeology and art history of Egypt. Steve is conducting excavations and survey at Abydos, focusing on the pyramid complex of Ahmose, founder of the Eighteenth Dynasty. This exciting field project has already started to yield important insights into a crucial period in Egyptian history — the expulsion of the Hyksos and the origins of the New Kingdom. Seth Richardson is an ancient historian whose research examines such topics as the collapse of the Old Babylonian state. Seth's studies of hundreds of unpublished cuneiform texts in the British Museum are showing that the once-powerful Babylonian state, founded by the great king Hammurabi, fragmented in the sixteenth century B.C. due to internal causes such as financial crises and an out-of-control military, rather than the traditional explanation of a Hittite invasion.

In Turkey, Aslıhan Yener is proceeding with her Atchana/Alalakh research project. This Middle and Late Bronze Age capital of the Amuq region is crucial for understanding the economic and political organization of the city-states of north Syria. The program of site mapping and documenting collections from the earlier excavations by Sir Leonard Woolley sets the stage for full-scale excavations, which are beginning in autumn 2003. This early excavation material was stored in the Hatay Museum in the modern city of Antakya (ancient Antioch) and in the Woolley dig house, which has miraculously survived intact for almost seventy years. We are extremely grateful to Joseph and Jeanette Neubauer, whose generous support makes possible this new excavation phase of the project.

Perhaps the most exciting development in Oriental Institute research is our return to Iran after a hiatus of almost a quarter century. The Iranian Prehistoric Project, co-directed by Abbas Alizadeh from the Oriental Institute and Nicholas Kouchoukos of the University of Chicago Anthropology Department, is the first American archaeological project in Iran since the Revolution. Abbas, Nick, and Tony Wilkinson of the Oriental Institute conducted archaeological and geomorphological survey work focusing on the fourth millennium B.C. archaeological landscape of Khuzestan, that region of southwestern Iran immediately adjacent to Sumer, or southern Mesopotamia. After completing his fieldwork, Abbas spent most of the year in Tehran, working at the National Museum to organize and shelve their collections of survey pottery while also assembling a "sherd library" of diagnostic ceramics from all major regions and chronological periods in Iran. This reference collection will prove to be an indispensable resource for all future archaeological survey research in Iran. It also marks the beginning of a new era of cooperation and partnership between American and Iranian scholars.

In Egypt, the Epigraphic Survey continues work in the Medinet Habu small Amun temple of Hatshepsut and Thutmose III. In addition to the ongoing process of recording, in 2002/2003 the Epigraphic Survey staff completed the digital scanning of all of the 17,099 large format photographs in the Chicago House archive. These images have now been copied onto CDs. One set now resides in the Oriental Institute archives, guaranteeing the preservation of this priceless visual record. The Epigraphic Survey also received a major grant of $95,000 from the World Monument Fund to support the Epigraphic Survey's conservation projects.

At home in Chicago, the Center for the Archaeology of the Middle Eastern Landscape (CAMEL) has continued its path-breaking work on the application of declassified satellite imagery to the reconstruction of archaeological landscapes in southeast Anatolia, north Syria, and Mesopotamia.

The three dictionary projects continue their steady progress. The Assyrian Dictionary is entering the final stretch. Three volumes are now in press, and the final volume is being written and edited. The projected completion date for this project is 2006. The completion of the Assyrian Dictionary, perhaps the single most important research tool for scholars of the ancient Mesopotamian textual record, will be marked and honored in 2005 by the convening in Chicago of the Rencontre Assyriologique Internationale. The prototype of the electronic version of the Hittite Dictionary — the P volume — is on the verge of completion. The Hittite Dictionary received a major bridging grant from the National Endowment for the Humanities for the coming year. The Demotic Dictionary now has eleven letter files online, and four more are ready for posting. Janet Johnson, the head of the Demotic Dictionary Project, was appointed to the Morton D. Hull Distinguished Service Professorship in recognition of her tremendous intellectual contributions to Demotic studies.

The Oriental Institute's Museum Education section has much to be proud of as well. In addition to their regular fare of educational programs, Carole Krucoff and her colleagues inspired and organized an extraordinary project — "Hip Hop Egypt" — in which students from the Kenwood Academy were given classes in Egyptian hieroglyphs, culture, and history as the background to use for their design and execution of a two part mural, titled "Ancient Egypt: A Hip Hop Perspective." The project was made possible through support of the Regents Park/University of Chicago Fine Arts Partnership. The Museum Education section is also to be congratulated for securing grants from the Fry and Polk Foundations in support of their innovative programs.

Finally, I am proud to highlight the active role that the Oriental Institute has played in responding to the looting and damage at the Iraq National Museum in Baghdad this past spring. McGuire Gibson has taken the lead in raising public awareness and in pressing the government of the United States to help track down and recover the stolen artifacts and help in the reconstruction efforts at the Museum. Clemens Reichel, aided by a dedicated group of volunteers, has established a website documenting the Iraq Museum holdings in general, and in particular, those 10,000 plus artifacts that can now be definitively established as stolen. We can only hope that this "cyber-alert" will help recover this lost Iraqi cultural patrimony.

Where are we going in the future? Karen Wilson and her colleagues are immediately starting on the installation of the East Wing of the Museum. This installation consists of three galleries: a gallery featuring the Assyrian reliefs from the private royal quarters at Khorsabad, the Herbolsheimer Syro-Anatolian Gallery, and the Haas Megiddo Gallery. At the same time, our research efforts in Egypt are expanding with Stephen Harvey's Abydos project. Most important of all, we are initiating new surveys, excavations, and museum projects in Iran. We are on the threshold of a new era of discovery in the lands of Elam and the Iranian plateau. I look forward to presenting the results of these exciting developments in next year's *Annual Report*.

IN MEMORIAM

FACULTY

Robert J. and Linda S. Braidwood

Robert Braidwood died peacefully in his sleep early on the morning of January 15, 2003, at the age of 95. His wife Linda, aged 93, followed a few hours later. It is difficult to overestimate the Braidwoods' professional stature, their impact on the archaeology of the Near East, and their role in archaeology as a general discipline. Their deaths mark the ending of an era.

Over the course of Bob Braidwood's long and distinguished career, he made numerous major contributions at every level — theory, methodology, and empirical data. As an educator, his textbook "Prehistoric Men" was tremendously influential in exposing several generations of students to the challenges of archaeology. More than almost anyone else, he exemplified archaeology at the Oriental Institute.

Bob was one of the first people to conduct and publish a systematic archaeological survey — "Mounds on the Plain of Antioch." His excavations at Kurdu, Dhahab, Ta'yinat, and Chatal Höyük in the Amuq plain — conducted under difficult conditions on the eve of World War II — established the basic chronological sequence for north Syria and southeast Anatolia: the sequence that remains in use more than six decades later.

Bob Braidwood's investigations of the Neolithic at Jarmo and related sites in the Zagros flanks pioneered the use of interdisciplinary research teams, bringing together natural scientists and archaeologists to study the origins of domestication and village life within their ecological context. He was the first to bring zooarchaeology and archaeobotany into the mainstream of archaeological research on these problems.

Bob Braidwood's work with Halet Çambel in the Joint Chicago-Istanbul Prehistoric Project not only resulted in the excavation of one of the most important Neolithic sites in the Near East, but also set the standard for real international collaboration with archaeologists from the Near East in investigating the past of their own countries.

Through the years, it is impossible to disentangle Bob Braidwood's contributions from those of his wife, Linda. The two of them were true intellectual partners in addition to their deep personal commitment to each other. Everyone who encountered them over the years was struck by the way they worked together as a team.

Although by her own preference less often in the public eye, Linda Braidwood was a major scholar and noted author in her own right. Her book "Digging Beyond the Tigris" is a wonderful example of both her deep knowledge of the Near East and her ability to convey the complexities and excitement of archaeology to the educated lay public.

Finally, Robert and Linda were generous and fundamentally decent people. They were good col-

Robert J. and Linda S. Braidwood

leagues and real mentors to generations of students and junior scholars. Virtually everyone with a long-term connection to the Oriental Institute has fond memories of the Braidwoods' generosity and hospitality, as exemplified by the numerous occasions when they were invited to the Braidwoods' home in La Porte for swimming, cookouts, and a general break from the stresses of the scholarly life.

We will miss Bob and Linda very much.

Gil J. Stein

FRIENDS

William A. Boone

William A. Boone, longtime volunteer at the Oriental Institute, passed away on August 3, 2002. William gave more than ten years of service as a docent to the Institute. William's interests outside of archaeology varied widely, including genealogy, playing the bagpipes, studying word derivation, and collecting and restoring vintage cars.

In his career, he served as president of Bell & Gossett, Co., and later International Telephone and Telegraph Co. Fluid Handling Division. William was preceded in death by two wives, Eleanor Gossett and Margaret Davis Gilgis. He is survived by his third wife, Florence, eight children, thirteen grandchildren, and three great-grandchildren.

George Joseph

George was a vital and interesting man, who was a wonderful friend to the Oriental Institute. A passionate Egyptophile and truly committed to the mission of the Oriental Institute, he served on the Executive Committee for the Legacy Campaign, which raised funds for the climate control project. He was a member of the Visiting Committee for almost seven years and resigned only when his health no longer allowed him to travel from his home in Oregon.

George's passion for Egyptology was not limited to service to the Oriental Institute. He was one of the driving forces behind the establishment of the Ancient Egypt Studies Association (AESA), bringing lecturers including the Oriental Institute's Emily Teeter, T. G. H. James of the British Museum, and Lanny Bell, former Director of Chicago House, to Oregon. I had the privilege of being a guest in the home of the Josephs when I spoke to the association.

His distinguished legal career is an additional tribute to George's character. He earned his J.D. from the University of Chicago Law School and his L.L.M from New York University. He taught law at several schools, worked in private practice, and served as Chief Judge of the Oregon Court of Appeals from 1981 until 1992.

Elizabeth and George Joseph

George died in Portland on Monday, June 23, 2003, of respiratory failure following pneumonia. He is survived by his wife, Elizabeth, their five children, thirteen grandchildren, and one great-grandchild.

George was a good friend to all of us at the Institute, and he is missed.

Carlotta Maher

Eleanor Ransom Swift

Eleanor Ransom Swift was a vital part of the Oriental Institute for many years. Whether accompanying her husband Gustavus F. Swift III, the first full time curator of the Oriental Institute, on excavations or volunteering in the Suq, she was always full of energy, honesty, and just plain spunk. She kept us all in order. Mrs. Swift died January 11, 2003 in her Hyde Park home.

Eleanor was raised by her mother and uncle in Denver, Colorado, after her father, a mining engineer, died before she was 5. There she adopted the western traits of pluck, determination, self-reliance, independence of spirit, and the frontier courage of meeting life head-on that lasted throughout her life. With this attitude, she headed off to Radcliffe where she graduated in 1939

magna cum laude in English. While at Radcliffe, she met her husband and they were later married and moved to Chicago.

She first traveled with her husband in 1951 to Iraq where he worked with Bob and Linda Braidwood at Jarmo. In the 1960s, she became a constant figure in Turkey while her husband was on the senior staff of the Sardis excavations. Undaunted that her family was not allowed to stay at the excavation compound, she set up house outside, learned Turkish, and did her shopping in town where her gregarious nature won the hearts of the village merchants.

Volunteerism was always a part of her life. She was an air raid warden for her neighborhood in Washington, D.C., during World War II, and went on to donate many years of service to the Chicago Child Care Society. Eleanor will be most remembered by us for her Mondays and Wednesdays in the Suq. She was always

Eleanor Ransom Swift

there, keeping us organized unless she was off with Georgie Maynard, another amazing Suq volunteer, on some unusual world tour — like the year they took the mail boat up the coast of Iceland.

She loved working in the Suq where she could handle 100 children at once with ease and understanding, while having the unique ability of being able to melt the most difficult of customers. She was also devoted to the students who worked in the Suq, making sure they had her extra tickets to the Lyric Opera or the Chicago Symphony, believing that an education in the arts was also important.

We who had the pleasure of knowing Eleanor Swift will never forget her.

Prepared by Denise Browning, with parts excerpted from the speech of Mrs. Swift's daughter, Alice Swift Riginos, at her memorial service January 26, 2003, at Montgomery Place.

RESEARCH

Overleaf. Plaque Showing a Harpist. Baked clay. Isin-Larsa/Old Babylonian Period (ca. 2000–1600 B.C.).
Purchased in Baghdad, Iraq, 1930. OIM A9345

PROJECT REPORTS

ABYDOS

Stephen P. Harvey

This year marks the initiation of the Oriental Institute's Ahmose and Tetisheri Project at Abydos, providing an important new opportunity for Institute students and researchers to be involved in archaeological fieldwork in Egypt. Operating under the aegis of the joint University of Pennsylvania-Yale-Institute of Fine Arts New York University Expedition to Abydos, our program of research also encourages a close link with a number of institutions and colleagues engaged in work at the site. Although this project marks the first time that the University of Chicago has actively supported excavation at Abydos, the Oriental Institute did play an early and important role in the publication of a landmark series of watercolor paintings that record the extraordinarily fine relief sculpture in the Abydos temple of King Seti I (ca. 1301–1287 B.C.). During a visit to that extraordinary temple in 1929, John D. Rockefeller was sufficiently impressed with the watercolor facsimile paintings and ink drawings then being produced by English artists Amice Calverley and Myrtle Broome to support their publication on a grand scale. Lavishly printed in deluxe folio volumes under the auspices of the Oriental Institute in collaboration with the Egypt Exploration Society, the highly accurate and colorful facsimiles produced by Calverley and Broome are themselves works of art, as well as essential resources for scholars studying Egyptian relief sculpture, painting, and religious iconography.

In antiquity, Abydos was revered as the center of the cult of the important god Osiris, who together with his sister/wife Isis and son Horus, formed a divine triad that was closely associated with the divine aspects of Egyptian kingship. Abydos is best known as the burial place of

Figure 1. View of the Ahmose pyramid mound at South Abydos

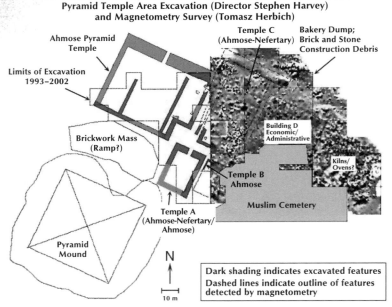

THE ORIENTAL INSTITUTE AHMOSE AND TETISHERI PROJECT 2002
Pyramid Temple Area Excavation (Director Stephen Harvey)
and Magnetometry Survey (Tomasz Herbich)

Ahmose Pyramid Temple

Limits of Excavation 1993–2002

Temple C (Ahmose-Nefertary)

Bakery Dump; Brick and Stone Construction Debris

Brickwork Mass (Ramp?)

Building D Economic/ Administrative

Kilns/ Ovens?

Temple B Ahmose

Temple A (Ahmose-Nefertary/ Ahmose)

Muslim Cemetery

Pyramid Mound

N

10 m

Dark shading indicates excavated features
Dashed lines indicate outline of features detected by magnetometry

Figure 2. Plan of Ahmose Pyramid Complex, showing features and structures revealed through excavation and magnetometry survey in 2002. Credits: Stephen Harvey/Tomasz Herbich

Egypt's first pharaohs, those rulers responsible for the political unification of the country ca. 3100 B.C. For millennia, Egypt's pharaohs built temples at Abydos to commemorate their link to these royal forbears, and to strengthen their identification with the sacred cults of Osiris and Horus. Over time, the broad popular appeal of the cult of Osiris and his growing significance in funerary ritual led Egyptians at all levels of society to leave behind monuments enabling their eternal communication with the god. One of the boldest and most extensive of these architectural statements was the memorial complex built at Abydos by King Ahmose (ca. 1550–1525 B.C.), the founder of Egypt's famed Eighteenth Dynasty of rulers.

Ahmose's great historical importance derives from his defeat of the Hyksos, a Canaanite ruling elite who established the capital of Avaris (modern Tell ed-Dab'a) in the eastern Delta. Following a century of Hyksos control of northern Egypt, a period during which the traditional dynasties of pharaohs ruled from their southern capital at Thebes (modern Luxor), Ahmose's army took Avaris, rapidly leading to the reunification of Egypt. Ahmose's subsequent military conquests in Palestine and Nubia resulted in the consolidation and expansion of a newly powerful Egyptian empire, the New Kingdom (Eighteenth to Twentieth Dynasties, ca. 1525–1085 B.C.). Despite Ahmose's place in history, no tomb or temple of this king has ever been discovered at Thebes, and thus his Abydos monuments, discovered by British archaeologists at the turn of the last century, take on a particular importance. Incorporating Egypt's last royal pyramid and pyramid temple, the Abydos complex of Ahmose also consisted of a variety of other structures dedicated in honor of the warrior king and his family, including a memorial pyramid built for his grandmother Queen Tetisheri. The nearby settlement and cemetery of workers and priests attached to Ahmose's posthumous cult provide a rare opportunity to examine an ancient cult place in its broader social context. Since 1993, I have directed a program of excavation and survey centered on understanding the rise of Ahmose's cult at Abydos and its decline three centuries later. The discussion below outlines some of our main research questions, as well as the intriguing results from our most recent season in 2002.

Project Background

My interest in Ahmose's monuments at Abydos was spurred while I was completing doctoral study at the University of Pennsylvania under the supervision of David O'Connor (now of the

Institute of Fine Arts, New York University), who since 1967 has directed research at Abydos together with William Kelly Simpson of Yale University. O'Connor and Simpson's work at Abydos has introduced a high standard of archaeological research to a site that, in the early days of exploration, had fallen victim to much unscientific plundering. Their work, and that of a second generation of researchers trained by them, has resulted in a series of surprising discoveries that have fundamentally altered scholarly perceptions of the site. Similarly, the discoveries made at the Predynastic and Early Dynastic cemetery of Abydos known as 'Umm el-Qa'ab by the German Archaeological Institute under Werner Kaiser and Günter Dreyer have transformed our views on the origins and date of the earliest hieroglyphic writing, the development of early kingship and administration, and Egypt's relations with contemporary cultures in the Near East. In searching for the subject of a long-term field project at Abydos, I was hoping to identify a site with considerable archaeological potential, and one that raised a series of compelling research questions.

Starting in 1988, I would use my days off while working on other projects at Abydos to wander south to examine the sandy 10 meter high ruin of Ahmose's pyramid (fig. 1). The vista from the top of Ahmose's pyramid is a commanding one, as it surveys the nearby cultivated fields at the edge of the Nile floodplain, as well as the limestone cliffs a kilometer away that mark the start of the plateau of the Sahara desert. Ahmose's architects conceived a grand series of royal monuments linking already ancient traditions of pyramid building to newer concepts developed at Thebes, all with reference to local alignments and processional routes at Abydos. Ahmose's pyramid, discovered in 1899 by the young British archaeologist Arthur C. Mace together with the ruins of a pyramid temple at its base, had received almost no scholarly attention since its discovery and seemed like a good candidate for re-examination. Mace had published photographs of only a few artifacts from the site, including some carved reliefs depicting the king. One discovery, a stela depicting a pharaoh of the Amarna period (some two centuries after Ahmose's death) standing next to the deified King Ahmose and his sister-wife Queen Ahmose-Nefertary, demonstrated the long survival of Ahmose's cult at Abydos.

After Mace's initial, brief exploration of the site, further exploration by Charles T. Currelly in 1902/1903 revealed a unique series of royal monuments that could be associated with the reign of Ahmose on the basis of stamped mudbricks bearing his name. These included the broad fieldstone and brick terraces of a temple built high against the limestone cliffs; a massive rock-cut tomb of a type better known from the Valley of the Kings at Thebes; and a second, smaller pyramid made of brick. In this last structure, Currelly found a 2 meter tall, elegantly carved dedicatory stela, the text of which detailed how Ahmose and his wife Ahmose-Nefertary chose to establish a pyramid at

Figure 3. Limestone pyramid casing block from Temple A. Photograph by Shawn Smejkal

Figure 4. View of Temple A (foreground) and Temple B (top right) at end of season. Photograph by Shawn Smejkal

Abydos in memory of their grandmother Tetisheri. Somewhat reminiscent of a legal contract, the text lays out the establishment of an economic foundation to be staffed with people, endowed with animals and supported by the produce of agricultural fields and groves. Currelly discovered traces of this support population in the form of a cemetery near the Ahmose pyramid, including the grave of a priest of Ahmose's temple cult named Pairy. He also located New Kingdom domestic remains in a nearby town, which he took to be a village purposefully built for the workers and priests of Ahmose's cult (although subsequent research does not support this view). Surprisingly, despite the importance and seeming promise of these finds, no further work was done after 1903. In all likelihood, this was due to the fragmentary nature of the finds, consisting of mere foundations of buildings, and the limited number of "important" artifacts discovered. Also, Mace and Currelly's brief reports (in *El Amrah and Abydos* and *Abydos III*) had long been assumed to be authoritative summaries reflecting the exhaustion of the site's archaeological potential. More recently, however, archaeologists have discovered the great value in returning for careful restudy of earlier excavations, especially employing modern technology and fresh research questions.

Reviewing the facts then known about Ahmose's constructions at Abydos, a number of mysteries remained. Why had Ahmose built so extensively at Abydos? In the absence of a known tomb or mortuary temple of Ahmose at Thebes, could either the stone-clad pyramid or the subterranean tomb at Abydos have been intended for Ahmose's burial? We also knew that the cult had survived for nearly three centuries after its founding; a stela from the time of Ramesses II (ca. 1287–1220 B.C.) demonstrated that a processional boat had served for local villagers as an oracle of the deified god-king Ahmose. The text of the stela described an appeal to Ahmose's sacred bark to provide an oracular judgment on a local dispute, demonstrating the posthumous role that Ahmose played in the local community. What processes were involved in the transformation of a royal, state-sponsored temple into an essentially local cult? The Ahmose complex at Abydos offered the chance to examine these processes in stratified contexts, and not just royal monuments, but support buildings, town, cemetery, kilns, and bakeries — all the features of an ancient Egyptian specialized settlement. Too often in the past, Egyptian temples were viewed in isolation from their archaeological and social contexts; in the worst cases, invaluable organic-rich strata documenting the life history of such institutions were summarily removed to expose stone walls and pavements. The Ahmose site provided a rare opportunity to study a temple and its varied and changing meanings alongside the community that supported it, all with reference to textual as well as archaeological evidence. In addition, the renewed excavation of the Ahmose monuments offered a chance to learn more about an extremely important transitional period in Egyptian history, one that is poorly documented at the key sites of Thebes and Memphis.

Initial Results of Excavation and Survey

Our first season of intensive work began in the spring of 1993, when we decided to focus our attention on re-excavating the pyramid temple of Ahmose discovered a century ago. Our primary

duty was the creation of the first-ever detailed map of the area, a task expertly accomplished by seasoned surveyor David Goodman, also allowing us to establish a grid for surface collection and excavation. Already within the first days of carrying out surface collection, it became clear that all parts of the concession held promise for renewed attention. In the area of the pyramid temple, a particular surprise was the high volume of fragments of carved and painted limestone that had once formed its walls and ceilings; only a handful of pieces had been mentioned in the original report. In addition, inscriptions and ceramic indicated that there was abundant material ranging over the entire period of use of site.

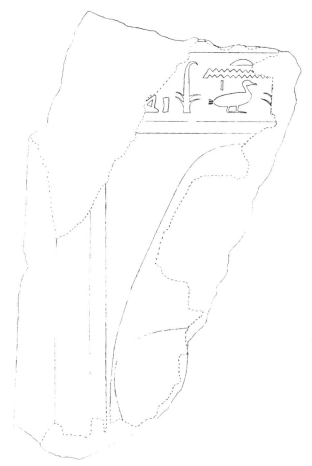

Within a few short weeks of excavation, we were overwhelmed with the volume of material deriving from contexts that had ostensibly been exhausted by Mace's excavations. In particular, we encountered more than 3,000 fragments of the limestone blocks that had once formed Ahmose's pyramid temple, some providing the potential to imagine the appearance of the temple's octagonal pillars, elaborate doorways, and starry ceiling. These fragments represented only a small percentage (less than 5 percent) of the temple's walls; most were only the edges or corners of blocks that had been

Figure 5. Fragment of a large limestone stela depicting a queen or goddess, with the title of "prince" in the text above. Drawing by Krisztian Vertes

Figure 6. Fragment of limestone relief showing the face of a pharaoh (Ahmose?)

carted away in antiquity for reuse in other buildings at Abydos, or (a more dispiriting thought) had perhaps been burned to make the essential ingredient of lime plaster. In many cases, however, even the remaining pieces of temple architecture were of extraordinary informational value. One large fragment depicting the falcon-headed deity Re-Horakhty even provided a direct join to the corner of a pillar illustrated in Mace's old report and now in the collections of the Metropolitan Museum, New York. Another piece provided the cartouche of King Amenhotep I, the son and successor of Ahmose, demonstrating that he had carried on with the decoration of his father's temple. Beyond the limestone evidence, we found that the walls enclosing the stone core of the temple had been constructed of a variety of types of bricks, most stamped with a range of inscriptions giving forms of the name of Ahmose, often followed by the epithet "beloved of Osiris." The varying thickness in walls, each built with a distinct type of inscribed brick, implied alterations in the temple plan and signaled more complexity than we had been led to expect from Mace's published plan.

Although the early excavators had certainly disturbed many stratified contexts in order to make their plan, perhaps by employing the outmoded practice of "following" walls in narrow trenches, it was also becoming increasingly clear that their excavation had not been exhaustive. Unfortunately, the fine desert sand at this site does not preserve the outlines of old excavation pits or trenches, and in many cases we could only reconstruct where and how deep Mace had worked on the basis of what features he had recorded. One clue of great value was our discovery of a number of oval foundation deposit pits made of brick, located at the base of walls that had been charted on Mace's plan. These features (though unfortunately plundered of their original dedicatory offerings) had never been seen by Mace, who would certainly have made note of them, as he did of other similar pits or caches.

The greatest discovery of the 1993 season was also the factor that demonstrated conclusively that Mace's work at the site, while seminal, had not been thorough. In an area on the eastern side of the temple, we began to encounter fragments of a small-scale battle narrative, including representations of horses and chariots (the earliest yet known in Egyptian art), archers, fallen enemies, and royal transport ships, all carved and painted in a lively style. The weapons, clothing, and beards of the enemies were those typical of Egyptian representations of Canaanites, and in all likelihood represent warriors fighting on behalf of Ahmose's Hyksos adversary. Conventional Egyptological wisdom up to that date held that complex battle depictions were not a feature of temple decoration until the end of the Eighteenth Dynasty, yet here we had what seemed to be vignettes carved at the very beginning of the dynasty. Scraps of hieroglyphic texts seemed to confirm our identification of these as scenes of Ahmose's Hyksos battles, including a mention of the Hyksos capital of Avaris, as well as a probable occurrence of the name of Apophis (Ipep), one of the last Hyksos kings. Longer portions of text, as well as additional parts of these battle scenes, could provide important information on Egyptian perceptions of contemporary events, as well as important insight into artistic strategies for depicting complex narratives. All evidence from the site points to the construction of Ahmose's Abydos monuments very late in the reign, possibly after year 22, and thus well after the conclusion of the Hyksos struggles.

In all, we opened a total of twenty excavation units (each 10×10 square meters) in 1993; the majority of these were located in the vicinity of Ahmose's pyramid temple. The analysis and recording of the high volume of finds from these units was a goal of our study season in 1996, funded in large part by the National Endowment for the Humanities. Together with a thorough study of the earlier excavations, these results were presented in my 1998 doctoral dissertation entitled "The Cults of King Ahmose at Abydos." Due to other professional obligations, however, we were only able to return for a field season in the (extremely hot!) summer of 2002.

The 2002 Season

Apart from the main area of the pyramid temple, our attention in 1993 had shifted to the area southeast of the structure discovered by Mace. Excavating there in the oddly asymmetrical southeastern corner of the pyramid temple, we had encountered the brick enclosure wall of a previously unknown building (Temple A; see fig. 2). Inscriptions on bricks once again proved extremely valuable here because the enclosure wall bore the stamp of Ahmose's Chief Treasurer Neferperet, a figure known from other sources to have been entrusted with quarrying and build-

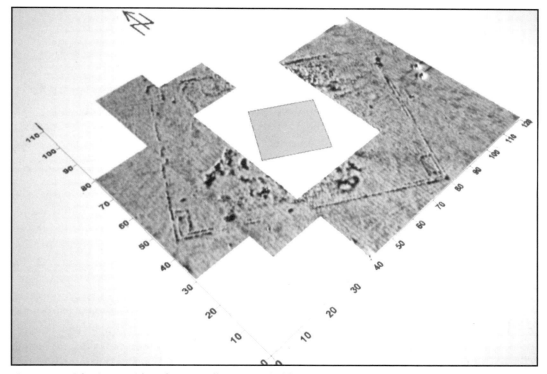

Figure 7. Tetisheri pyramid enclosure walls, as revealed by magnetometry. Credit: Tomasz Herbich

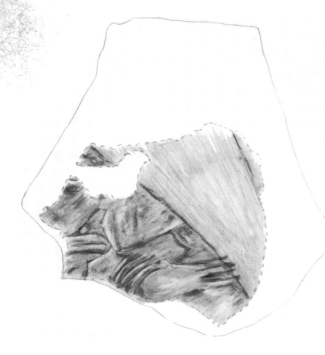

Figure 8. Limestone relief fragment, possibly depicting a heap of severed hands. Drawing by Krisztian Vertes

ing activities late in Ahmose's reign. The interior walls were formed in part of bricks stamped with Ahmose-Nefertary's name and titles, while other bricks provided Ahmose's cartouche. Due to time limitations, we were only able to excavate a portion of the outer room and doorway of this structure, and we were unsure of its function. Considering the presence of bricks stamped with the Ahmose-Nefertary's name, and the discovery of several fragments of private stelae depicting a queen in a vulture headdress, I had postulated that it perhaps was a shrine dedicated to Ahmose-Nefertary. The suggestion that the enclosure might prove to contain a subsidiary pyramid was based purely on the proximity of this new building to the immense, stone-clad pyramid ascribed to Ahmose.

Accordingly, a major goal of work in 2002 was the continued excavation of this structure, which required the removal of more than 5 meters of sandy overburden in most areas. We opened up an area of 350 square meters in this area, revealing the foundations of a building approximately 28 meters long and 19 meters wide (fig. 2). Underneath volumes of sand and limestone boulders, some with quarry marks, we encountered mud surfaces across the interior of the enclosure, covered with a massive volume of New Kingdom offering pottery. No stone foundations were found *in situ* in the rear portion of the structure, though several massive blocks found in the lowest levels of the excavation were clearly pyramid casing blocks with an outer face at a steep angle of about 65 degrees (fig. 3). Since this finding corresponds closely to Mace's written descriptions of the casing of the main Ahmose pyramid, these blocks may derive from the Ahmose pyramid itself, though alternatively they might come from an additional, as yet undiscovered smaller pyramid in the vicinity. Based on its advanced state of destruction, the function of this structure could unfortunately not be clearly determined, although its location alongside the main Ahmose pyramid may yet prove to be meaningful.

The discovery of a previously unsuspected royal structure in 1993 implied that further exploration beyond the pyramid temple was warranted. A large area (about 0.6 hectare) to the east of Ahmose's temple had intrigued me since my first visits to the site, as it was covered with New Kingdom ceramic and other small finds. In 2002, we decided to explore the eastern periphery of the main pyramid temple using two methods: traditional excavation and magnetometric subsurface survey, carried out by Dr. Tomasz Herbich of the Polish Institute, with the assistance of Piotr Kolodziejczyk. Excavation provided the first surprise in the form of a corner of yet another mudbrick enclosure no more than 7 meters to the east of the main pyramid temple, and 5 meters to the north of Temple A (fig. 4). Like this last building, the new structure (now dubbed Temple B) also was constructed of bricks naming "The God's Wife, Daughter of a King, Wife and Mother of a King, Ahmose Nefertary." Magnetometry carried out adjacent to Temple B indicates that it had dimensions of 25 × 40 meters, with what seems to be a massive, 40 meter wide pylon located to its north. Over 1,000 fragments of decorated limestone temple relief, votive stelae, and parts of statues found in 2002 point to the existence of a decorated structure within this brick enclosure. Evidence for cultic activity into at least the reign of Ramesses II could be demonstrated through inscriptions of that ruler, as well as from abundant evidence for votive pottery and other cult objects of Ramesside date. Especially intriguing was the discovery of the fragment of a large limestone stela in sunk relief, bearing the image of a woman, and above it the phrase "king's son" (fig. 5). Originally the scale of this stela would have been very large (over 1.5 meters), and it is likely that it dates to the early Eighteenth Dynasty on stylistic and paleographic grounds. Fragments of small votive stela found within this building indicate the presence of a cult of the royal family of Ahmose down to the Ramesside era. Additionally, hundreds of fragments of decorated limestone found within this structure probably derive from the decoration of its now-vanished stone building, including parts of a carved and painted doorway that may have carried the titles of Ahmose-Nefertary, and the representation of a pharaoh's face (fig. 6).

The discovery since 1993 of two structures clearly associated with Queen Ahmose-Nefertary strengthens the already powerful impression of South Abydos as a center for royal attention in this period that would have rivaled (and might possibly have eclipsed) building projects of these rulers at Thebes. It is interesting to consider the prominent role that Ahmose-Nefertary seems to have played in royal projects, as evidenced by her mention on the Tetisheri stela from Abydos and the presence of her name and titles alongside those of Ahmose on two inscriptions announcing the reopening in Ahmose's regnal year 22 of limestone quarries at el-Ma'asara (near Cairo). This last text is particularly fascinating, as it details the construction of temples throughout Egypt entrusted to the Chief Treasurer Neferperet, the same individual whose name occurs repeatedly on the bricks forming the exterior wall of Temple A. Only rarely do archaeologists have such satisfying textual confirmation of agency at both the royal and private levels.

Two additional buildings were located in 2002 in the area to the east of Ahmose's pyramid temple, both sharing the alignment of the other early Eighteenth Dynasty structures, bringing the total count of known structures in this area to five. To the east of Temple A, the narrow corner of a small building was excavated, associated with King Ahmose on the basis of brick stamps. Only a small portion of this structure (Temple C) was excavated, and its form and function will remain unclear until it is excavated further in the coming season of work. However, its location alongside Temple A and its position near the pyramid of Ahmose may imply that it has a funerary or commemorative function. The other structure (Building D) was far more massive, at least 35 × 40 meters in size, and located just beyond Temple C. Based on debris from temple bakeries encountered nearby in 1993, Building D might represent an administrative or production center for the Ahmose cult. The area to its east may contain kilns or ovens, to judge from the strong magnetic response of remains buried below the surface. Excavation is planned in coming seasons for these areas, which may be among the most informative in terms of the economy and daily functioning of the Ahmose temple.

Figure 9. Fragments of relief showing the figure of a pharaoh standing before the rudder stanchion of a ship or processional bark. (Abydos fragments placed against outline of a later king for comparison)

The Pyramid of Queen Tetisheri

In addition to our work last summer in the area of the Ahmose pyramid, we ventured farther into the desert to investigate the environs of the pyramid shrine of Queen Tetisheri. Although Charles Currelly discovered the actual pyramid shrine in 1902, there encountering the famous Tetisheri stela now in the Cairo Museum, no earlier researcher had found any trace of brick enclosures or additional structures in this area. While attempting to build a perimeter fence to protect the site from encroachment in 1996, our worker's tools hit some ancient mudbricks. Suspecting that we may have located an enclosure wall of some sort, we asked Dr. Herbich and his assistant to conduct magnetometry survey, and the results were extremely satisfying (fig. 7). A massive 90×70 meter enclosure wall of brick was detected very clearly, with small structures of unknown function in three corners, each building measuring about 5×8 meters. The text of the Tetisheri stela mentions the construction of both a pyramid (Egyptian *mer*) and an enclosure (Egyptian *hut)*, providing textual confirmation of both features. We intend to investigate the enclosure's corner structures in the coming seasons in hopes of determining the function of this unique ritual complex.

In addition to excavation, analysis was conducted on ceramic deriving from 1993 work on the Ahmose Pyramid Temple and Temple A of Ahmose-Nefertary. Julia Budka of the University of Vienna, a specialist in New Kingdom ceramic with extensive experience at Elephantine and Tell el-Dab'a, was responsible for the analysis of material also from last season and was able to document a large number of imported wares, in addition to Egyptian ceramic types of the Eighteenth and Nineteenth Dynasties. A large number of diagnostic sherds were drawn and photographed for future study. In addition to ceramic study, all major finds from the 2002 season were recorded in a database, drawn, and photographed in color and black and white. Fragments of relief sculpture were carefully studied in terms of style, color, and relation to finds from the 1993 season. Interestingly, a number of pieces of limestone were discovered that might belong to the "Hyksos" battle narrative. These include what may prove to be the earliest known representation of a heap of severed enemies' hands on the battlefield (fig. 8), an image well known in Ramesside temple battle scenes. Of great interest was a small piece showing triangular battlements, perhaps from a fortress, above which appears the head of a soldier wearing a helmet. This fragment may well relate to a scene of the siege of a fortress, the presence of which was indicated in 1993 by a fragment depicting archers firing arrows at a steep angle. Also, a number of fragments were recorded from scenes of large and small-scale boats. One of these (fig. 9), depicting a pharaoh (possibly Ahmose) wearing a *shendyet*-kilt and standing directly in front the rudder stanchion of a ship, may represent a royal or divine processional bark, rather than a scene from the battle narrative. Ahmose's processional bark was most likely housed at South Abydos, and received public veneration during its journeys to stations in the precinct of Osiris and in other royal temples.

The exciting discoveries of last summer, discussed above, have exponentially expanded the size and significance of the Ahmose complex at Abydos, meaning that the project that we are bringing to the Oriental Institute has tremendous future potential. We anticipate a productive season of excavation during Winter Quarter 2004 (January to March). Our first job will be selective excavation of monuments recovered by magnetometry, while in coming seasons we plan on partial excavation of the Ahmose pyramid, as well as the investigation of the nearby New Kingdom settlement. Further down the road, we intend to re-excavate and conserve Ahmose's subterranean tomb, and to tackle the excavation of the massive foundations of Ahmose's Terrace Temple, as well as the investigation of an oval structure of unknown function identified by

Currelly only as a "Roman Farm." Based on our experience thus far, the temple and tomb complex of Ahmose, together with the economic and settlement components that surround it, will continue to yield many surprises in the years to come.

Acknowledgments

In all of these pursuits, the interest, support, and assistance of a number of people and institutions must be acknowledged. First, thanks go to Dr. Zahi Hawass, Secretary General of the Supreme Council of Antiquities (SCA) of Egypt; Dr. Magdy el-Ghandour, Chairman of the Permanent Committee on Archaeological Expeditions of the SCA; and Dr. Yahya el-Masry for their continued support and interest. In Sohag Governorate, I am grateful to Mr. Ahmed el-Khattib, as well as to Miss Aziza Sayed Hassan of the Balliana office of the SCA. I would especially like to thank Mr. Mahmoud Ahmed Yussuf for his able assistance as our inspector last season. Mme. Amira Khattab of the American Research Center in Egypt was particularly invaluable to our efforts, as were many members of her staff. Our international team included Dr. Tomasz Herbich and Piotr Kolodziejczyk, Magnetometry; Michelle Marlar, Andrew Bednarski, and Amanda Leenerts, Site Supervisors; Jane Hill, Surveyor and Site Supervisor; Heather Reeves, Registrar; Krisztian Vertes and Elizabeth (Dee) Turman, Artists; Shawn Smejkal, Photographer; and Julia Budka, Ceramicist.

In the United States, William Kelly Simpson of Yale University and David O'Connor of the Institute of Fine Arts, New York University, must be singled out for their constant support on all levels. I also thank Lorelei Corcoran, Director of the Institute of Egyptian Art and Archaeology of the University of Memphis, and her staff and students for their financial, administrative, and logistical assistance. Support for last season's work derived from the Institute of Fine Arts, New York University, and from the Institute of Egyptian Art and Archaeology of the University of Memphis, as well as from an anonymous donor. Support in previous seasons is gratefully acknowledged from Yale University, the National Science Foundation, the Samuel H. Kress Foundation (through a grant to the American Research Center in Egypt), and the National Endowment for the Humanities.

AMUQ VALLEY REGIONAL PROJECTS

K. Aslıhan Yener

Tell Atchana (Alalakh) 2002

Over the last three seasons (2000, 2001, and 2002), the Amuq Valley Regional Project (AVRP) teams from the Oriental Institute at the University of Chicago conducted multi-disciplinary investigations at Tell Atchana, ancient Alalakh, prior to the resumption of excavations in the fall of 2003. This preliminary work served to comprehensively document the status of the site and finds excavated for the British Museum and Oxford University by Sir Leonard Woolley from 1936 to 1949 with a gap during World War II. I will be greatly aided in the newly formulated Oriental Institute Expedition to Alalakh by the expertise of Associate Director, David Schloen of the Oriental Institute, who has written extensively on Late Bronze Age socio-economic history. David's long years of experience excavating in Israel at Ashkelon complements, and will potentially build conceptual bridges with, my own northern Anatolia focus.

Figure 1. Egyptianizing ivory box. Tell Atchana, Hatay Archaeological Museum Depot. Photograph by K. A. Yener

While Alalakh was the Middle and Late Bronze Age capital of the Mukish kingdom, as the Amuq was known at that time, Tell Atchana is only one of several Amuq sites that are now targeted for reinvestigation. The AVRP was conceived in 1995 as a series of coordinated excavations and field projects located in the most southern state of Turkey, Hatay. The original path-breaking University of Chicago "Syro-Hittite" Plain of Antioch surveys, led by Robert J. Braidwood, recorded Tell Atchana as site no. 136. It and subsequent Oriental Institute excavations at Tells Chatal Höyük, Judaidah, Kurdu, and Ta'yinat, established a sequence that has played a fundamental role in defining the archaeology of this and neighboring regions. The eighth season of the broad-based AVRP concentrated on four main operations:

1. Field operations included the continuation of map making at Atchana mound with the total station. In addition, Tony Wilkinson (AVRP survey director) and Jesse Casana (Department of Near Eastern Languages and Civilizations Ph.D. candidate) continued the geoarchaeological and archaeological sweep of the Amuq valley and its surrounding hillsides;

2. Yener and NELC students resumed the inventory of collections from Tell Atchana and the 1930s Oriental Institute excavations (Tells Ta'yinat, Kurdu, Chatal Höyük, and Judaidah) housed in the Hatay Archaeological Museum in Antakya. The inventory also integrated the Atchana collections with the depot of Sir Leonard Woolley's dig house, reopened in 2001, into the database;

3. Important infrastructural issues were addressed prior to the excavation of Tell Atchana (ancient Alalakh). Attention was focused on establishing the excavation headquarters on land in proximity to the mound; and

4. Ta'yinat and Kurdu excavation teams resumed their survey and study seasons.

Operation 1: Mapping Atchana

A small rump team finished shooting the last surveying locations to clarify gaps in the Atchana
topographical map. In 2001 and 2002, our mapping teams completed shooting in a combined total of 3,725 points. Almost the entirety of the
mound was covered, with special emphasis in the
old Woolley excavation areas in the northeastern
tip of the mound. This coverage allowed us to superimpose digitized images of the excavated architecture for a composite map — something
lacking in the Woolley publications (see forthcoming AVRP monograph). The referenced
points were mainly anchored on architecturally
prominent nodes, such as the Level VII gate
stone blocks, as well as the columns and stair-
case cornerstones of the *Bit Hilani* Style Level
IV palace.

*Figure 2. Horseshoe-shaped copper based ingot. Tell
Atchana, Hatay Archaeological Museum Depot.
Photograph by K. A. Yener*

Both published and newly obtained archaeological evidence were utilized to create scale
models of the capital, Alalakh, level by level, spanning most of the second millennium B.C. The
eight composite settlement layouts encapsulate the spatial organization of the city and provide a
powerful tool with which to resolve many architecture-related questions prior to excavation.
These questions will be answered by first setting out the historical framework and then comprehensively reviewing the archaeological evidence and literature for both. The reconstructed city
plans provide benchmarks from which future excavation trenches will be targeted and a range of
other specialized problem-oriented research designs can be based.

Operation 2: Documenting Finds

An important 2002 activity focused on documenting shelf-loads of finds left in storage originating from the Woolley excavations over fifty years ago. Back in 2001, our Oriental Institute
teams had found bags of these study materials stored in the long-inaccessible and dilapidated dig
house depot on top of Tell Atchana (see *2001/2002 Annual Report*, pp.
16–17). Eighty-six crates of study materials, probably from the post
World War II seasons, were subsequently moved to safer storage at the
Mustafa Kemal University in Antakya. The sherds, seals, glass, faience,
ivory (fig. 1), metals, and other artifacts were photographed and entered
into a workable database in anticipation of additional finds from upcoming excavation seasons. The Turkish collections are being scanned and
photographed, and efforts are being made to make them available through
our XML system for Textual and Archaeological Research database,
XSTAR: http://www-oi.uchicago.edu/OI/PROJ/XSTAR/XSTAR.html

Given my enduring interest in metals, the storage depots at the Hatay
Archaeological Museum and Woolley dig house provided ample research
materials. A five kilogram horseshoe shaped copper ingot (fig. 2), slag,
molds, crucibles, and the disk-shaped ingots (see ibid., fig. 6) found last
year increased the evidence of metals processed and housed in the Alalakh

*Figure 3. Lion-shaped stone
weight. Tell Atchana, Hatay
Archaeological Museum
Depot. Photograph by
Necmi Burgaç*

Figure 4. Horse painting on a sherd from a Mycenaean pictorial style amphoroid crater. Tell Atchana, Woolley Dig House Depot. Photograph by R. Koehl

palaces. Alalakh's proximity to vital mineral and timber resources in the Amanus and Taurus Mountains gave rise to questions regarding the procurement, shipping, processing, and distribution of raw materials and finished products. For example, what production and exchange systems underlay local metal smiths, woodworkers, ivory workers, and others engaged in specialized manufacturing? Was there a major specialized production of bronze supported by the palace or were they private entrepreneurs? What are some of the systems of weights and measurements used at the site (fig. 3) and can they provide information on regional and international commercial practices? These and other related topics on specialized craft production are now the focus of several doctoral dissertations on Atchana based materials.

Atchana ceramic specialist, R. Koehl, pointed to several important Anatolian and Aegean issues stemming from the stored sherd collections. Among several items of archaeological interest we encountered in the depots were unpublished fragments of a Mycenaean pictorial style amphoroid crater depicting horses (fig. 4). Small stirrup jar (fig. 5) and vertical globular flask sherds were also found in abundance, which reflects a distribution pattern typical of the imported Mycenaean pottery found in Levantine contexts. Koehl noted that, in the Levant, only Ugarit had yielded a larger number of Aegean pottery and that its relative frequency at Tell Atchana might suggest that trade between the Aegean and the Levant was organized to reflect local preferences for specific Mycenaean commodities stored in these vessels. Also, numerous sherds of so-called red lustrous wheel-made ware brought to mind issues regarding their provenience and whether they are Hittite, non-Hittite Anatolian, or Cypriot. Equally important is a number of Hittite artifacts such as a clay model of a liver used for omens (fig. 6) and a stela with a hieroglyphic inscription identifying the figure as Tudhaliya who is now thought to be a nephew of Hittite Great King Mursili II (fig. 7) and perhaps the royal governor of Alalakh. The relationship of the capital of the Hittites, Hattuša, with this distant sector of their empire is an intriguing avenue which we will explore more fully.

Figure 5. Mycenaean stirrup jar. Tell Atchana, Hatay Archaeological Museum Depot. Photograph by Necmi Burgaç

While the processing of artifacts from the Woolley dig house depot continued, the Hatay Archaeological Museum was in the throes of reinstalling its pre-classical galleries. Urgently invited to aid in their efforts, our teams helped reorganize, redesign, and reinstall the display cases, selecting from thousands of finds stemming from the early twentieth century excavations in the Amuq. Marble statues from the Princeton excavations at classical Antioch, ritual altars and sculpture from Alalakh (figs. 8–9), cylinder seals from Tell Judaidah and Chatal Höyük, gold and sophisticated bronzes from Tell

Ta'yinat, and countless exquisite ceramics from all periods and from all areas of the Near East were all part of these museum collections. A preliminary selection of artifacts was completed and decisions about display layouts were roughed out for the interior designers in a "virtual gallery" created by Steve Batiuk. A large-scale poster to display in the galleries was composed for each site excavated in the state of Hatay (Atchana, Tell Ta'yinat, Tell Kurdu, Orontes Delta and Al-Mina, and Kinet Höyük). Copious photographs and text in English and Turkish on the poster provided information about the excavation, the finds, and the relative chronologies.

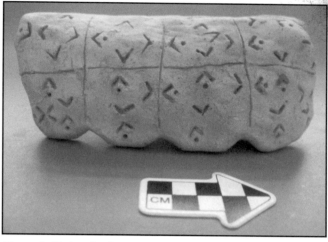

Figure 6. Hittite clay liver omen model. Tell Atchana, Hatay Archaeological Museum Depot. Photograph by K. A. Yener

Jacob Lauinger (NELC Ph.D. candidate and staff philologist) studied the tablets from Atchana and other sites housed at the museum. Having provided translations for a large selection of important cuneiform tablets (fig. 10), he was asked to design the layout of the tablet display case. A cursory inventory of Alalakh-related publications revealed that 274 tablets had already been published as copies or translations, but that 519 tablet fragments found were as yet unpublished. Over a thousand digital photographs were taken of the tablets, and a month was spent in the museum and Woolley depots documenting the tablets and other collections.

Operation 3: The AVRP Dig House Compound

With generous funding from the Oriental Institute, three prefabricated buildings had been purchased last year from a first-rate company in Ankara, PreKons. The first building is a staff dormitory unit capable of sleeping twenty-four and is provided with four bathrooms. The second is a laboratory building with dining room and kitchen facilities. The third is a two-room container for use as the director's office.

Our new headquarters were well on their way to being completed when events related to the impending Iraq War, as well as massive floods, destruction of crop fields in the Amuq, and denial of a permit to erect our buildings on top of the mound intervened. By a stroke of good fortune, we narrowly missed losing all three buildings to an extensive flood in the Amuq plain that drowned several people and caused widespread loss of property during winter. Unusually heavy rainfall and the emergency release of the dam floodgates on the Orontes River, over the border in Syria, inundated the valley, turning the mounds into an island archipelago in the recreated Lake of Antioch. But the apocalyptic clouds had a silver lining. Luckily, the prefabricated dig house panels had been waiting in a warehouse in

Figure 7. Stele depicting Tudhaliya. Tell Atchana, Hatay Archaeological Museum Depot (Woolley 1955)

Figure 8. Diorite bust, perhaps of King Yarim Lim. Tell Atchana, Hatay Archaeological Museum Depot. Photograph by K. A. Yener

Ankara until a location for our excavation compound had been established. The floods (fig. 11) caused unforeseen scheduling delays and various heroic efforts to finish projects before excavations began were recounted by team members. To meet a critical deadline, Arslanoğlu and Temiz rowed a canoe out to the island(!) of Atchana in order to complete the architectural drawings of Woolley's dig house, slated for a permit for restoration as a historical heritage site. Fortunately, for the two women, the Black Sea folk living in the village of Tayfur Sökmen knew all about boats and where to find them, and came to their rescue by providing a canoe from the Mediterranean coastal city of Iskenderun.

Concerned by our dig house predicament, the regional governor (*kaymakam*) of the Reyhanlı area finally found us a plot of land, located three kilometers to the east of Atchana and far from the threat of floodwaters to rent. Accordingly, the expedition compound will be a beacon of three, brightly-colored buildings in burgundy and yellow set in a background of green cotton fields. Two additional rented houses provide storage for the collections from the expeditions of Atchana, Ta'yinat, Kurdu, and the AVRP survey, thus making them accessible for research during study seasons. Our neighborhood of archaeologists is now situated on the eastern edge of Tayfur Sökmen village, so-named after the first and only president of the Republic of the Hatay in 1938. A townhouse located in downtown Antakya across the street from the museum will also serve as a visitors' center and city headquarters.

Operation 4: AVRP Surveys and Excavations at Other Amuq Sites

Recent surveys at Tell Ta'yinat were directed by Tim Harrison from the University of Toronto. A parallel inventory program proceeded to document artifacts excavated from the previous Oriental Institute excavations at the site. This massive Iron Age capital, perhaps Kunulua, located 700 meters away from Atchana, is slated for excavations in 2004.

Similarly, a study season was scheduled for Tell Kurdu, to be led by its new field directors, Fokke Gerritsen, former NELC Masters Degree student, and Rana Özbal, of Northwestern University. Teams working on this important Halaf and Ubaid period Chalcolithic site (ca. 5700-4300 B.C.) continued processing finds from previous excavation seasons and will resume excavations in the near future.

Figure 9. Lion sculptures from temple entrance. Tell Atchana, Hatay Archaeological Museum Depot. Photograph by K. A. Yener

Every effort is being made to share resources and dovetail schedules in AVRP's busiest excavation seasons. To that end, excavations at Tells Atchana and Ta'yinat will be staggered so that only one site will be excavated per year, while the other will process finds. Given the differences in university academic systems, the Ta'yinat team will usually be in the field during the summer months and Atchana teams will excavate during the fall months. By so doing, visitors to the Amuq will find an excavation in progress every year.

In conclusion, the AVRP program is poised for the simultaneous excavation of three major sites, building on its origin as a regional survey in 1995. Attention has now turned to the full-scale investigations at Tell Atchana, Tell Ta'yinat, and Tell Kurdu. Not to be outdone, the regional survey will redirect attention to the mountain resource areas and the highlands. The higher elevations hold great potential for research, given the multitude of copper and gold mines, forests, rock quarries, and summer pasturage for pastoral nomads. The results of these surveys and excavations will have compelling implications for other regions. Especially important are the transitions from early state formations, as well as important shifts from the Early Bronze Age and its regional states to the empires of the second and first millennium B.C.

Figure 10. Cuneiform tablet. Tell Atchana, Hatay Archaeological Museum Depot. Photograph by C. Klinger

Acknowledgments: The 2002 AVRP Tell Atchana staff included the following: K. Aslıhan Yener, Project Director; Jacob Lauinger, Christina Klinger (University of Chicago); Steven Batiuk (University of Toronto); Hatice Pamir, Tülin Arslanoğlu, Mine Temiz (Mustafa Kemal University, Antakya); Robert Koehl, Ivan Zadunaisky (Hunter College, New York); and Brenda Craddock (U.K.). The research was supported by grants from the Institute of Aegean Prehistory, members of the Oriental Institute, and numerous private donors. Heartfelt thanks go to the "Friends of the Amuq" Committee in Chicago (Sel Yackley, Ayhan Lash, Emel Singer, Ercan Alp, Muammer Akgun, Matt Argon, Jim Stoynoff, Yuksel Selçukoğlu, Katie Miller, Fatoş Aktaş, and Meral Bensch) for their untiring efforts. The research was conducted under the auspices of the Turkish Ministry of Culture, Directorate General of Monuments and Museums. Spe-

Figure 11. Floodwaters surrounding Tell Atchana, ancient Alalakh, winter 2002. Photograph by T. Arslanoğlu

cial acknowledgment and thanks go to the Hatay Archaeological Museum Acting Director Aslı Tuncer and Archaeologists Ömer Çelik and Faruk Kılınç. Special thanks are also given to Haluk Ipek and Miktat Doganlar of the Mustafa Kemal University for their help and guidance.

CAMEL

Tony J. Wilkinson

CAMEL stands for Center for the Archaeology of the Middle Eastern Landscape. This is somewhat of an overstatement because it is by no means a center but rather is a small laboratory in the basement of the Oriental Institute (my own little Bletchley Park) that processes large quantities of data that once were considered to be secret. Nevertheless, despite its modest scale, since its foundation in 1998 the lab has been the home of a number of interesting archaeological developments (fig. 1). Activities conducted under the general umbrella of CAMEL include the study of the landscapes of highland Yemen (see our web page: http://www-oi.uchicago.edu/OI/PROJ/CAMEL/Main.html), the development of Geographical Information Systems (GIS) databases of various archaeological surveys, and, most importantly, building up a large collection of high quality satellite images from the Cold War era. These image collections have provided a remarkable and invaluable source of information on the development of the ancient Near Eastern landscapes.

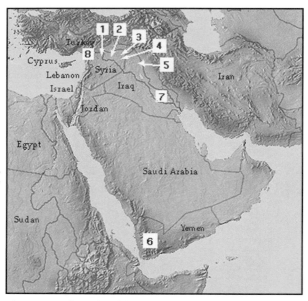

Figure 1. Projects involving CAMEL: (1) Tell es-Sweyhat, (2) Balikh Valley, (3) Tell Beydar, (4) Hamoukar, (5) Ashur Area, (6) Dhamar Project, Yemen, (7) Southern Mesopotamia

In our mission statement we declare: "At CAMEL we aim to analyze and understand the ancient Near Eastern landscape by combining both traditional on-the-ground archaeological surveys with remote-sensing methods such as satellite imagery and aerial photograph analysis. In addition our research methods include geoarchaeological studies of buried landscapes and environmental change, and the use of texts to provide information on human use of the land. Although much of our work does entail the reconstruction of demographic histories and economic landscapes, we are also seeking an understanding of the various ways in which people related to their landscapes. An extension of the CAMEL approach to landscape is a modeling program which is attempting to show how a Bronze Age Near Eastern Society provisioned itself with food, and how in the long term such strategies might have varied according to fluctuations in climate.

Such modeling techniques, that harness the capabilities of GIS with powerful crop and demographic models, are currently being developed as a CAMEL-related project in conjunction with the Division of Information Sciences at the Argonne National Laboratory, Argonne, Illinois."

The lab itself is housed within the archaeology laboratory in the basement of the Oriental Institute within my own laboratory. We must thank Annette Klein who contributed the funding for the creation of this space, as well as grants from the University of Chicago which contributed to the initial purchase of the computers and software. Thanks must also go to William Sumner whose vision enabled these laboratories to be established in the basement of the Oriental Institute.

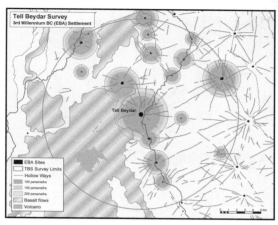

Figure 2. GIS reconstruction of the Bronze Age landscape around Tell Beydar, Syria. Processed by Jason Ur

A huge vote of thanks must also go to John Sanders who, at the outset, supplied the expertise and advice on the development of this lab and whose skills continue to enable it to function.

Regular readers of the *Annual Report* will by now be familiar with the significance of landscape archaeology, but it is useful to be able to show just how the techniques of satellite remote sensing and Geographical Information Systems (GIS) are proving to be such powerful analytical

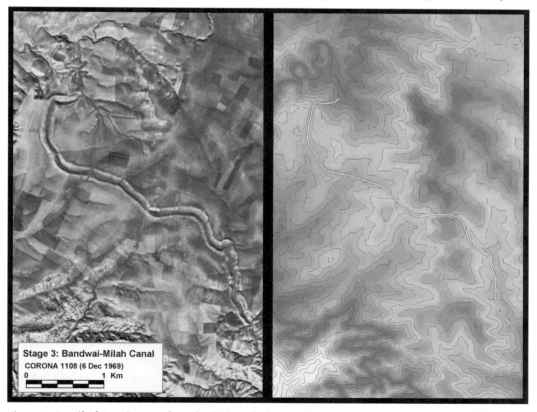

Figure 3. Detail of Assyrian canal north of Nineveh showing its course projected on a topographic map generated via a GIS. Processed by Jason Ur (courtesy of U.S. Geological Survey, used with permission)

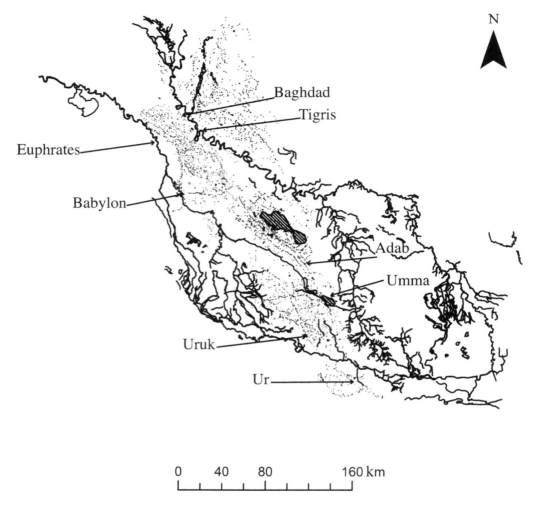

Figure 4. The pattern of archaeological sites in southern Mesopotamia, Based on data from the original surveys of Robert McC. Adams, McGuire Gibson, Henry Wright, Hans Nissen, and others and replotted by Carrie Hritz by means of a Geographical Information System

tools. GIS enable different types of mapped information to be stored as a series of "layers" that can then be analyzed and manipulated together so as to display them in new ways or to provide new data combinations. It is therefore possible to superimpose distributions of archaeological sites on, for example, soil maps to determine favored locations for settlement development; to calculate the areas of archaeological sites; estimate the amount of cultivated land around sites of a given period; as well as to ask questions such as the distance to nearest water sources or nearest neighbors. When employed in conjunction with information on the physical environment and the landscape derived from satellite images, GIS can provide an excellent means of manipulating the large spatial data sets gathered during survey. For this reason alone, Geographical Information Systems will prove to be indispensable in landscape analysis in the future, and, because the Oriental Institute has long been a center for archaeological survey, these techniques will become indispensable for the future of the Institute.

An example of the application of GIS to northern Syria should demonstrate some of the potential of these new methodologies. Archaeologists frequently employ the term "city-states" rather loosely to the scatter of settlements and polities that appeared in Mesopotamia during the Bronze Age. However, it is sometimes difficult to understand precisely what type of settlement systems that are being refereed to. In the rain-fed north of Upper Mesopotamia, the classic tells form a relatively even scatter across a landscape. In the last two or three years, Jason Ur has been working assiduously to understand more about these systems of settlement. Jason's analyses provide reconstructions of the landscapes around tells, as well as estimates of the economic infrastructure that enabled them to grow and survive. The recently released CORONA satellite images (Cold War satellite images declassified in 2001) enable him to recognize the routes of ancient tracks or pathways that radiated out from the Bronze Age tells. Most importantly, they allow him to demonstrate how these routes enable the reconstruction of the pattern of cultivated lands around each of these sites. Because archaeological surveys have demonstrated that the tells in this part of northern Syria and Iraq are dated to the third millennium B.C., we are able to estimate

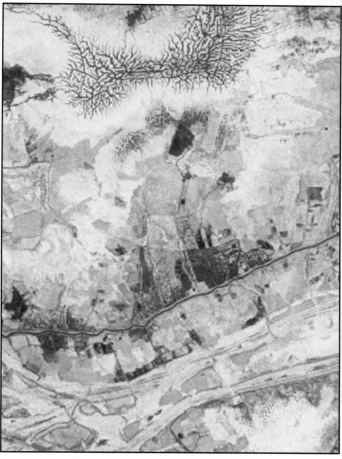

Figure 5. Detail of the landscape around Babylon as captured by a CORONA satellite image during the early 1970s. Note the distinctive soil pattern of gilgae features to the top and the ancient and recent canal traces at the base of the image and a little above respectively. Processed by Carrie Hritz (courtesy U.S. Geological Survey, used with permission)

the size of Bronze Age cultivated areas. This can be undertaken using three different approaches. First we can estimate the area of cultivation from the point where the tracks from the village settlements disappear or fade out (fig. 2). Next we can calculate the population of the settlements from their surface area on the satellite images or by means of field survey. From this figure, we can then estimate the amount of staple foods required to feed the population, and from this demand we can estimate the area of cultivated land required to produce those crops. The figures show these various estimates combined with a third factor, namely the area of land that could be cultivated by the plow teams referred to in cuneiform texts from the nearby site of Tell Beydar. Magnus Widell's analysis of the textual sources provides this additional estimate. These estimates suggest that these tells were surrounded with just enough cultivated land to support the community housed within the settlement. Although such analyses were not impossible using traditional techniques, they become much more efficient using GIS. Moreover, without the crucial information supplied by the satellite images (namely the points where the local tracks fade out), we would be without one of the fundamental data sources for reconstructing these 5,000 year old

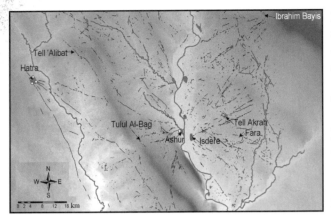

Figure 6. The road system radiating from the Assyrian capital of Ashur, superimposed on a topographic map. Processed by Mark Altaweel

landscapes. Even more important, I feel, is that GIS enable us to bring together and analyze evidence from archaeological field survey, excavations, satellite image analysis, and cuneiform texts within the same framework.

During the 1950s, 1960s, and 1970s, Robert McC. Adams and a number of colleagues here at the Oriental Institute undertook a grand sweep of archaeological surveys throughout the Mesopotamian plains and adjacent regions of Iran. With the advent of GIS, we are now able to take data from these surveys and re-analyze it against a backdrop of information derived from soil surveys, satellite images, and the changing pattern of past land use as provided by various forms of mapping over the last century or so. Carrie Hritz is currently analyzing an impressive database derived from the earlier surveys and is demonstrating just how densely the ancient Mesopotamian plains were populated (fig. 4). Not only was the density of settlements remarkably high, but also (as has long been known by the original surveyors of this landscape) these settlements are arranged in distinctive alignments that follow the patterns of former channels. Evidence of the actual channels is also forthcoming from the spoil banks that line some of the channels, as illustrated on an additional image from the neighborhood of Babylon (fig. 5).

Although the field of Assyriology has a long and illustrious history, it is unfortunate that until recently our understanding of the archaeology of everyday life of Assyrian communities has been rather meager. Now, Mark Altaweel (Department of Near Eastern Languages and Civilizations (NELC) student, CAMEL member) is contributing to our knowledge of the infrastructure of the Assyrian Empire. Specifically, around the early capital of Ashur, Mark has been able to recognize a remarkable pattern of roads that radiate from the capital city (fig. 6). Some of these are almost certainly of Assyrian date. Others, for example, the feature leading to the major Parthian city of Hatra, were clearly in use during or until Parthian times, that is into the early first millennium A.D. Such research adds considerably to our knowledge of how the Assyrian empire actually functioned.

Figure 7. Three-dimensional image of the Assyrian capital of Nimrud with detail of Assyrian canal (right foreground). Produced by draping a Corona satellite image over a digital terrain model of the Tigris Valley. Processed by Mark Altaweel (Corona image courtesy of U.S. Geological Survey, used with permission)

Other types of imaging provide new ways of looking at the landscape. For example, this dramatic three-dimensional view of the site of Nimrud demonstrates rather convincingly how the canal associated with the Nagub tunnel winds around the contours of the Tigris valley to bring water into the Assyrian capital of Nimrud (fig. 7).

In the west of the Fertile Crescent, Jesse Casana has been using CORONA images to study the archaeological resources of the Amuq Plain on behalf of the

Figure 8. Three-dimensional view of the Amuq Valley, showing landscape features visible on the surface of the plain. Processed by Jesse Casana (Corona image courtesy of U.S. Geological Survey, used with permission)

Amuq Valley Regional Project (fig. 8). Today, especially in summer when much of the valley floor is blanketed by a thick carpet of irrigated cotton, it is very difficult to recognize archaeological sites. Fortunately, the CORONA images were taken during the peak of the Cold War during the late 1960s and the early 1970s when agricultural systems were much less intensive. As a result, Jesse has been able to discern the faint soil or vegetation marks of numerous small archaeological sites. Significantly, many of these have eluded archaeological survey, both the original surveys of the late Robert Braidwood and our own more detailed studies.

One by-product of our work might be termed "applied archaeology." We have all witnessed the disastrous consequences of the looting of the Iraq Museum, but it is important to appreciate that in recent months the archaeological sites of Iraq have also suffered considerably, both from looting and from the ravages of war. Satellite images, taken over a period of some forty years (i.e., since the early 1960s), therefore provide a crucial and invaluable tool for monitoring archaeological sites as well as their preservation or loss. War is not the only force that results in the loss or damage to archaeological sites. These can be destroyed as a result of the expansion of agricultural lands or the development of roads, suburbs, and other forms of industrial urban land use. Satellite images are therefore ideally suited for the long-term assessment and monitoring of archaeological sites. Clearly this type of reconnaissance is particularly useful once the date and size of a site are known from field surveys. After this, it is then possible to monitor the recent life history (or the demise) of archaeological sites and to establish when they are under threat from encroaching developments or when they first started to be plundered. As McGuire Gibson points out, many sites in southern Mesopotamia have been so heavily plundered in the last few months that they now resemble waffles. Such types of damage is readily recognizable on high resolution satellite images, and these techniques therefore should contribute in future to the safe-guarding of archaeological heritage throughout the Near East.

CHICAGO ASSYRIAN DICTIONARY

Martha T. Roth

During 2002/2003, the staff of the Chicago Assyrian Dictionary (CAD) worked on the four remaining volumes of the dictionary, P, T, Ṭ, and U/W. Martha T. Roth, the Editor-in-Charge, devoted most of her attention to the P and Ṭ Volumes.

A major accomplishment this year was sending the Ṭ Volume out to the typesetter. We now have three volumes being typeset, P, T, and Ṭ, and the last remaining volume, U/W, is being written and edited. Roth spent autumn and winter reading the checked volume of Ṭ, evaluating all the changes, corrections, and suggestions that emerged from the checking process and from the comments of our outside consultant W. G. Lambert of the University of Birmingham and of the members of the editorial board. Research Associates Tim Collins, Gertrud Farber, Jennie Myers, and Joan Goodnick Westenholz labored in the preparation of Ṭ; our new colleague, Christopher Woods, fielded the occasional Sumerological query. The corrected final manuscript, prepared by our Manuscript Editor Linda McLarnan, was sent to Eisenbrauns for typesetting in April 2003. Eisenbrauns began work immediately on receiving the volume, and the CAD has already received the first set of galleys. These galleys were distributed in June to the editorial board members and our outside consultants to enhance their summer reading pleasure.

The members of the Editorial Board, Robert D. Biggs, John A. Brinkman, Miguel Civil, Walter Farber, Erica Reiner, Martha T. Roth, and Matthew W. Stolper, and our Consultants, Simo Parpola of the University of Helsinki and Klaas R. Veenhof of the University of Leiden, completed reading and commenting on the 1,108 first galleys of the P volume. Roth, with Research Associates Tim Collins and Jennie Myers, incorporated these comments into a corrected copy, which was returned to the typesetter. By June, we returned 900 of the first galleys, and those galleys have been set as page proofs. Additionally, Eisenbrauns has set all of the T Volume as first galleys, and we have page proofs for the first 250 galleys.

With the Ṭ Volume out the door and temporarily off her desk, Roth has been able to return to editing the final volume in the set, U/W. In this stage, she reads through the available draft manuscript of each word, evaluates the organization, and adds new references. Most of the draft manuscript for this volume has been prepared by Joan Goodnick Westenholz (Jerusalem), Hermann Hunger (University of Vienna), and Erica Reiner (Oriental Institute). Staff and visitors will continue to write draft articles for U/W during the coming year.

During 2002/2003, the CAD was assisted by visiting scholar Joan Westenholz and by Research Associates Tim Collins, Gertrud Farber, and Jennie Myers. Westenholz, on leave from her job as chief curator at the Bible Lands Museum Jerusalem, was with us for the summer and fall of 2002 and wrote many articles including *urigallu* "divine standard, staff" and *ūru* "roof." Collins wrote articles for the Ṭ and U/W Volumes, including *urpu* "cloud" and *uršu* "bedroom," and assisted Roth with the editing of P and Ṭ. Farber assisted with any queries involving lexical texts. Myers helped with the editing of P and Ṭ and the proofreading of P and T. Additionally, she, with the assistance of her husband Christopher Woods, produced a beautiful baby boy, Alexander Tristan Woods, on Mother's Day, May 11, 2003. Matthew Saba, a first-year student in the College, generously volunteered his time to the CAD during the academic year through the College Research Opportunities Program, and Jonathan Earling, after completing his first year in the College, began contributing his talents in June 2003.

CHICAGO DEMOTIC DICTIONARY

Janet H. Johnson

The staff of the Chicago Demotic Dictionary Project, Thomas Dousa, François Gaudard, and I, have continued the time-consuming job of checking and double-checking every entry and every reference included in the Dictionary. We have been ably assisted this year by several volunteers. Anne Nelson, David Berger, and David Frankhauser verified and corrected bibliographic entries for us; David Berger also began the laborious job of "reading" the thousands of cards in the dictionary files to make sure that they are all still in alphabetical order. Alejandro Botta has continued to be our expert on interconnections between Demotic and various Northwest Semitic languages.

As noted in previous *Annual Reports*, discussions with Gene Gragg, then Director of the Oriental Institute, and with Thomas Urban, of the Oriental Institute Publications Office, led us to decide to post completed files on the Internet in order to make them available around the world without waiting for the completion of the rest of the dictionary. There are at present eleven letter-files posted on the web, each containing the full entry for one letter of the Demotic "alphabet." In addition, there is an introduction to the dictionary, explaining its layout and the conventions used in preparing individual entries. Also included are supplementary files providing lists of abbreviations, including bibliographic abbreviations and abbreviations used in referring to individual texts. Last year, we added a file called "Problematic Entries," calling on colleagues around the world to help us resolve problems of reading and meaning.

I am delighted to say that this is beginning to happen. At the beginning of this academic year, the 8th International Congress of Demotists was held in Würzburg. My status report on the dictionary highlighted how much we have accomplished and stressed our need for assistance to resolve the numerous problems which remain. I illustrated this point with several specific examples on which we were currently working. I received some immediate feedback from participants about those particular questions. Even more importantly, we are now regularly receiving comments and suggestions for additions or corrections to the letters (and problems file) which are posted online. Indeed, two of our German colleagues, Friedhelm Hoffmann and Joachim Quack, have been extremely helpful in pointing out typos, noting alternatives, and providing unpublished or recently published references. All additions and corrections are entered into the "master" file kept on the Macintosh computer in the Demotic Dictionary office. Eventually, updated Portable Document Format (PDF) files of letters which have been posted will be prepared and the old files archived electronically (so that they can be accessed on request, to check the original version).

In addition to the eleven letter-files currently online, there are four more files prepared for electronic publishing for which all the problems which had been identified over the years have now been addressed and resolved, if possible; all the scans and hand copies have been prepared; all the cross-references have been entered; and the final proofread has been completed. The "Problematic Entries" file continues to grow and an updated version of that file is also ready to be posted. Those five files will be posted beginning this summer, as the Publications Office finds time to do their checks and prepare the online documents. Perhaps a few statistics would be useful. The thirteen files which are online amount to almost 825 pages: the introduction and lists of abbreviations are 65 pages long, the eleven letter-files are almost 700 pages total,[1] and the file containing problematic entries is almost 60 pages long. There have been over 7,000 "hits" on the CDD (Chicago Demotic Dictionary) web-page during the last year and over 1,500 people have downloaded the "prologue" (introduction and abbreviations) during that time. The nine letter-files which have been up for over a year have been downloaded an average of 700 times during the current academic year (and, on average, about 1,700 times overall). The two letter-files posted in the fall of 2002 have been downloaded 1,500 and 850 times, respectively. But what is very heartening for us is that the "Problematic Entries" file, which was posted last spring, was downloaded over 1,400 times this year (and over 2,100 times in total). That means that a lot of people are thinking about our problems, and there is a good chance some of them will be solved.

The four letter-files which are ready for the Publications Office are larger, on average,[2] and amount to another 475 pages. That means that, once these four letter-files are posted, we will have over 1,150 pages, accounting for over half the letters of the Demotic alphabet, completed and available. For practical reasons, many of the first letters to be finished were the letters with the smallest number of entries, and the letter-files for several of the remaining nine letters will be much bigger than the letter-files completed so far — they range from 150 to 260 pages each as they currently stand and amount to another 1,150 pages overall. And so we will continue to work our way through these nine long letter-files, trying to resolve problems, incorporate all the scans and hand copies, make all the cross-references, and generally proofread one more time.

I have, over the years, talked about different aspects of dictionary making and of the range of vocabulary attested in Demotic. Many of you may find it interesting to know how the Egyptians conceptualized their own language/writing systems. At the end of the Decree of Canopus, one of the so-called "trilingual" decrees set up by the Egyptian priesthood to honor various Ptolemaic rulers, it is stated that various officials are supposed to write the text of the decree on a monument of stone or copper to be posted in the open areas of the first, second, and third class temples of Egypt. It further indicates that the text is to be written in the "writing of the 'house of life,' document-writing, and the writing of the Greeks." The "house of life" was an institution associated with temples, serving as a scriptorium, library, and center for performance of rituals. The writing of the "house of life" was hieroglyphs, the script used in the topmost inscription of

---

1. And range in size from F, only ten pages long, and Y, only fifteen pages, to ꜣ (*aleph*), 110 pages long, and Ḏ, 100 pages.

2. Although G is only 75 pages long, Q is 100 and ꜥ (*ayin*) and N are 150 each.

the trilingual. In the Rosetta Stone, another of these trilingual decrees in honor of Ptolemaic rulers, the hieroglyphs are called the "script of the divine word." The Demotic section, in the middle of the decree, is here, and elsewhere, referred to as "document-writing." This name reflects the fact that Demotic, when it first came into use, was used exclusively for personal documents (letters, contracts, and so on). Gradually Demotic replaced hieratic (a cursive script derived from hieroglyphs) for administrative documents and then for literary, including religious, texts. Hieroglyphs continued to be used for formal monumental inscriptions. Most classical Greek authors who discussed Egyptian scripts distinguished between a "sacred" script (hieroglyphs and hieratic) and a "popular" (Herodotus's δημοτικά) script. Greek texts written in Egypt usually distinguished two Egyptian scripts, the sacred and the "Egyptian" (as in the above-mentioned Canopus Decree). Clement of Alexandria, writing in the second or third century of our era, distinguished all three Egyptian scripts: ἱερογλυφική "hieroglyphic," ἱερατική "hieratic," and ἐπιστολογραφική "epistolary."

Greek was not, of course, the only non-Egyptian language and script with which Demotic-writing Egyptians came into contact. During the time of the Persian Empire, before 330 B.C. and before Alexander and the Ptolemies, Aramaic was the lingua franca of the Near East. Numerous documents written in Aramaic have been found in Egypt. Many of these were personal documents written by or for Persian administrators or Aramaic-speaking immigrants or settlers in Egypt, especially the communities of mercenaries settled at various posts throughout Egypt (including the Jewish colony at Elephantine). But some official documents were also written in Aramaic. One such document was a summary of the laws of Egypt, drafted by senior Egyptian "soldiers, priests, and scribes" at the request of the Persian King Darius. Although no copy of this "code" of the laws of Egypt has been preserved, a reference to its composition is found in a short Demotic text (currently in the Bibliothèque Nationale in Paris) which notes that copies were prepared in the "writing of (As)syria" (i.e., Aramaic) and in "document writing" (i.e., Demotic). One assumes that this compilation was made to enable Persian administrators to run Egypt, but it is important to note that they were to do so according to Egyptian law and custom.

I must end this report on what is, for the Demotic Dictionary, a sad note. Tom Dousa, who has been the mainstay of the Dictionary for many years, has now moved to Indiana to pursue a career in library science. Tom's mastery of the difficult Demotic script, his intensive and extensive bibliographic knowledge, and his meticulous attention to detail have helped make the Dictionary the great resource it has become. He will be greatly missed for his academic contributions and for himself — his warm collegiality, his generosity, and his great sense of humor. We wish him all the best as he moves forward in his new career.

CHICAGO HITTITE DICTIONARY

Theo van den Hout

At the Chicago Hittite Dictionary (CHD) we had a good and productive year. As usual, work on the dictionary proceeded at various levels. Harry Hoffner and Theo van den Hout met regularly to transform first or intermediate drafts of words for the next fascicle or installment that is due. Such sessions are prepared by van den Hout, who makes all the necessary changes and checks practically all references in a draft and then passes it on to Hoffner for comments and additions. In the process, our outside consultants Gary Beckman (Ann Arbor, University of Michigan), Craig Melchert (Chapel Hill, University of North Carolina), and Gernot Wilhelm (Julius-Maximilians-Universität, Würzburg, Germany) are regularly queried. In their meetings, Hoffner and van den Hout establish a definitive text. Richard Beal, one of our two Senior Research Associates (SRA), implements all changes in the computer version of the draft so that the dictionary entry is ready to go! Van den Hout and Hoffner have reached almost the end of the enormous amount of Hittite words starting in *šar-*. This means that our goal to publish the second fascicle of the letter Š of about the same size as Š/1 (208 pages) in 2004 is right on track.

Meanwhile Senior Research Associates Richard Beal and Oğuz Soysal continued writing first drafts of words for our next letter T. The T volume will be even larger than the Š volume and it is important that as much as possible is ready in first draft by the time we publish the last installment of Š and start preparing for T/1 (2006–2007). In this, Richard and Oğuz received very valuable help from our guest Research Associate, Alice Mouton. Alice is a Ph.D. student from Paris in the very final stages of her dissertation (Paris-Leiden) who joined us in January 2003 for one calendar year. She received a Programme Lavoisier scholarship from the French Minis-

Research Associate Alice Mouton and visiting graduate student Petra Goedegebuure

try of Foreign Affairs. In her characteristically enthusiastic manner, she has helped us in many ways and has, among other things, written many first drafts already.

Kathleen Mineck, our new half-time staff member, continued the work of keeping up our file collection. She is well known to the Oriental Institute community and a Ph.D. student in the department. Newly published texts were entered by her into the CHD server and cards were made ready to be parsed and filed. In between, Kathleen assists van den Hout in specific queries concerning final drafts on which he is working. Students working for the CHD this year and doing the parsing and filing work were Natasha Bershadsky, Dennis Campbell, and Andrei Chatskov.

Sadly, Hripsime Haroutunian, the predecessor of Kathleen Mineck, who had been on the dictionary team for almost ten, years left us in the fall of 2002 to become lecturer for Armenian here at the University of Chicago. We greatly appreciate everything she has done for us and meant to the CHD during all those years. We wish her all the best in her new job!

Thanks to Sandra Schloen, substantial progress has been made on the electronic version of the Chicago Hittite Dictionary. A representative sample of almost one hundred entries of the P volume has been converted to XML format and stored efficiently in a Tamino (Internet-based) database. These entries can be displayed in a live document view which mimics the format of the printed version but provides additional features like content-based, color-coded links and cross-references. A Java-based interface is currently being developed to provide tools for navigating, querying, and viewing the data.

We had several visitors again this year: Petra Goedegebuure from the University of Amsterdam was here during the month of November to do some final checking on the material for her dissertation. Billie-Jean Collins, from Emory University and previous Research Associate on the CHD, visited us and consulted the files in December. Willemijn Waal from Amsterdam and Andrei Chatskov from St. Petersburg consulted our files and used the Research Archives to work on their respective Master's Theses. Both were at the Oriental Institute for a full quarter. Ian Rutherford came from the University of Reading in Great Britain.

Together with our Director of Development Debora Donato, both Hoffner and van den Hout went to Los Angeles for the April 4 premiere of the movie *The Hittites* by Tolga Örnek (for which, see *2001/2002 Annual Report*, pp. 30–31). We expect this documentary will raise public awareness of the Hittites and their history, which should be a great help to us in our fund raising efforts for the coming years. This brings us to last year's highlight: we received another grant from the National Endowment for the Humanities (NEH) for the year 2003/2004. That will be our last regular NEH grant before we submit the Challenge Grant in November!

DIYALA PROJECT

Clemens D. Reichel

Despite many obstacles and challenges during the year 2002/2003, we moved substantially closer to our goal of electronically publishing all the 15,000 objects from Tell Agrab, Tell Asmar, Ishchali, and Khafaje, four sites excavated by the Oriental Institute in the Diyala Region in Iraq between 1930 and 1936.

This has been a difficult year for our project, first and foremost due to the tragic events that happened in Iraq. Months before the war started, scholars publicly expressed concern about the threats that military combat poses, not only to archaeological sites but also to museums (for the impact of the war in Iraq on archaeological sites and the looting of the Iraq Museum, see McGuire Gibson's Nippur and Iraq at Time of War and my Iraq Museum Project in this *Annual Report*). Our worst fears seemed to have come true in the days following April 9, when newspaper reports and initial television clips suggested a total loss of the Iraq Museum's collection. Such a catastrophe, too staggering for an archaeologist to grasp, would also have meant a loss of 50% of the Diyala material (ca. 8,000 objects), including most the finest pieces from these excavations. Thanks to the foresight of the museum staff, who removed many objects from the exhibition or stored them off-site before the war, the initial estimates fortunately turned out to be too high. Yet, there is no reason to celebrate. Some 12,000 objects are currently (July 2003) confirmed to have disappeared from the museum's storerooms, among them 4,875 cylinder seals. This is a particularly tragic loss for Mesopotamian scholarship. Often made of precious stone (e.g., lapis lazuli, hematite, jasper, and carnelian) and decorated with elaborate designs, cylinder seals have been major collectors' items ever since interest in the ancient Near East awoke. As a result, most of the seals known today (no statistics have ever been published but 90% or more seems like a reasonably cautious guess) came from the antiquities market. This leaves many questions open concerning their provenience, chronological placement, as well as their authenticity. The cylinder seals at the Iraq Museum represented the largest collection of properly excavated Mesopotamian seals, which explains why their loss or decimation is so devastating to us.

To those of us who are working on the Diyala material there is a personal component to this tragedy. Excavations on other sites in Iraq such as Ur, Uruk, Nippur, Girsu, Assur, and Nuzi have recovered truly spectacular seals. However, in terms of absolute numbers, periods, and styles represented, the corpus of 1,235 seals recovered in the Diyala excavations remains unmatched. In fact, the Diyala seals still are the backbone for Mesopotamia's seal chronology between 3300 and 1800 B.C. The significance of this corpus was not lost on Henri Frankfort, the field director of the Diyala expeditions, who in 1955 published the monograph *Stratified Cylinder Seals from the Diyala Region* in the Oriental Institute Publication series (OIP 72). Even now, reading the words "stratified" and "cylinder seals" in sequence may strike some scholars as odd — for too long seals have been treated and published as art objects in museums, far removed from the dirt that once covered and dated them. We can barely imagine the impact that Frankfort's decision to publish the Diyala seals *not* sorted by iconographic themes and stylistic dates *but by archaeological site, level, and locus* must have had on scholarship. Its long-term effect may not even have been clear to Frankfort, but we are certainly more than grateful for his visionary idea. Since 1955, the correlation between stylistic dates (such as Jemdet Nasr, Mesilim, or Fara style) and absolute year dates has been subject to substantial realignments, which makes cross comparisons between seals from different sites, let alone with objects from other artifact categories, difficult if not impossible. The Diyala seals remain one of the few *cor-*

pora for which chronology can be re-evaluated based on its archaeological sequence and where chronological, as well as functional, correlations with other artifact categories such as reliefs, sculpture, and pottery from the same context can be studied. It is therefore more than distressing to learn that as many as 600 of these seals — about half of this corpus — may have been lost in the looting of the Iraq Museum. Needless to say, we expect that other artifact categories have been affected by the museum looting as well — as yet we still have little information as to which objects have been looted or damaged.

Such is the impact that the tragic events in Iraq have left on us. Our ongoing database work, despite the upheavals of the last year and many sidetracks, still proceeded with success. This is largely thanks to George Sundell, who joined our project in the fall of 2000 and who has been working on the transfer of the Diyala database to a new, web-compatible layout with Oracle 9-i as its back-end application. As described in last year's report, George and I have been working on a new layout that will allow systematic searches while preserving the data integrity of the original records with all its idiosyncrasies. By creating a virtual archive on the web, including not only photographs and descriptions of objects but also all the archival material such as field plans, diaries, and locus cards, users will be able to evaluate and question our own interpretations. Access to all the archival Diyala material through the web will allow primary research to be conducted on this material without the necessity of travel to Chicago.

Laying out such a model in theory was one step. Implementing it is quite another matter, as we learned in the course of the last year. Naturally, we anticipated that numerous problems would show up during this process. While all of them have so far been solved, they forced us to do a lot of rethinking in the way we structure and link our data. A database layout is based on logically and systematically defined relationships between distinct elements of information, and its success is dependent on consistency in data entry. Last fall, we ran into problems when we started to work on archaeological provenience data, information concerning the find context of the objects. Figure 1 illustrates some of the issues with which we had to deal. It shows an isometric view and two sections of a hypothetical excavation area (Area A), in which two consecutive levels (Level I and II) are exposed. Both Level I and II contain distinct, different buildings, whose rooms are labeled with locus numbers. In most recording systems a locus number is kept unique and not reused at a lower level. If index tables for the correlation between locus numbers-to-level and level-to-locus numbers are available, a unique locus number also identifies the level at which the room with this number was found. So much for the theory. Three typical situations, mapped out in figure 1 in isometric and section view and marked contexts *a–c,* show how the reality in the Diyala field recording could differ from the theory:

> *a* — a room (Locus 1) in Level I overlays two rooms (Locus 2 and 3) at Level II.

> *b* — a room (Locus 4) in Level I largely overlaps a room in Level II. While the change of level was observed and recorded, the locus number was not changed for some reason. Although at different levels, both rooms are labeled Locus 4.

> *c* — The dashed line between Level I and II indicates that the change between these levels was not noticed and therefore not recorded during the excavation. The rooms at both levels are labeled Locus 5.

Such differences in archaeological field observations impact the level of detail to which the archaeological provenience of an object can be narrowed. In context *a,* the locus numbers are unique within the area. An object recorded from Locus 1 *has* to be from Level I, while an object from Locus 3 *has* to be from Level II, even if the level is not spelled out in the object register.

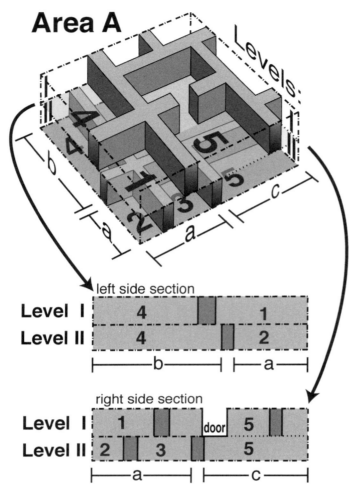

left side section

Level I 4 1
Level II 4 2

right side section

Level I .... 1 .... door 5
Level II .... 2 .... 3 5

Figure 1. ARCHAEOLOGICAL REALITIES encountered during an excavation often result in notable inconsistencies in the recording of features. This isometric view of a hypothetical excavation area (A) with two superimposed archaeological levels (I and II) shows three contexts with different recording scenarios, also shown in two sections. In a the difference in level was noted and different locus numbers were used for the rooms in the Level I and II; in b the levels were kept separate but the locus number was not changed when penetrating into Level II; in c the change from Level A to B remained unobserved, making it impossible to separate the archaeological material from this context by levels. Such different qualities in digging and recording complicate the systematic processing of archaeological data in a computer database

The uniqueness of locus numbers is missing in contexts *b* and *c*. In *b*, the change of levels was noticed and recorded, so objects can be assigned to their proper level and building despite the ambiguity of the locus number. In *c*, however, no level was recorded at all, making it impossible to distinguish an artifact assemblage by level and building in this case. When trying to create a structural layout for an archaeological database (fig. 2), the lack of uniqueness in some values and the occasional absence of other values have their consequences. Traditional models assume a hierarchy of site subdivisions ordered by area, level and locus (fig. 2.1), areas are divided into levels and levels into loci. Such a layout could easily be adapted into a relational database, if levels names are kept unique within areas and locus numbers are unique within both areas and levels. However, as figure 2.2 shows, only context *a* with its unique locus numbers per level meets this demand. In context *b* the locus number is not unique to a level, creating an ambiguity in the data structure. Since no level was recorded for context *c* it would be impossible to link area and locus in the layout given in figure 2.

Quite clearly, the Diyala archaeological sequence required a more flexible layout. While the sequence had to be systematic and searchable it also had to reflect the idiosyncrasies of individual excavators and the differences in the quality of the original records. It took George and me several attempts and a clear departure from our own traditional concept of how to structure archaeological data to come up with a satisfying solution. The model we chose to employ is shown in figure 3. Instead of putting area, levels, and loci into separate, hierarchically linked tables we now put them all into one table (called "Object Table") that contains their names and descriptive elements. A separate table ("Relationship Table") expresses links between objects and the nature of their relationship. Area A and Level I, for example, can be linked and their relationship expressed as "Area A 'contains' Level I." Area A also "contains" Level II, while the relationship between Levels I and II is that "Level I 'is above' Level II." The attraction of this layout is its flexibility. The relationship between Area A and Locus 5 from context *c* can now be defined by the expression "Area A 'contains' Locus 5" even if no level has been recorded. All known relationships between units of site subdivisions can be expressed systematically without losing idiosyncrasies in data recording, but none of them is mandatory. The possibilities in expressing relationships are almost endless — relationships between loci could be expressed (e.g., "Locus 2 'abuts' Locus 3"); features found within a locus (e.g., pits, hearths, benches) could be added as a further subdivision of a locus into the Object Table; features that extend into several loci (e.g., drains) can be linked to any locus that they pass through without duplicating descriptions. Multiple relationships can also be expressed — a locus, for example, can "contain" a drain but also be "cut" by it. Control mechanisms can be turned on to prevent contradiction if requested (e.g., a level that is "above" another level cannot also be "below" it) but can also be disabled to faithfully reflect contradictions as they are found in the field notes.

This example shows one of the typical daily challenges that one encounters when trying to enter "old" data into a computer database systematically. Physically, we may have shifted from paper to electronic data a while ago, yet we are still learning how to overcome the restrictions that the two-dimensional data layout on paper once imposed. To some this work may seem tedious, but most archaeological data from the Near East is "old data" from excavations that were undertaken long before the common use of computers in archaeology. The lessons learned with the Diyala material will be more than useful for other web-based publication projects.

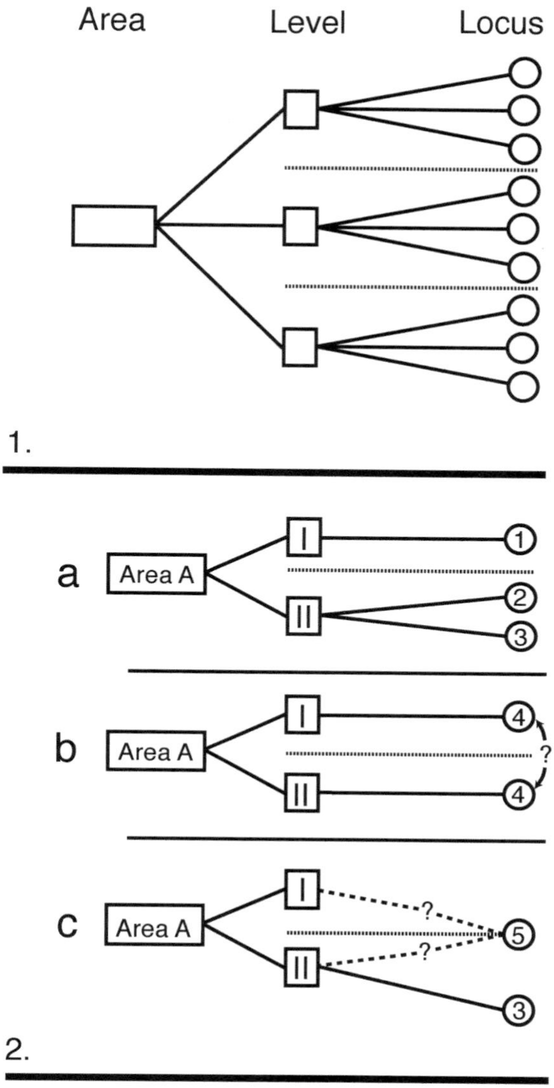

Figure 2.1–2. TRADITIONAL ARCHAEOLOGICAL DATA MODELS (fig. 2.1) rely on a hierarchical relationship between area, level, and locus. Figure 2.2, which displays data models for contexts a–c recorded in figure 1, shows, however, that only context a can be processed and linked properly in this layout; the evidence from b creates an ambiguity in the data structure since the locus number is not unique to a level; in c the absence of a recorded level precludes any link between area and locus

At this point, the data transferal of the archaeological material is nearing its end. Parts of the physical object descriptions have already been transferred, others still need to be dealt with, though most of it should be accomplished within the next year. A major challenge remains in the addition of digital photographs and scans. The recent events in Iraq have changed our outlook

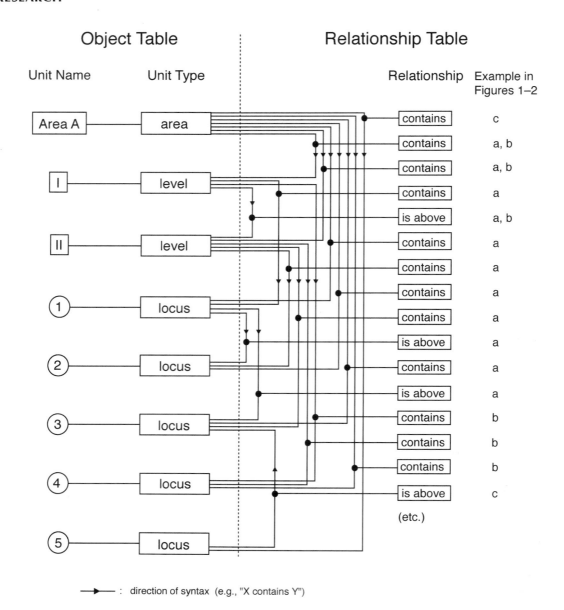

Figure 3. *AN OBJECT-ORIENTED DATABASE allows the entry of archaeological data without a strict hierarchical layout. The left side shows site subdivisions (here area, levels, and locus numbers from contexts a to c in fig. 1) that have been entered into an object table; relationships between these entries are expressed by links via a relationship table on the right side, that contains expressions of relationships. Since no link is mandatory and no relationship is dependent on the presence of another one, the idiosyncrasies of archaeological field records can be reflected faithfully without losing the ability to do systematic future data searches*

concerning the photographs of the Diyala objects. Whether destined for Chicago or the Iraq Museum, almost all objects were photographed during the 1930s excavations using a large-format camera. Between 1996 and 1998, these images were scanned by a Diyala Project volunteer. Since we did not have the technological means to scan negatives of this size, they were scanned from photographic prints. A scanner capable of handling large-format negatives became available in 1998 in the University of Chicago's Digital Media Lab. We mainly scanned the negatives of excavation photographs — only negatives of object photographs for which no print could be found were also scanned. We immediately recognized the by-far-superior quality of these scans compared to those from photographic prints. By that time, however, Betsy Kremers and I had already started to take new photographs of Diyala objects at the Oriental Institute, which were scanned by a professional lab and burned onto CDs. The quality of these new images, taken with 35 mm single lens reflex cameras and macro lenses, clearly surpassed those from the 1930s, which often contained more than a dozen objects in one photograph. We decided to re-photograph wherever possible and, as a first step, to concentrate on the documentation of the Oriental Institute Diyala material. We had hoped that sooner or later the political situation in Iraq would improve, the embargo following the 1991 Gulf War would be lifted, and we would be able to re-photograph the Diyala material in Baghdad as well. The looting of the Iraq Museum obviously forced us to rethink this plan. With so much uncertainty left as to which objects have been stolen, the old field photographs are, at least for the time being, our main and sometimes only image source for Diyala objects in the Iraq Museum. For the moment we will "content" ourselves with the positives of those photographs that we have already scanned. However, we will soon start to scan the original negatives in order to have these images at the best possible quality. Due to insufficient fixation while in the field, some of these negatives have deteriorated over time. Digital imagery helps reduce these effects and remove scratches or fingerprints. Figure 4, a photograph of three stone vessels, gives an example of a typical Diyala negative; figure 5 shows the positive of a cleaned-up high-resolution scan of the negative featuring two of these vessels. Even if photographs taken from other angles would be necessary for exhaustive publication, these objects can be considered as adequately documented.

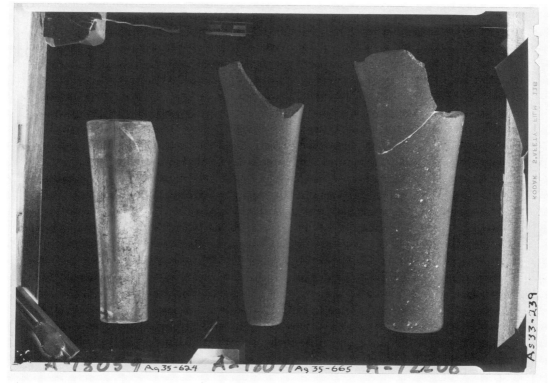

Figure 4. A DIYALA FIELD NEGATIVE showing three stone vessels. The field numbers of the objects were added in handwriting, to which the museum numbers were added later. The negative has suffered numerous scratches and shows cracks and signs of brittleness along its edges

Figure 5. A DIGITAL POSITIVE of two of the stone vessels shown in figure 4. Digital modifications can help significantly reduce the effect of aging and handling on the image quality found in old negatives

Thanks to Betsy's tireless work, the photographic documentation of Diyala objects at the Oriental Institute itself has been progressing well and so far resulted in about 6,500 new photographs. Photographs were taken with a 35 mm SLR on black and white film; these images were then scanned by a professional lab and returned to us on CDs. This system had worked well for us and resulted in excellent pictures, but a significant drop in prices for digital SLRs recently encouraged us to upgrade to a Nikon digital SLR with a macro lens. With an image size of 6.1 Megapixel, the photographs taken with it are of a high resolution and of publication quality. Working with this camera will speed up photography dramatically and allow for a much faster turnover, since images will now be available for immediate use.

We are currently trying to raise sufficient funds to upgrade our computer equipment, hire student assistants, and pay programmers to work on the browser interface for the database. While plenty of work remains to be done, we hope to launch a first version of the Diyala website within 2003/2004. Launching this site, however, will just be the beginning of a process that we anticipate to take years. Once it is up and running, scholars worldwide will be able to study this material and undertake a more detailed analysis of object categories, which will give us a chance to update our site and add information as it becomes available. Many field notes, catalogues, object cards, and plans still need to be scanned and added to the "Virtual Diyala Archive" in the next few years. As can be seen from this report, launching an electronic publication of this size poses substantial logistical challenges. Unlike a book publication it will also require maintenance, frequent software and data updates, and, therefore, a long-term commitment by the Oriental Institute to host and maintain it. In this respect, the Diyala Project will be a first — both a milestone and test case. Hopefully, it will soon be followed by other electronic publications of this kind.

The financial contributions of numerous private donors have supported the Diyala Project this year. To all of them go our most heartfelt thanks for their generosity.

EPIGRAPHIC SURVEY

W. Raymond Johnson

The Epigraphic Survey completed its seventy-ninth, six-month field season in Luxor, Egypt, on April 15, 2003. Epigraphic and conservation work continued at Medinet Habu in the small Amun temple of Hatshepsut and Thutmose III, in the Hatshepsut sanctuaries, and the bark sanctuary and ambulatory of Thutmose III. Paint collation and large-format final publication photography continued in the two central Hatshepsut sanctuaries after the painted reliefs were cleaned by the conservation crew. Restoration work was completed on the rooftop of the entire Eighteenth Dynasty temple, including channels and drain spouts for directing rainwater off the roof. New sandstone flooring was completed in the central sanctuary room, two floor slabs were laid in the northwesternmost "naos" room, and sandstone wall patches were placed in the back central sanctuary. At Luxor Temple, 227 meters of new damp-coursed brick storage and treatment platforms were constructed for the decorated sandstone wall fragments formerly on the ground, 6,311 decorated wall fragments were raised from the damp ground onto the new mastabas, and 80 meters of covered aluminum framing were installed over selected wall fragment treatment and storage platforms for additional protection of deteriorating wall fragments awaiting treatment. Analysis suggests that a considerable amount of the fragmentary material at Luxor Temple was quarried in the Middle Ages from the Mut Temple precinct at Karnak.

Small Amun Temple of Hatshepsut and Thutmose III at Medinet Habu

The epigraphic team continued its ongoing documentation work in the Medinet Habu small Amun temple of Hatshepsut and Thutmose III from October 21, 2002 to April 15, 2003, and made excellent progress on all fronts (fig. 1). One new Egyptologist / Epigrapher, Jen Kimpton, was trained on-site this season, and she also very capably supervised the Chicago House library. The primary epigraphic work of the season focused on material for volumes 1 and 2 of the small Amun temple publication series. Penciling, inking, and collating of facsimile drawings took place in the Eighteenth Dynasty bark sanctuary and ambulatory, including the façade, for volume 2. The paint collation of the six interior chapels, the focus of volume 1, also continued; the front central sanctuary was completed, and paint collation was begun in the back central sanctuary. In all, seventeen drawings from these two rooms were paint collated by the artists and epigraphers, then reviewed and passed by the director for publication (fig. 2). Staff

Figure 1. Epigraphers Brett McClain and Randy Shonkwiler collating at the small Amun temple, Medinet Habu. Digital photograph by Ray Johnson

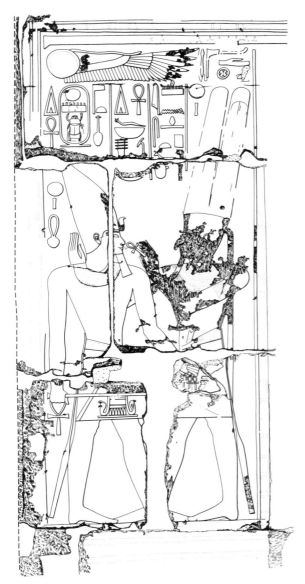

Figure 2. Inscribed wall surface MHB 32, front central sanctuary, west wall left side, small temple of Amun at Medinet Habu. Hatshepsut (name changed to Thutmose III) being offered life by Amun. Facsimile drawing by Sue Osgood and Margaret De Jong. Photograph by Yarko Kobylecky

Photographer Yarko Kobylecky, assisted by Photograph Archives Assistant Ellie Smith and Photo Archivist Sue Lezon, photographed pre- and post-conservation sanctuary walls with 4 × 5 B&W and color transparency film in the two central sanctuaries for the volume 1 publication. Our schedule calls for all of the material for this volume to be finished by the end of next season, and production of that volume to begin next summer.

A total of thirty-nine new drawings for volumes 1 and 2 of the small Amun temple series were penciled at the wall by Artists Tina Di Cerbo, Margaret De Jong (fig. 3), Susan Osgood, and Will Schenck — assisted occasionally at the hard-to-reach places by Assistant to the Director Emily Napolitano — and eleven new drawings were inked. Eleven additional drawings were collated by Epigraphers J. Brett McClain, Harold Hays, Randy Shonkwiler, and Jen Kimpton at the wall, and the artists transferred corrections to eighteen drawings that were checked and passed by the epigraphers. Director's checks were completed by me on twenty drawings, which are now ready for publication.

Egyptologist / Artist Tina Di Cerbo compiled a database this season of all the known graffiti in the Medinet Habu precinct, including over 1,450 individual entries with negative numbers, locations, and descriptions. This was a process begun by the Epigraphic Survey more than seventy years ago, but never completed. William Edgerton's publication, *Medinet Habu Graffiti Facsimiles* (OIP 36; Chicago, 1937), and Heinz Thissen's *Die demotischen Graffiti von Medinet Habu: Zeugnisse zu Tempel und Kult im Ptolemaïschen Ägypten* (Demotische Studien 10; Sommerhausen, 1989) present a sample of this material, although luckily much more of it was actually photographed in the past. Tina is matching graffiti to photographs, identifying new ones, plotting the locations on key plans, and continuing the facsimile documentation of the material for eventual publication (fig. 4). In addition, Tina compiled another illustrated database for use as a paleographical reference by the artists and epigraphers based on scanned finished drawings for volumes 1 and 2 of the small Amun temple. The electronic paleography includes hieroglyphic signs (by Gardiner number), examples of cartouches, human and divine figures, and iconographic elements printed out for use on-site at the temple.

This season marked the seventh year of a grant approved by the Supreme Council of Antiquities from the Egyptian Antiquities Project of the American Research Center for documentation and conservation of the small Amun temple at Medinet Habu. As in past years, this season's conservation work focused on the rooftop over the Eighteenth Dynasty temple and inside the painted chapels. Senior Conservator Lotfi Hassan and Conservators Adel Aziz Andraws, Nahed Samir, and Lamia Hadidy completed the cleaning of the painted reliefs in the two middle sanctuary chambers with excellent results (fig. 5). They extracted salts from the lower wall sections where the humidity was greatest and replaced deteriorated mortar where necessary between the wall courses with hydraulic lime and sandstone powder in distilled water. Sepiolite and distilled water poultices were applied effectively to wall surfaces for cleaning and desalination. Organic solvents used in the cleaning process included Butylamine, Dimethyl Sulphoxide, and Dimethyle Formamide, depending on the nature of the dirt and deposit on the stone surface. Paraloid B72 and Paraloid 44 were used as surface consolidation of the paint layer in selected areas. On the west wall of the front sanctuary, left side (MHB 32; see fig. 2), a small sandstone fragment preserving the king's hand grasping *ankh*-signs was re-affixed to its original position on the wall. Artist Margaret DeJong added that detail to the facsimile drawing, after which it went through the normal collation process.

This spring, Stonecutter Dany Roy completed the restoration and stabilization of the small Amun temple sanctuary roof, one of the major goals of the grant project (fig. 6). He completed the grouting of the entire Eighteenth Dynasty temple roof area and the restoration of missing roof blocks over the bark sanctuary and ambulatory. In all, thirty-five new sandstone slabs (covering approximately 5 square meters in total surface) were laid over the bark sanctuary this season, and sixteen original sandstone blocks were dismantled and reinstalled. In addition, he installed three new stainless steel drain spouts which now direct rainwater off the roof, two off the south side and one off the north. Dany stabilized the westernmost roof block over the bark sanctuary by reinforcing it with five stainless steel dowels set in araldite (two 1 cm in diameter, 70 cm in length; and three 1 cm in diameter, 25 cm long). Dany also stabilized a roof block in the back central sanctuary with four stainless steel dowels set in araldite (two 2 cm in diameter and 100 cm in length; two 0.5 cm in diameter by 30 cm in length).

In the front central sanctuary, Dany laid two last floor slabs (95 × 55 × 15 cm; and 85 × 75 × 15 cm), which completes the new flooring for that chamber (fig. 7). In the

Figure 3. Epigraphic Survey Artist Margaret DeJong penciling at the small Amun temple bark sanctuary, Medinet Habu. Digital photograph by Ray Johnson

Figure 4. Tina Di Cerbo copying graffiti in the small Amun temple front central sanctuary, Medinet Habu. Digital photograph by Ray Johnson

back central sanctuary, he carved and placed two sandstone wall patches in the bottom eastern section of the south wall (40 × 27 × 8 cm; and 40 × 25 × 8 cm). In the northwesternmost sanctuary, the "naos room," Dany laid two new floor blocks (40 × 27 cm and 40 × 25 cm), both 8 cm thick. He also carved a new sandstone threshold slab for the new entryway to the sanctuary area with an emplacement for the new doorway that will be installed next season. Dany also designed and began the installation of the aluminum framing of the new skylight over the first chamber, which will be completed next fall.

Luxor Temple

This year marked the end of the grant approved by the Supreme Council of Antiquities from the Egyptian Antiquities Project (EAP) of the American Research Center in Egypt (ARCE), for the protection and consolidation of deteriorating decorated sandstone wall fragments at Luxor Temple. Our sincerest thanks go to ARCE and EAP for this invaluable assistance, which has allowed the preservation of thousands of wall fragments for future analysis and restoration. Stone Conservators John Stewart and Hiroko Kariya are preparing the final report for the six seasons of treatment funded by the grant. Because of the Iraq war, Field Conservator Hiroko had to postpone her return to Luxor to monitor the condition of the treated material until next fall.

With the assistance of a Robert Wilson matching grant and the World Monuments Fund (WMF), the Epigraphic Survey successfully completed the second year of a two-year funded program to raise all of the decorated stone wall fragments in the Luxor Temple precinct up off the wet ground onto protective, damp-coursed platforms designated by category. The results were spectacular. This season, 216 additional meters of damp-coursed storage and treatment mastabas were constructed in ordered, numbered rows around the temple precinct south of the Abul Haggag mosque on the east (fig. 8), directly east of the Colonnade Hall, and west of the Ramesside first court by the Roman gateway. An 11 meter platform was constructed at the southern end of the precinct. 6,311 decorated wall fragments (not counting the thousands of uninscribed blocks) were raised from the ground onto the new, damp-coursed platforms for storage, conservation, and analysis (fig. 9), including over 3,000 Akhenaten *talatat* blocks. In the west area, nine new platforms were constructed between the Roman gate and the fragments of the partly reassembled Ramesses II granodiorite colossus, with ample space intentionally left around the colossus for any future restoration work there. Thanks to the diligence of Blockyard Assistant Jamie Riley (my right hand at Luxor Temple) and our remarkable workmen Mohamed, Mustafa, Saoud, Saber, Sayid, Hassan, and Ali, we were able to accomplish all of our goals for the season, and then some! We still have some large blocks to raise next season, but the bulk of the protective work is done. My heartfelt thanks to WMF for its vital assistance at this critical time.

There were surprises. This winter, during the sorting process, over two hundred decorated fragments were isolated for reassembly in the blockyard east of the Amenhotep III sun court. The categories included square Hathor pillars inscribed for Ramesses III, parts of a Kushite doorway, and several Ptolemaic gateway sections (fig. 10), one group inscribed for Ptolemy II, and another for Ptolemy VIII. All of the blocks were photographed by Staff Photographer Yarko Kobylecky, assisted by Ellie Smith. Preliminary analysis of this material indicates that it was quarried in the medieval period from the Temple of Mut, two and a half kilometers to the north! The bases of the Hathor pillars and the Ptolemy VIII gate, for instance, still survive *in situ*. While it has long been known that Karnak had been partly quarried for building stone in the medieval period — the *talatat* blocks, for example, found at Luxor Temple were quarried from Horemheb's Karnak pylons where they had been reused after Akhenaten's death — the pinpointing of Mut Temple as another major source for building stone has not been made until now and is a very exciting discovery with some far-reaching implications.

Much of the fragmentary wall material in the Luxor Temple blockyard was quarried from Luxor Temple itself, and many groups from all sections of the temple can be reassembled and eventually put back on the temple walls, thereby restoring beautiful, long-vanished wall scenes and architectural details. There is exciting potential for the material from Karnak eventually to be returned to its original site, once it has been documented, analyzed, and reassembled in the Luxor Temple blockyard. And if the bases of the original walls cannot be determined or do not survive, our plan calls for the fragment groups to be reconstructed either at Mut Temple or in the Luxor Temple blockyard, which has been designed to function as an open-air museum for reassembled groups. I have been in touch with the current excavators of Mut Temple, Richard Fazzini of the Brooklyn Museum and Betsy Bryan of Johns Hopkins, and will coordinate any and all future efforts with them.

The priority for the last two seasons in Luxor Temple has been the protective storage of the fragmentary wall material stored around the temple, essential for its long-term preservation. Now that this has largely been accomplished, during the next field season the Epigraphic Survey will begin the process of dismantling fragment rows stacked in the east long ago, which are all mixed up, with the bulk of the decorated surfaces inaccessible. Our goal is to sort and store them by category, to document each one and consoli-

Figure 5. Conservators Nahed Samir and Lotfi Hassan cleaning the painted reliefs of the back central sanctuary, small Amun temple, Medinet Habu. Digital photograph by Ray Johnson

Figure 6. Dany Roy and Chicago House workmen doing restoration work on the roof of the small Amun temple, Medinet Habu. Digital photograph by Ray Johnson

date them when necessary, and to reassemble all reconstructible groups. As we do so, we will learn more about where the material came from and to where we will eventually return it. This is a project that will definitely grow more interesting with every passing year!

At the end of this season 80 meters of fiberglass-covered aluminum framing (fig. 11) were installed over selected wall fragment treatment and storage platforms in the Luxor Temple eastern blockyard areas for additional protection of deteriorating wall fragments. Almost a thousand decaying fragments are now housed on protected "hospital" platforms awaiting future consolidation. Sadly, when we uncovered the bottommost layer of blocks in the row of Akhenaten *talatat* piled against the length of the eastern exterior wall of the Colonnade Hall, we found them so decayed they could not be moved. Our conservators determined that leaving them exposed to the air would activate the migration of salts and insure their rapid disintegration. So 108 decorated Akhenaten *talatat* were carefully photographed in B&W, color print, and slide film *in situ* and were then reburied with their original soil to re-establish a stable environment, i.e., a balance of salt in the blocks and soil around them. When the Epigraphic Survey soon inaugurates a new expanded wall-fragment consolidation program at Luxor Temple, we will uncover the blocks, consolidate them, and store them properly.

Luxor Temple Structural Condition Study

During the last three seasons, Chicago House has sponsored a study of the structural stability of the Luxor Temple monument in light of changed environmental conditions that are adversely affecting the ancient monuments all over Egypt. The steady rise of salt-laden groundwater is a particular problem. This study has been generously supported for the last two seasons by our

Robert Wilson matching grant and the World Monuments Fund. From December 3 to 12, 2002, Structural Engineer Conor Power continued his monitoring of the temple structure. He reported to us that no additional cracks have opened up during the last year, nor has there been any discernible movement in the pylons recorded in the two crack monitors ("calibrated telltales") we placed on the south wall of the East Pylon and its upper west side door opening. No significant changes were noted in the Colonnade Hall walls or column-architrave structure, nor was there any noticeable change in efflorescence levels. No changes were noted in the rest of the temple complex. It should be noted that the plumb bobs and targets that were installed last season (one by the Epigraphic Survey and two by SWECO) had all been moved, and the Chicago House plumb bob had been completely replaced. The targets all required re-affixing to the pavement and realigning by Jamie Riley, and they will now be monitored on a regular basis.

Chicago House

It is a great pleasure to announce a major milestone in the digital duplication and backup program of the Chicago House Photo Archives. The digital scanning of all of the large format negatives in our Luxor archive (17,099 of them) was finished in April, resulting in 242 CDs that are now in the U.S. (another set remains in Luxor). These CDs, a digital duplicate of the Chicago House archive, are being transferred to Chicago in batches this summer and permanently housed in the Oriental Institute Museum Archives. Photo Archivist Sue Lezon, who has painstakingly coordinated the entire effort, is currently finishing the careful checking of each image and the converting of each scanned images into thumbnails for our new, illustrated Chicago House Photo Archives database, the first version of which will also be turned over to the Oriental Insti-

Figure 7. New sandstone floor and newly cleaned walls, front central sanctuary, small Amun temple, Medinet Habu. Digital photograph by Ray Johnson

Figure 8. Newly constructed blockyard east of the Colonnade Hall, Luxor Temple. Digital photograph by Ray Johnson

tute later this summer, another happy milestone. In these uncertain times, this new technology has allowed us the assurance that priceless and unique information formerly accessible only in Luxor is now also available here. The scanned images and database will now allow the Oriental Institute Museum Archives to assess exactly what negatives are solely to be found in Luxor, and what are in Chicago. Our long-term, ultimate goal is to make sure that hard copy duplicates of all of the negatives in Luxor are also in Chicago; the database and digital images will greatly facilitate that effort. In addition, 430 CDs of our 35 mm archive are also back in the U.S. (1,218 rolls of film and 32,900 images) and will also be transferred to Chicago once they have been checked and added to the new Chicago House 35 mm database. Thanks to Photo Archives Assistant Ellie Smith for the careful entering of all that data. The scanning of that part of the Chicago House Photo Archives is still incomplete and will continue next season.

The Chicago House Library was supervised this winter, starting at the beginning of December, by Epigrapher/Librarian Jen Kimpton. She was assisted during the month of January by volunteer Meg Dorman (who also kindly helped out in the Photo Archives). During the season, Jen accessioned 199 new publications, including journals, series, and monographs; maintained subscriptions and standing orders; conserved and repaired books; and assisted library patrons weekday afternoons and all day Friday. At the beginning of the season, Assistant to the Director Emily Napolitano capably supervised the library until Jen arrived, and in the course of the winter, gave twenty-three library tours to interested groups and friends. Emily ran the office and maintained the house — including daily food procurement — with maximum efficiency and ensured the smooth running of our whole operation, for which she is owed special thanks. Finance Manager Safinaz Ouri assisted by Accountant Marlene Sarwat Nassim continued to firmly oversee the financial end of our operation. The devaluation of the Egyptian Pound and poor stock market returns this winter had Safi working overtime occasionally, but thanks to her great skill we still managed to stay within our reduced budget!

Helen and Jean Jacquet were with us in Luxor from mid-November until the end of the season. During the winter Helen worked with Emily Napolitano and Tom Urban on refinements for her *Graffiti from the Khonsu Temple Roof at Karnak: A Manifestation of Personal Piety* (Khonsu Temple 3). Katherine Strange Burke, under Tom Urban's supervision, has scanned the nearly 700 pieces of artwork and finished the page layout in PageMaker, and we expect to print this landmark volume before we return to Luxor. Congratulations to Helen on this exciting culmination of nearly fifty years of work.

Because of ill health, our beloved Dr. Henri Riad remained in Cairo this season with his family and was missed terribly by us in Luxor. But Henri received a wonderful honor this winter. In December, he was celebrated as the oldest living former director of the Egyptian Museum, Cairo, and received a trophy in the form of the goddess Maat from Egyptian First Lady Susanne Mubarak at the centenary celebration of the museum (fig. 12). We are very proud of Henri and rejoice with him at this well-deserved recognition.

On a sadder note, when we returned to Luxor in October, we learned of the passing of our well-loved former *safragi* Shafei and Second Cook Abdel Zaher, both long retired. They were venerable institutions unto themselves and had been part of the Chicago House family for over thirty years, from the time of George Hughes and Charles Nims. Now their children and even grandchildren work for us, continuing the long tradition, but no one can ever replace those two.

Figure 9. Chicago House workmen and SCA inspector moving blocks in the west area, Luxor Temple. Digital photograph by Ray Johnson

Figure 10. Newly reassembled wall fragment group, Ptolemaic king offering to the goddess Mut (seated) and accompanying goddesses, Luxor Temple eastern blockyard. Digital photograph by Ray Johnson

The month of April saw another chapter in the history of Chicago House come to a quiet close with the death of our beloved Chief Engineer, "Bosh Mohandis" Saleh Shahat Soliman, who was 86 (fig. 13). Hired full time by Kent Weeks in the mid-1970s, Saleh was one of those brilliant mechanics that is needed and longed for by every expedition in the field. He kept Chicago House maintained and running smoothly for more than thirty years and was a surrogate "Papa" to many of us. He will be missed beyond words.

We were very fortunate that the events in Iraq did not negatively impact our operation in Luxor. Despite the widespread unhappiness with American policies throughout the Mideast, at no time did we feel any threat, and we were able to continue our work and finish our normal work season. For that we are extremely grateful and look forward to another year of fruitful work and collaboration with our Egyptian friends and colleagues. Here's to a more peaceful 2004!

The professional staff for the 2002/2003 season, besides the Field Director, consisted of J. Brett McClain, Harold Hays, and Randy Shonkwiler as Epigraphers; Jen Kimpton as Epigrapher and Librarian; Christina Di Cerbo, Margaret De Jong, Susan Osgood, and Will Schenck as Artists; Yarko Kobylecky as Staff Photographer; Susan Lezon as Photo Archivist and Photographer; Emily Napolitano as Assistant to the Director and Office Manager; Jill Carlotta Maher as Assistant to the Director; Safinaz Ouri as Finance Manager; Marlin Sarwat Nassim as Accountant; Elinor Smith as Photo Archives and Library Assistant; Margaret Dorman as Photo Archives and Library Volunteer; and Saleh Shehat Suleiman as Chief Engineer. Lotfi Hassan, Adel Aziz

Andraws, Nahed Samir, and Lamia Hadidy worked with us as Conservators; Jamie Riley worked as Blockyard Supervisor; Dany Roy as Stonecutter; and Conor Power, P.E., as Structural Engineer Consultant. Special thanks go to Drs. Helen and Jean Jacquet who lent their considerable expertise to our work.

To our partners in preservation, the Supreme Council of Antiquities, we owe a special debt of thanks for our extraordinarily productive collaboration this season: especially to Dr. Zahi Hawass, Secretary General of the SCA; Dr. Magdy El-Ghandour, General Director of Foreign Missions; Dr. Sabry Abdel Aziz, General Director of Antiquities for Upper and Lower Egypt; Dr. Mohamed Abdel Fattah Abdel Ghani, Director General of Upper Egypt; Drs. Holeil Ghaly and Mohamed El-Bialy, General Directors of Luxor and Southern Upper Egypt respectively; Dr. Ali Asfar, General Director for the West Bank of Luxor; Dr. Mohamed Assem and Mr. Bakit, Directors of Karnak / Luxor Temples respectively; Dr. Atteya Radwan, General Director of Excavations in the Egyptian Antiquities sector; Mme. Nawal, Chief Inspector of Luxor Temple; and Mme. Sanaa, Director of the Luxor Museum. Sincerest thanks must go to our small army of inspectors over the course of our six-month field season; at Medinet Habu: Mr. Ahmed Ezz El-Din Ismail; Mr. Mohsen Ismail Ali Yousef; and Mr. Mohsen Helmi Yousef Badawi. And at Luxor Temple: Mr. Abdul Satar Badri Mohamed Hameed; Ms. Hanem Sadeek Kenawy Mahmoud; Mr. Mustafa Mohamed Mohamed El-Soghayer; and Ms. Manal Mohamed El-Sayed. It was a tremendous pleasure working with them all. Heartfelt thanks to all our friends and colleagues for helping make our field season so very productive this year.

Figure 11. Aluminum and fiberglass covered "mastaba" platform for protected storage of deteriorating sandstone wall fragments, Luxor Temple eastern blockyard. Digital photograph by Ray Johnson

Figure 12. Dr. Henri Riad and "Maat" lifetime achievement award. Cairo, January 2003. Digital photograph by Ray Johnson

Figure 13. Chief Engineer "Bosh Mohandis" Saleh Shahat Soliman. Chicago House, 2001. Digital photograph by Ray Johnson

At this time I would like to express my sincerest thanks once again to the many friends of the Oriental Institute whose support has allowed us to continue our vital documentation and conservation work. Special thanks must go to the American Ambassador to Egypt, the Honorable David Welch; the former Ambassador to Egypt, the Honorable Daniel Charles Kurtzer, and Sheila Kurtzer; Reno Harnish, Deputy Chief of Mission of the U.S. Embassy in Cairo, and Leslie Harnish; Elizabeth Thornhill of the U.S. Embassy; Bill Pearson of the United States Agency for International Development and Genie Pearson; Exa Snow; Ahmed Ezz, EZZ Group, Cairo; David and Carlotta Maher; David and Nan Ray; Mark Rudkin; Dr. Barbara Mertz; Daniel Lindley and Lucia Woods Lindley; Dr. Marjorie M. Fisher; Eric and Andrea Colombel; Piers Litherland; Dr. Fred Giles; Marjorie B. Kiewit; Nancy LaSalle; Tom and Linda Heagy; Debora Long; Donald Oster; Dr. William Kelly Simpson; Kelly and Di Grodzins; Bob and Anne Hamada; Dr. Ben Harer; Dr. Roxie Walker; Louis Byron, Jr.; Dr. Irene Bierman, Dr. Jere Bacharach, Dr. Bob Springborg, Mary Sadek, Amir Abdel Hamid, and Amira Khattab of the American Research Center in Egypt; Dr. Chip Vincent, Dr. Jarek Dobrolowski, Cynthia Schartzer, and Janie Abdul-Aziz of the Egyptian Antiquities Project; Dr. Michael Jones of the Antiquities Development Project; and all of our friends back home at the Oriental Institute. I must also express special gratitude to British Petroleum, the Getty Grant Program of the J. Paul Getty Trust, LaSalle National Bank, Mobil Oil, the American Research Center in Egypt, and the World Monuments Fund for their invaluable support. Thank you!

Members of the Oriental Institute and other friends of Chicago House are welcome to stop by to see us. We suggest that you write or call in advance to schedule a meeting that is convenient

Figure 14. Staff photograph by Yarko Kobylecky. Chicago House, Luxor, Egypt

to all. Chicago House is open from October 15 until April 15, and closed Saturday afternoons and Sundays. Our address in Egypt: Chicago House, Corniche el-Nil, Luxor, Egypt. The phone number is (from the U.S.A.) 011-20-95-37-2525; fax 011-20-95-38-1620.

The Epigraphic Survey home page is at:

http://www-oi.uchicago.edu/OI/PROJ/EPI/Epigraphic.html

GIZA PLATEAU MAPPING PROJECT

Mark Lehner

2003 STUDY SEASON

During the 2003 season of the Giza Plateau Mapping Project (January 8–May 31), the team focused on preparing the tremendous amount of material from our previous seasons (especially the intensive clearing, mapping, and excavations from 1999 through 2002) for analysis and publication. Excavation was limited to clearing two trenches west of the soccer field of the Abu Hol Sports Club to determine if our Fourth Dynasty site continued that far south. We also mapped the newly excavated areas of the Aswan obelisk quarry where the Supreme Council of Antiquities has been working.

Site Work

In our last excavation season (2002), we found that the Fourth Dynasty settlement we have been working on since 1988 continued south beyond our excavations under the modern Abu Hol Sports Club. We cleared 25 meters of what proved to be the back end of a huge royal administrative building in the southeast corner of the site. The rest of the royal building obviously lay under the soccer field that runs south of our excavations.

This season, Chief Inspector Mansour Bureik asked us to peel back the sandy overburden in two places immediately west of the soccer field south of our site to ascertain if the ancient settlement continues this far south and west. We had good reason to anticipate finding settlement here. Our first excavations on the site in 1988/89 were in Area AA, about 75 meters west of the northwest corner of the soccer field. We found a substantial building, probably for storage, with what looked like part of a large house. Between this area and the soccer field, an ancient mudbrick wall has protruded, since about 1983, from the area where the sand diggers from the riding stables had removed the overburden. This wall and pottery scatters in the area were among the first clues that the overburden hid substantial settlement remains from the Pyramid Age.

Trench SFW-1

Our first trench, SFW (Soccer Field West)-1, about 10 × 15 meters, cut through overburden several meters thick, mostly deposited along the west side of the soccer field since the early 1990s. Just as soon as the workers, supervised by Mohsen Kamal, lifted the sandy overburden, marl lines and brick patterns of ancient plastered walls appeared. The walls enclose rectangular rooms and courtyards, 2.5 to 3.0 meters wide, and a small bin such as we have seen in houses within the Gallery Complex. Dark ash-filled spaces could have been cooking areas. The organization appears to be more regular than in the Eastern Town, the village-like settlement that we found last year on the eastern side of the site. The settlement on the west could be a more formally laid out extramural town (outside the Enclosure Wall around the Gallery Complex). The buildings that we excavated in 1988/89 probably belong to this part of the town (see figs. 1–3).

Trench SFW-2

The second exploratory trench (SFW-2), also 10 × 15 meters, was at the far southern end of the soccer field right up against its west wall. The workers, supervised again by Mohsen Kamal, dug

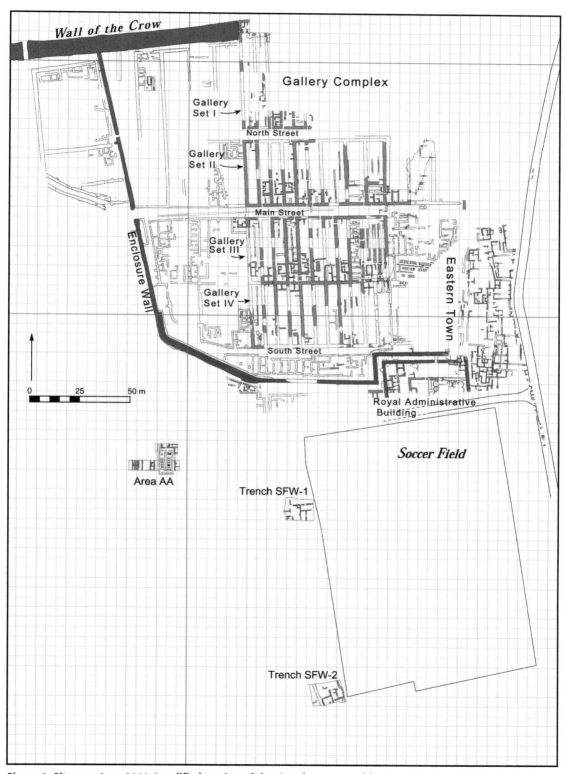

Figure 1. Site map June 2003 (modified version of the site plan prepared by Peggy Sanders, Archaeological Graphics Services)

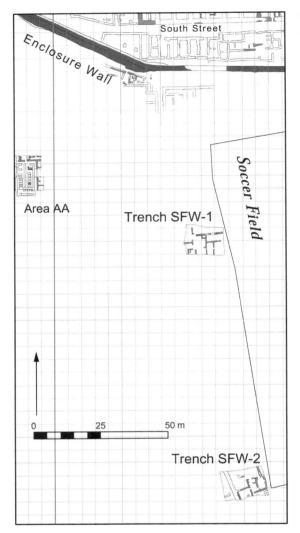

Figure 2. Map detail, plan of trenches SFW-1 and SFW-2

through thick layers of gray and black ash from recent burning of stable dumping, then a layer of clean sand, to expose the surface of the ancient ruins (see fig. 4).

These Old Kingdom ruins include a field-stone wall, 1.50 meters thick, that stands high above the surrounding mud mass along the western end of SFW-2. The wall runs at a pronounced angle west of north, similar to the angle of the Enclosure Wall west of the Gallery Complex. On the west side of the field-stone wall, in the few meters between it and the boundary of the trench, there are traces of thinner fieldstone walls that may be remnants of a bakery, as suggested by a thick ash deposit in the far southern corner of the trench.

Thin mudbrick walls, with marl plastered faces, are attached to the east side of the large fieldstone wall. They form a square court, 5.20 meters (10 ancient royal cubits) wide east to west. Traces of other walls show in a wide, shallow depression north of the court. More mudbrick walls to the east of the court could belong to a house, about 5 × 6 meters.

On the far east side of the trench, thicker mudbrick walls run along and just south of the soccer field. These, like the fieldstone wall on the west, stand high above the more sunken ruins in between, so that initially we thought the two walls might form a wide avenue running north to south. But the sunken corridor appears to be filled with courts and houses.

The second trench (SFW-2) extends the ancient city ruins more than 150 meters south of the southern limit of our excavations up to the end of our last season, 2002 (with the exception of isolated Area AA). We now know that the ancient settlement extends for a length, north to south, of more than 350 meters, and with a width of 260 meters, covers more than 9 hectares.

Surveying and Mapping the Unfinished Obelisk Quarry

Last year, the Supreme Council of Antiquities (SCA) excavated nearly 100,000 cubic meters of debris at the site of the Unfinished Obelisk in Aswan revealing massive trenches where New Kingdom workmen literally pounded out possibly as many as five of the largest obelisks ever, probably for the Eighteenth Dynasty king, Thutmose III. In October 2002, Dr. Zahi Hawass asked the Giza Plateau Mapping Project to help prepare a large-scale map to document all the cultural features, as well as natural joints, fissures, and major outcrops in the quarry trenches. Both the cultural and natural features offer important information about the quarry work (see fig. 5).

All over the quarry there are red painted marks and lines remaining from the notation of ancient granite workers and surveyors. Every stage of Bronze Age granite working is represented in the quarry. In the Bronze Age, quarrymen removed shapes such as obelisks from the bedrock using deep trenches that they pounded out of the rock with dolerite hammer stones. The various stages of Iron Age quarrying are also seen in parts of the quarry. During that era, quarrymen had the aid of small wedges to split large pieces. Iron Age quarrymen left long lines of wedge sockets where they removed pieces in various parts of the quarry.

Natural features, such as fissures, are also informative. The ancient quarrymen recognized and skillfully exploited such geological realties in order to extract obelisks as long as 32 meters, weighing more than 400 tons, without cracking and breaking, after scores of laborers had spent months pounding them out of the solid bedrock.

Survey

To help document these important natural and cultural features, we scheduled three weeks to capture all the details of a boulder-strewn series of quarried areas comprising 250 × 150 meters, the size of our whole cleared area at Giza where we have spent three years mapping part of an ancient settlement.

Ana Tavares designed the survey and Tobias Tonner was our computer technician and database manager. With Stephanie Durning and Mark Lehner as sketchers and point takers, we went to Aswan with two total stations. Mohsen Kamel and Mary Anne Murray joined us for a short period.

Our approach was to sketch large tracts of the quarry by eye, somewhat to scale (about 1:200 or thereabouts) but measured only by pacing. With the total stations, and using a survey control network of points already established by SCA surveyor Mohammed Ali, we then "shot" hundreds of points on the sketches — outlines of boulders, major corners, trenches, ancient pounding patches, "spines" left where large blocks and obelisks had been snapped off. Back in our "office" at the Cleopatra Hotel, right in the heart of Aswan's busy Market Street district, Tobias Tonner printed out the points against the local Aswan grid established by the Swiss-German archaeological mission. We then used the point plots to correct our sketches, bringing them true to scale. Sometimes we took the corrected drawings back for more points, and further corrections. Altogether we surveyed more than 10,000 points.

Meanwhile the inspectors from the SCA continued to map the detailed masonry fea-

Figure 3. Trench SFW-1, looking east toward the Abu Hol Sports Club soccer field

Figure 4. Trench SFW-2, looking northwest toward the pyramids. A large stone wall is visible on the left side of the photograph

tures at 1:50, as they had been doing during the several months before we arrived. Their excellent maps greatly advanced the work. We could reduce them by half to 1:100 and lock them into our overall map, which saved us from having to map such minute detail.

In this way we are compiling a map of the entire mass of granite comprising the north and south quarry trenches. We designated major topographical areas, such as West Ridge; the main quarry trenches north and south; major removal areas; features of major quarry works including pounding patches, or cavities left by large block removals; and specific contexts such as exploratory "proofing holes" or spines where a block was snapped free.

We are still working on drawing up the overall map, at scales of 1:100 and 1:200, which we will deliver to the SCA for their development of the site for tourist visits, as well as further archaeological documentation.

Acknowledgments

For a very successful season, we are grateful to Dr. Zahi Hawass, Undersecretary of State and Secretary General of the Supreme Council of Antiquities. We thank Mr. Adel Hussein, Director of Giza, and Mr. Mansour Bureik, Chief Inspector of Giza. We thank Mr. Naser Ramadan and Mr. Gaber Abd al-Dayim who represented the Supreme Council of Antiquities at the excavation site, and their assistants, Mr. Tamer Shawqi and Mr. Shazli Ahmed, as well as Mr. Ahmed Eiz who served as our inspector in the storeroom. Reis Sobhi supervised the workmen who cleared our backfill from last season and refilled the excavations at the end of this season.

We could not have carried out this work without the major support of Ann Lurie, David Koch, Jon Jerde, and Peter Norton. We also appreciate the loyal support of Robert Lowdermilk, Glen Dash, Matthew McCauley, Bruce Ludwig, Ann Thompson, Fred and Suzanne Rheinstein, Sandford and Betty Sigoloff, Victor and Nancy Moss, David Goodman, Marjorie Fisher, Alice Hyman, Don Kunz, Richard Redding, Lora Lehner, Bonnie Sampsell, Art and Bonnie McClure, and Charles Rigano.

Our crew this season was an international team that included the following individuals: Mark Lehner, Harvard Semitic Museum and the University of Chicago, Director; Mary Anne Murray, Institute of Archaeology, University College, London, Assistant Director and Archaeobotanist; Mohsen Kamal, University of California, Los Angeles, Assistant Director and Archaeologist; Ana Tavares, Centre de recherches archéologiques, (CNRS) Valbonne, Object Registrar, Surveyor, and Archaeologist; Tobias Tonner, University of Tübingen, Database Manager and Ar-

Figure 5. Members of the Giza Plateau Mapping Project surveying in the Aswan obelisk quarry with the Supreme Council of Antiquities. In the foreground Ana Tavares works with the total station

chaeologist; Richard Redding, Michigan Museum of Natural History, Faunal Analyst; Cordula Werschkun, University of Tübingen, Lithics Analyst; John Nolan, University of Chicago, Epigrapher; Anna Wodzinska, University of Warzaw, Ceramicist; Jessica Holst Kaiser and Johnny Karlsson, Osteo-Archaeologists; Caroline Hebron, University College, London, David Swan, Firat Archaeological Services, Johnny Karlsson, Artists; Stephanie Durning, Firat Archaeological Services, Archivist; Fiona Baker and Paul Sharman, Firat Archaeological Services, Lauren Bruning, Ashraf Abd al-Aziz, Supreme Council of Antiquities, Conny Meister, Angela Milward Jones, Archaeologists.

HAMOUKAR

McGuire Gibson

The continuation of research at Hamoukar, originally scheduled to take place in fall 2002, was postponed because we thought the Iraq war would begin in October. Since we did not want to be eight kilometers from the Iraqi border when war broke out, we postponed until spring 2003. The war, when it came in the spring, prevented our work once again. Currently, we are planning to resume digging in the spring of 2004.

Figure 1. Area B Burnt Building, from south. Hamoukar, Syria

With all my energy concentrated on the Iraq crisis, I cannot say that I have gotten much done on the analysis of our findings at this remarkable site, which saw the development of one of the earliest cities in the early fourth millennium B.C. However, Clemens Reichel, in preparation for some public lectures, refined his analysis of the findspots of seal impressions from the Burnt Building we excavated in Area B (figs. 1–5). And I understand from my co-director in Syria, Dr. Amr al-Azm, that substantial progress has been made on the analysis of the seeds collected from

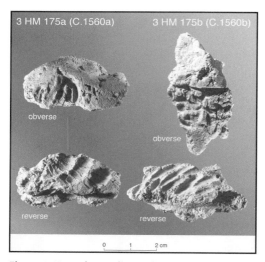

Figure 2. Two clay sealings, showing stamp seal impression on their obverses and impressions of basketry and string on their reverses. These sealings were applied on either boxes or baskets

Figure 3. Jar stopper: clay lumps such as this one were inserted into the neck of jars to close them and prevent spillage or unauthorized access to the content of the vessel. Most jar stoppers bear the impression of one or more seals on their tops

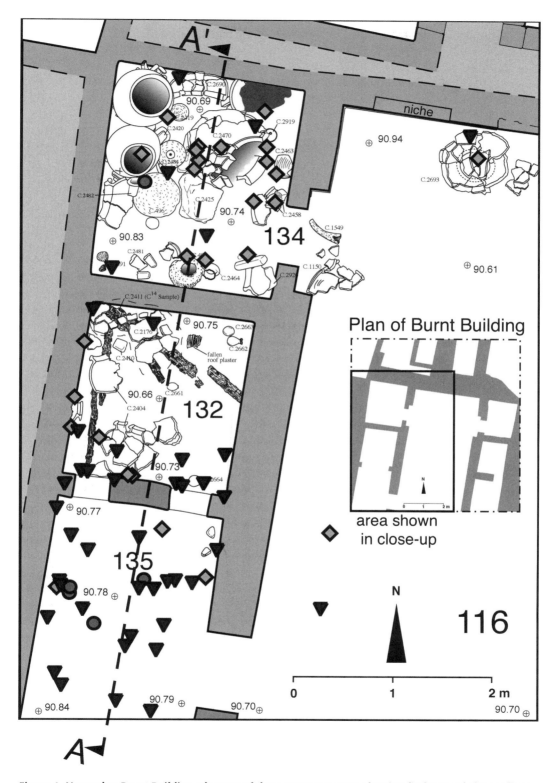

Figure 4. Hamoukar Burnt Building, close-up of three western rooms, showing findspots of clay sealings. For explanation of symbols and Section View A-A', see figure 5

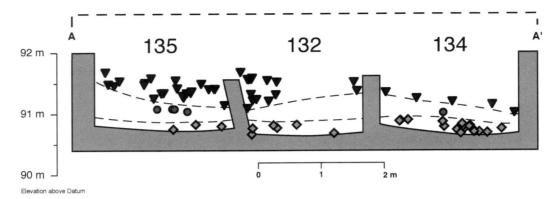

92 m

91 m

90 m

Elevation above Datum

Figure 5. Section view A-A' (location marked in fig. 4): showing spatial distribution of clay sealings in destruction debris as recovered during excavation. Sealings from ground floor and upper floor context are identified by different symbols. Hamoukar Burnt Building

the site. Jason Ur's work on the settlement history of Hamoukar and the area around it has been incorporated into the study of a much larger area, so that he can now show road systems linking northern Iraq and much of northern Syria. In this research, he is making increasingly sophisticated use of satellite images, remote sensing, and Geographical Information Systems (GIS) technology.

We have been making inquiries about geomagnetic surveying of the site of Hamoukar. When done in the right circumstances, patterns of resistance and non-resistance can show ancient buried walls, baked brick pavements, pits, and other features that are not otherwise visible. This technique, which works best on stone or baked brick walls, has been refined in recent years so that even unbaked mudbrick walls can show up dramatically. The advantage to the excavator is that one can make decisions about where to dig most effectively. Hamoukar is a very good candidate for such treatment since it has a very large lower town that has well-built houses dating from about 2200 B.C., almost directly under the present surface. Some of these houses proved to be rich in finds, having been abandoned with most of their contents left in place. Although the site is more famous for its early city remains, these houses of the last part of the third millennium B.C. also deserve investigation since they will help to answer one of the major questions in North Syrian archaeology: did the cities of that time come to a sudden end or was there a gradual process? One scholar, Harvey Weiss of Yale, has suggested that all of northeastern Syria was abandoned at the

ARCHAEOLOGICAL DETECTIVE WORK: The function of many of the 250 clay sealings found in the debris of the Burnt Building was difficult to explain at first. Many of them were basket sealings (fig. 2), not jar sealings (fig. 3), as the large number of storage vessels found in these rooms would have suggested. The building's pristine, undisturbed find context called for extra care in field mapping. During the excavation the findspots and elevation of sealing in the destruction debris was recorded very carefully; this data was later added to the plan of the building. Both plan and section of the building's three western rooms (figs. 4–5) show that the sealings actually belonged to two distinct assemblages, the ground floor and an upper floor which had collapsed during the destruction of the building by fire. Almost all basket sealings belonged to the upper floor assemblage, resolving the apparent contradiction between container and sealing. The evidence shown here lends empirical proof to the notion that there was a second floor on the building. Drawings by Clemens Reichel

end of the Akkadian period (2200 B.C.) and he has proposed the following causes in different articles: (a) volcanic action, (b) meteoric impact, or (c) a shift in the global weather pattern. There is some evidence at Hamoukar, as at some other sites, that there was a continuation of settlement beyond the Akkadian period, so our evidence could be critical in addressing the proposed collapse.

Plans are underway to mount the next season of excavations, and next year's report be should as exciting as those of previous seasons at Hamoukar. We anticipate working on both fourth millennium and third millennium levels, completely exposing the Burnt Building of Area B and making more progress on the third millennium public building of Area C, and we will begin real planning for the geomagnetic survey.

I would like to thank the Friends of Hamoukar for their generosity in the past and for their help in the future. We will be in touch.

IRAQ MUSEUM PROJECT

Clemens D. Reichel

The events in Iraq during March and April 2003 (see separate report Nippur and Iraq at Time of War by McGuire Gibson), notably the looting of the Iraq Museum between April 9 and 11, drew numerous responses from scholars at the Oriental Institute, which led to the formation of the Oriental Institute's Iraq Museum Project.

The initial grief and anger within the Oriental Institute over the looting of the museum was soon paired with a feeling of being overwhelmed by the worldwide reaction that followed in the days thereafter. We received hundreds of phone calls and thousands of e-mails from people who were shocked and appalled by this atrocious act and who volunteered their help in any capacity to recover the stolen objects. By that time, scholars on the Ancient Near East (ANE) Mailing List were already engaged in an intense debate about a proper response from the scholarly world, and the idea of some kind of a database of stolen artifacts was mentioned repeatedly. McGuire Gibson had started a project providing government and customs agencies with sample photographs and descriptions of key artifact types. As reports of a total loss of the museum's holdings were coming in — which thankfully turned out not to be true — pressure was mounting to build a much more comprehensive computer database with a web interface that scholars, police, and customs officials alike could access worldwide. Following our initial pitch announcing this plan on several e-mail lists, we were encouraged by colleagues around the world to start building the database. Less than a week after the looting, an Iraq Museum Workshop convened at the Oriental Institute, where many of the objectives for the project were developed. Aside from myself, regular participants of these meetings included Gil J. Stein (Director, Oriental Institute), McGuire Gibson (Professor of Mesopotamian Archaeology), Charles E. Jones (Research Archivist and Bibliographer), John Sanders (Head, Computer Lab), Nicholas Kouchoukos (Professor, Department of Anthropology), and Moain Sadeq (Director of Antiquities for the Gaza Strip and Fulbright Scholar at the Oriental Institute in 2002/2003).

In publishing data on the stolen objects from the Iraq Museum as a web-based computer database, we incorporated lessons learned after the looting of several Iraqi museums following the Gulf War in 1991. Between 1992 and 1996, three booklets entitled *Lost Heritage* were published by American Association for Research in Baghdad, the British School of Archaeology, and the Japanese Archaeological Mission, providing photographs and descriptions of stolen objects. These booklets were intended to help academics, antiquities dealers, and auction houses determine if a suspicious item on the antiquities market was in fact stolen from one of Iraq's museums. Although these booklets were well intended, they were doomed to limited success. These booklets were not circulated widely enough to have a real impact; once they went out of print, they were not reprinted. Some object photographs could only be supplied by the Iraqi Department of Antiquities *after* the booklets were published and were therefore not included. As we were painfully reminded again in the past few months, there are many dynamic factors in a museum looting. Objects that were thought to be stolen turned out to be misplaced or were returned; others were only later identified as truly missing. While paper publications do not provide the flexibility for frequent changes, a computer database does. This point was not missed by some of the contributors to the booklets, but at the time access to the Internet was still relatively uncommon, modem speeds were slow, and most computers were ill equipped to handle graphic files.

Twelve years later, after another Iraq war and museum looting, the technology to build such a database and make it available via web browsers is commonly available. From its outset, time was an essential factor in this project. It was only through an exceptional team spirit that it got off the ground so swiftly. By April 18 — only seven days after the museum looting was reported worldwide — John Sanders launched Lost Treasures of Iraq, a new webpage that became the web outlet for most Iraq-related activities at the Oriental Institute (see Computer Laboratory report). At its earliest stage, Lost Treasures already hosted a precursor to the later database consisting of an illustrated index of the most important objects from the Iraq Museum. In the meantime, we had started building a relational database which was made available on the website on May 13. See:

Lost Treasures of Iraq — http://www-oi.uchicago.edu/OI/IRAQ/iraq.html

Iraq Museum Database — http://www-oi.uchicago.edu/OI/IRAQ/Iraqdatabasehome.htm

The speed at which we were able to proceed was only possible because of the help that we got — unsolicited and unparalleled. In the first few days after the museum looting, our own graduate students lined up at our doors offering help. The shock and disbelief in their faces at what looked like the annihilation of our field of work and their line of study is still a vivid memory. Graduate students have little time and even less money (and our project, less than three days old then, had no budget to pay *anyone*), yet none of this was an issue or even mentioned at that point. Those students, notably Carrie Hritz, Mark Altaweel, Alexandra Witsell, and Leslie Schramer, deserve an extra thank you for being such exceptionally good sports and for working unpaid overtime in scanning and data entry. From late April onward, these jobs were taken over by volunteers. Two names deserve special mention here. Alim Khan patiently entered the data for the Diyala cylinder seals. It was Karen Terras, however, who for the last four months has made the Iraq Museum Project an almost full-time mission. To mention everything that she has accomplished would be almost impossible — it ranges from entering data on thousands of Nimrud ivories to scanning images of ivories, cylinder seals, and other artifacts. Karen has a background in art history, data management, and text editing, so she took it upon herself to edit many of the scholarly descriptions of objects and to simplify them for a non-academic audience — anyone who ever has tried to run a data management project on a shoestring budget will know what kind of a help this is! From day one of the crisis, Charles E. Jones, who is also moderator of the ANE mailing list, has been actively involved in our efforts. Jones has summarized his efforts following the Iraq Museum looting in a separate report (see Research Archives). Soon after the looting he launched IraqCrisis, a moderated discussion list on events relating to Iraq's antiquities [http://www-oi.uchicago.edu/OI/IRAQ/iraqcrisis.html], which by most scholars' accounts has become one of the best news lists on current events regarding Iraq's antiquities. As the Oriental Institute's Research Archivist and Bibliographer, Jones went through endless numbers of books, excerpting Iraq Museum numbers with publication reference. This list, which by now contains over 12,000 entries, is published on the Oriental Institute's website [http://www-oi.uchicago.edu/OI/IRAQ/iraq_bibliography.html] and will soon be linked to the object database. This site also contains data concerning Iraq's destroyed libraries and manuscript collection — not

Figure 1. Looted objects returned to the Iraq Museum in May 2003. Photograph by McGuire Gibson

a main research focus of the Oriental Institute, but as it becomes more and more apparent, a cultural tragedy of this war that exceeds the Iraq Museum looting in its horrendousness and long-term impact.

The question has been asked repeatedly — why should such a database be compiled at the Oriental Institute? Numerous reasons could be given here — the Oriental Institute has assembled one of the largest groups of scholars involved in the study of Mesopotamian archaeology. Additionally, web-based publication projects such as the Diyala Project (see separate report) have given us a significant edge in computer-based data management. Certainly the most important argument is our own long-standing tradition of archaeological projects in Iraq. Some of the most important excavations in Iraq, such as Nippur, Tell Asmar, Khafaje, Tell Agrab, and Ishchali, have been undertaken by the Oriental Institute. These excavations, which were crucial in establishing the chronological backbone for Mesopotamian archaeology, resulted in the recovery of thousands of objects that were divided between the Iraq Museum and the Oriental Institute. All of these objects were catalogued during the excavation and most of them photographed and/or drawn in the field. As a result, the Oriental Institute has a visual record of these objects, whether they are housed in Baghdad or Chicago. At present, we can digitally publish this kind of information for 8,500 Iraq Museum objects originating from the Diyala excavations. Together with all the finds from other Oriental Institute excavations in Iraq, especially from Nippur and Khorsabad, this figure may increase to almost 20,000.

Our own excavation material, however, is just one of the resources at our disposal. In the weeks following the looting of the Iraq Museum, scholars and publishers from around the world have offered to contribute material, both published and unpublished, to our database. Some of the finest photographs of objects in the Iraq Museum are published in Eva Strommenger's monograph *Fünf Jahrtausende Mesopotamien* (Munich: Hirmer Verlag, 1962). Hirmer not only generously allowed us to use these images for our database but also sent us a list of unpublished object photographs that had been taken in the Iraq Museum. Several members of the British School of Archaeology supplied us with their own data. Georgina Herrmann (Institute of Archaeology/University of London) provided us with thousands of digitized photographs of Nimrud ivories (many thanks to Stuart Laidlaw for scanning them at the Institute's photolab). Harriet Martin gave us her photographs of all Abu Salabikh cylinder seals in the Iraq Museum found before 1990. Nicholas Postgate (Cambridge University) sent us photographs and drawings of over 1,000 objects missing after the 1991 Gulf War, many of them not included in the *Lost Heritage* booklets. Other contributors or people willing to contribute include (and I simply cannot list everyone) Carol Meyer (Chicago), Karen Radner (Munich), David Stronach (Berkeley), Lynn Dodd Schwartz (University of Southern California), Leigh-Ann Bedal (Penn State, Erie), Marilyn Jenkins-Madina (Metropolitan Museum of Art), Timothy Potts (Kimbell Art Museum), and Elizabeth Stone (State University of New York, Stonybrook). In short, we have been flooded with data; the main challenge now is to sort it quickly and make it available on the web.

Having spent the last eight years of my life on building the Diyala Project database (see separate report), a relational database for archaeological objects that will soon be accessible as a web-based publication, it was probably inevitable that the construction of the Iraq Museum database fell into my hands. But comparing these projects feels like comparing apples and oranges.

Art Auction by Chicago Artists to Benefit the Iraq Museum Project

In late April, a group of Chicago artists approached the Oriental Institute with an offer to help raise money to aid the recovery of objects stolen from the Iraq Museum. Soon after establishing contact, the artists decided to support the Iraq Museum Project with an art auction. Eighty-one artists, including many of Chicago's best-known names, participated in the effort by donating, and in many cases specially creating, artworks for this auction.

A preview of the artwork was held at Gillock Gallery in Evanston on June 7, 2003. The auction took place on June 14, 2003, at Gallery Mornea in Evanston, with a press preview and artists' reception held on June 13. The auction raised almost $10,000 in support of the project.

This great success would have been impossible without the unfaltering commitment of time and effort by numerous individuals, most notably Bert Menco (organizer of the auction), Michael Monar (Director, Gallery Mornea), Richard Davis (Manager, Gallery Mornea), Connie Gillock (Director, Gillock Gallery), Mickie Weiss, Fern Bogot, Grant Signs, and Mo Cahill. Thanks to all of them, not only for their support before, during, and after the auction, but also for their continued friendship, which has become a source of inspiration to us in our work. Thanks also to the contributing artists for donating their artwork to support our cause.

A list of the contributing artists can be found at http://www-oi.uchicago.edu/OI/IRAQ/artistsrespond.html

Gallery Mornea is located at 624 Davis Street, Evanston; telephone: 847-864-1906.

Gillock Gallery is located at 930 Ridge Avenue, Evanston; telephone: 847-864-3799.

The core of the Diyala Project is a database that contains both published and unpublished data on archaeological objects found during the Diyala excavations. Since this web-based database is intended to be both a final publication as well as an expandable research tool, the data resolution in it has to be very fine, the layout sophisticated, and its database backend very well structured. By contrast, the Iraq Museum database is neither intended as a primary publication nor as a research facility. Its most important function is to help the recovery of objects from the Iraq Museum by providing basic information such as images, materials, and measurements that will allow a visual match should such an object be recovered. What at first looked like doing more of the same — another archaeological database — turned out to be a challenge of a very different kind. This database is intended less for a scholarly audience than for anyone who might encounter a stolen object from the Iraq Museum — anyone from a customs official to the cleaning personnel working for an unscrupulous antiquities dealer. Therefore, any description and categorization has to be simple, descriptive, and easily understandable. Regardless of how hard one tries to avoid the pitfalls, this is where a scholar runs into trouble. Scholars are likely to identify objects with terms relating to their function, not their appearance.

Take the term "cylinder seal," for example. Part of this term is descriptive since the object itself is of cylindrical shape, but the "seal" component is fully interpretive. A viewer may recognize figurative designs on the object and realize that an impression of it could be made into soft material, yet the identification as a "seal" is based on external, "scholarly" information. Similar pitfalls exist for many other terms that we are accustomed to, such as "cuneiform text," "bulla," "votive plaque," "mace-head," "boundary stone," none of which gives a lay person any clear concept of what to expect visually. In short, we had to take off our scholarly glasses and learn to re-type objects based on simple, vi-

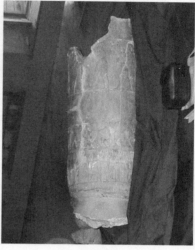

Figure 2. Warka Vase (left) as seen in the Iraq Museum before the war and (right) broken after being returned to the museum on June 12 (left side: E. Strommenger, Fünf Jahrtausende Mesopotamien, fig. 19; right side: photograph acquired by McGuire Gibson, used with permission)

sual characteristics. Quite often this was easier said than done. What object category, for example, does the famous Warka Vase fall into (fig. 2)? Since it has clearly identifiable relief decoration, some people might classify it as a "relief," while others would probably call it a "stone vessel." Different people are likely to look for the same object under different categories, so it is vital that an object be categorized by multiple entries. For example, take the well-known Nimrud ivories: scholars tend to refer to these artifacts, which were found at the site of Nimrud in Assyrian palaces dating from the ninth and eighth century B.C., as "ivories," but while most of them are panels with reliefed decoration, others are actually sculpted in the round. While they fall into the same material category, they represent two distinct artifact categories, "relief" and "sculpture." In a database, a reliefed ivory panel therefore has to be found under two different categories, "ivory" and "relief." But this is only the tip of the iceberg. Presenting all ivories on one webpage would be logistically impossible — imagine how long it would take for a page with several thousand thumbnail photographs to load! And how easy would it be to find an object without a more refined breakdown into sub-categories? This is where things get very tricky. *Ivories from Nimrud*, the scholarly publication series, presents these objects either sorted by archaeological findspot or by stylistic "schools." Such categorizations, however essential for scholarly work, offer no aid to a lay person in recognizing and identifying an object. We had no other choice but to come up with our own typology based on visual characteristics. The results can be seen in figure 3. The left side (a) shows an overview of the present layout of our "ivory" page [http://www-oi.uchicago.edu/OI/IRAQ/ivory.htm]. Every entry represents an easily recognizable iconographic element (such as "Male Figure, Standing," "Male Figure, Kneeling,"

"Sphinx," "Griffin," "Scarab Beetle," "Sacred Tree," "Floral Designs," etc.), each illustrated by an example to its right. Clicking on one of them (here shown for the entry "Griffin" in fig. 3) will show thumbnails of all entries currently available in the database (b). Clicking on a thumbnail opens the individual page for this object (c). For a "scholarly" publication, such a data layout would be unsatisfactory. However, we believe that this visually-orientated presentation makes it possible for non-specialists to locate objects in our database even if they are unaware of names, functions, or cultural significance.

With about 300 entries, the ivories represent our largest group of objects posted so far, yet over 1,000 are still to follow. Some 600 to 700 seals, mostly from the Diyala, Nippur, and Abu Salabikh, are to be posted next. They will join a representative (though by no means exhaustive) display of statues and statuettes, stone vessels, reliefs, gold and bronze items, and terra-cottas that have already been posted.

At this point, I finally have to address two crucial and often asked questions: What is the significance (or even necessity) of this site in light of the ever changing numbers of lost items from the Iraq Museum? And what will its eventual scope and purpose be? The initial estimates given by the press in April, which predicted a total loss of the museum's collection (ca. 170,000 objects), were exaggerated. Yet, some press reports that have come out since May are equally misleading. A list of thirty to forty items, first published in late April based on information from Iraq Museum officials, has often been referred to as exhaustive list of missing items. Based on this, certain parties accused scholars and Iraq Museum officials of "hysteria" and "disinformation." But this list reflects *only* objects stolen from the museum galleries. As anyone who works in a museum knows, only a tiny fraction of a museum's holdings are typically on display. Most items remain in storerooms. While not accessible to the public, a museum's storerooms represent its real data pool for scholarly research. And this is where tragedy truly hit the Iraq Museum. The storerooms were broken into and several of them plundered. Since many items were taken off their shelves and are therefore misplaced or broken, it will take a long time to determine what is really missing. Moreover, the museum registry was devastated during the looting. The current loss estimates are approximations by specialists who had worked on certain artifact types in the museum and were familiar with its collection. These numbers are far from being final, but the general tendency is not encouraging. Some objects have been returned in the weeks following the looting (fig. 1). A UNESCO spokesperson reported in late May that 2,000–3,000 objects were still unaccounted for, but the numbers kept rising in June. They took a dramatic step up when in mid-June it was noted that, contrary to earlier reports, virtually all of the Iraq Museum's cylinder seals excavated before 1990 are missing. By late July, the official figure of missing objects had moved up to 12,000 with no indication of any finality. In short, there really is no reason for us to relax. But how do we reconcile these changing figures with our work on the Iraq Museum Database? With few exceptions, we have at present no way of establishing definitively which objects are missing and which objects have been located. By the time a final list is made available, however, many items may well have disappeared into private collections. The time to act is *now*. Our solution to this dilemma is a re-definition of the corpus in our database: all objects in it are known to be property of the Iraq Museum (and in this statement we do also include items that were stolen during looting after the 1991 war). The presence of an object in our database does not necessarily imply that it has been stolen. Should any of the objects be seen outside of Iraq, except in the context of a traveling exhibit, law enforcement should be contacted immediately. We are aware of the potential shortcoming of a list that is by far longer than the actual list of stolen items, but at present we feel that our resources in manpower and equipment are best used in adding more information than in spending time to re-examine the database

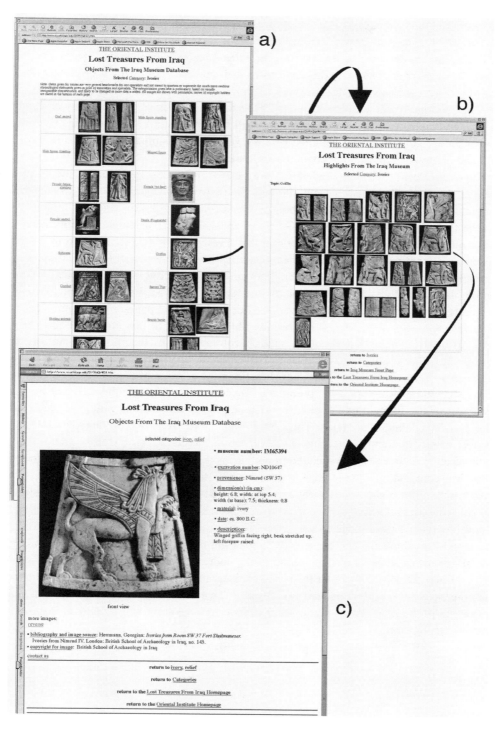

Figure 3. A set of screens from the Iraq Museum Database Project's Webpage, showing possible set of navigational steps from (a) a category page ("Ivories") with a listing of its sub-categories to (b) a sub-category page (iconographic motiv of "Griffin"), showing thumbnails of all entered objects belonging to this group, and (c) a description of an individual object

for objects that may or may not have been recovered. After all, what good would it do to add an object to the database six months from now once its theft is finally confirmed, if authorities could have intervened when it was on the antiquities market? Items that are recovered will be successively annotated, including descriptions of their current status. This is important since not every object returned was actually intact. The famous Warka Vase, for example, the relief scenes of which give one of the earliest accounts of the Mesopotamian picture of the world, was returned in mid-June but was severely damaged with its top register broken off (fig. 3). Although fragments are said to have been returned with the vase, it is possible that some pieces have gone astray and might eventually show up on the art market.

In summary, while we have made great progress over the past few months, plenty of work remains to be done. We hope that our site will soon move to the University of Chicago's Network Servicing and Information Technology Department. An Innovative Technology Grant from the Provost's Office, written by Gil Stein and Nicholas Kouchoukos, will enable us to transfer the database into a different environment. Presently the data is managed in a database program on a local machine; the data then gets scripted to the website. By definition, the data presented on the web is always an "older" backup, no matter how recent the update was done. Soon the database itself will be available online; data that is added or edited will be available immediately. This new layout will also replace our current static pages with dynamic pages, allowing much more individualized and refined object queries. In this effort, we have enjoyed great help from Nicholas Kouchoukos, an archaeologist in the Department of Anthropology, whose interests are closely related to ours. His expertise in building web-accessible databases using open source code has been extremely helpful in the creation of the design for this project.

This account must be somewhat preliminary since events that shape the nature of the project are still unfolding. I would like to close by thanking the people who so generously have helped this project financially, in particular Tony and Lawrie Dean for their very generous contribution. The most memorable and unprecedented contribution, however, came from a group of people who themselves have a very personal bond with artwork — artists. Devastated by the looting of the Iraq Museum and feeling the need to do something to help in the recovery of these priceless artifacts, a group of eighty-one Chicago artists donated countless hours of time, materials, and skills to create artworks that were sold during a special auction at Gallery Mornea in Evanston on June 13 to benefit our project (see inset). This event raised close to $10,000, a sensational success and a sizable sum that has greatly helped the financing our project. Truly, the money raised at this event played a distant second to the unprecedented nature of the event — as Bert Menco, a Chicago artist and one of the key organizers of the event, expressed it, "… the Artists helped the Art with the work of their own hands." Thanks to him, to the organizers at Gallery Mornea, and to the artists themselves. Their support and devotion will remain an inspiration to us in our ongoing work.

ISLAMIC ARCHAEOLOGY

Donald Whitcomb

The discipline of Islamic archaeology may be less familiar to members of the Oriental Institute, which describes itself as devoted to the art and archaeology of the ancient Near East. Research in this period began with the first field projects in the 1930s, tangential to work at Alishar Tepe, the Amuq, Nippur, and Medinet Habu (Jeme), and the special focus of later projects as E. F. Schmidt's work at Rayy and Istakhr and Robert McC. Adams work in the Diyala, Abu Sarifa, and Jundi Shapur. These projects contributed Islamic artifacts to the museum's large holdings of Arabic papyri, bookbindings, and tombstones, originally on display in Breasted's "Persian and Islamic Hall." Building on this tradition, the Oriental Institute has supported Islamic field projects at Quseir al-Qadim, Luxor, Aqaba, and most recently Hadir Qinnasrin, with a growing number of students benefiting from these opportunities to specialize in this relatively new field.

One of the most enduring ideas of Breasted is the concept of the "Fertile Crescent." Aqaba lies at a pivotal juncture along this zone of incipient civilization. This site has made major contributions toward understanding the formative period of Islamic civilization in the seventh century. The city plan and artifacts testify to the gradual transformation from late Byzantine into early Islamic styles. This parallels the emergence of Islamic political and cultural identity in the time of the first caliphs and the Umayyad dynasty. This is the beginning of a new age and not the end of antiquity, as more often depicted here in the Oriental Institute. The emergence of Islamic civilization, which is no clearer than the emergence of the Sumerians or the Old Kingdom, demands the attentions of archaeological research. Islamic archaeology presents a prime opportunity to address historical questions from complementary textual and archaeological evidence.

Quseir al-Qadim

In early November, Alka Patel, University of Michigan, organized an Interdisciplinary Workshop entitled, "Communities and Commodities: Western India and the Indian Ocean (11th–15th Centuries)." This provided an opportunity to present the resist-dyed textiles recovered in the Quseir al-Qadim excavations. The research of Ruth Barnes on the block-printed textiles from western India, located in the Kelsey museum (1993), is paralleled by a closely similar collection in the Oriental Institute. More importantly, this excavated corpus provides the first and largest body of evidence, closely datable and with architectural (and thus social) contexts. There is

some irony that the Quseir textiles are becoming the most important, or at least best known, result of these excavations.

A corpus of documents and textiles from one residence, called the Sheikh's house, may be narrowly dated to the first half of the thirteenth century. This artifactual assemblage features a wide range of ceramics, glass, coins, and evidence of foodstuffs, both used and stored in the residence and warehouse. Recent studies of the Quseir

letters by Li Guo (in *Journal of Near Eastern Studies* 1999, 2001) begin the description of the family of Sheikh Abu Mufarrij, who participated in the "kinship network" that was part of a Muslim commercial hegemony. This combination of artifacts and documentation allows an extremely detailed examination of this trading community, its relationship with the Geniza and archaeology of Fustat, and its role in the larger picture of Indian Ocean history. A preliminary article on the interrelationship of architectural context, artifacts, and documentation was written by the author with Katherine Strange Burke (doctoral candidate in the Department of Near Eastern Languages and Civilizations [NELC]), who will pursue the details of this subject in her dissertation.

Aqaba and Its Castle

Archaeological research has brought to light the early Islamic city of Ayla in the heart of the modern city of Aqaba. This archaeological site was occupied during a pivotal historical period (from ca. A.D. 650 to about A.D. 1100). The broader occupation pattern at Aqaba was a sequence of settlements, generally moving from northwest to the southeast. The early phases of archaeological research at Aqaba tended to focus on its foundation, on the potential significance of one of the earliest Islamic cities as a key to understanding the beginnings of this advance in urbanism. More recently, interest has shifted to the collapse of this city, or perhaps better, the causes of change to the newer settlement around the castle.

The latest events in the early Islamic port may be bracketed by the visit of the great geographer al-Muqaddasi (ca. 985), when he discerned the last phase of its early Islamic prosperity. This literary account may be contrasted with the archaeological evidence of massive destruction, the results of the earthquake of 1068, which sealed the fate of this settlement at a time when the shores of the Red Sea were dominated by the Fatimid dynasty of Egypt. This environment was one of political and economic instability, graphically demonstrated in the hoard of dinars from

Sijilmasa, perhaps lost during the bedouin sack of the town in 1024. The events of the millennium are an opportune moment to seek new historical understandings from archaeology.

When the site of early Islamic Ayla was abandoned in the early twelfth century, settlement shifted to the castle, known now as Aqaba castle. This fortified structure is located about one kilometer southeast at the mouth of the Wadi Shalala; the structure may be Crusader or, more likely, Ayyubid in origin. The present remains are mostly Mamluk and Ottoman. The author has argued that the castle and its surrounding settlement was called Aqabat Ayla in the medieval period. This name persisted until the fourteenth century, when the ruins of Ayla were no longer extant, and the name contracted to Aqaba. The modern city of Aqaba expanded from this village around the castle only in the last few decades.

While settlement in this region had certainly declined from the early Islamic urban center of Ayla, a continuity of human occupation was guaranteed in the constants of abundant freshwater, agricultural, and marine resources, combined with the economic incentive of seasonal activity provisioning pilgrims. The study of this castle has begun with two seasons in 2000 and 2001, under the direction of Johnny De Meulemeester, Denys Pringle, and Sawsan al-Fakhri. A larger season, with the participation of several NELC students, was postponed due to the recent conflict in the Gulf. One hopes that the larger settlement history, a splendid example of the utilization of archaeological and documentary resources in a regional context, will continue to amplify the discoveries in early Islamic Ayla.

Khirbet al-Karak

This small site is well known as Beth Yerah, an important early Bronze Age settlement on the southern shore of Lake Tiberias. The Oriental Institute's involvement in this site began in 1952/1953, when Pinhas Delougaz and Richard C. Haines excavated a Byzantine church beneath an "Arab building." Last year's *Annual Report* presented the startling discovery that this building was part of an early Islamic settlement called Sinnabra. A preliminary article outlining this analysis appeared in *al-Usur al-Wusta* 14.1.

More recently, the Israeli archaeologist, Rafael Greenberg, has returned to Khirbet al-Karak for new excavations. He reports much new information about the Islamic materials, as well as additional records in the stores of the Israel Antiquity Authority. Closer to home (in the Oriental Institute storerooms), NELC student Gabrielle Novacek has begun systematically examining the Bronze Age collections from this site; she reports finding more Islamic materials in this search. One hopes that a cooperative project may be possible at this multi-period site in the near future.

A30411

Jundi Shapur

Last February, Robert McC. Adams and many other archaeologists who worked in Khuzestan many years ago gathered for a Landscape Archaeology workshop in the Oriental Institute. I presented a paper praising Adams's contribution to Islamic archaeology in Iraq and Iran and followed this with the display of a small collection of ceramics from Jundi Shapur. In 1963, Adams turned his attention briefly from the long history of development of settlement and agricultural infrastructure in the Mesopotamian alluvium toward the adjacent region of Khuzestan in southwestern Iran. In one campaign, he mapped and excavated soundings on a city founded by Shapur

I in the mid-third century A.D. The site was located not far from the Oriental Institute excavations at Chogha Mish. Adams recorded the formidable ruins of Jundi Shapur, extending some 3.0 km by 1.5 km and laid out in an orthogonal fashion described as a chess board some seven hundred years later.

The brief excavations conducted by Adams at Jundi Shapur were too limited to reveal Sasanian monuments and communities, especially its medical school and Christian churches. Likewise, the continuations of the medical school and astronomical observatory, and social interactions within the early Islamic city, could not be located and these social achievements were denigrated as a long cultural decline. Last year, Abbas Alizadeh and Nick Kouchoukos began a program to return to Khuzestan on behalf of the Oriental Institute to continue the study of ancient settlements and irrigation systems. Abbas has prepared a solid foundation for this renewed investigation in his efforts to publish Kantor's work at Chogha Mish and (soon) Chogha Bonut, as well as his own archaeological research there. Like Adams before them, interest in the great Sasanian irrigation schemes lead naturally to the immense city of Jundi Shapur. In the spring season of research in Khuzestan, I hope to visit Iran and explore the possibility of resuming archaeological investigation at Jundi Shapur.

As part of these preparations, the Jundi Shapur sherds have been thoroughly studied. They proved interesting enough, colored glazes are always pleasant to handle, that they became teaching tools for a ceramics class that I taught this spring. A fine ceramic spout in the shape of a bull's head, a symbol of the potential interests of this Sasanian and early Islamic city, will be featured *in News & Notes*, Fall 2003, No. 179.

A Meeting in Berlin

The International Congress on the Archaeology of the Ancient Near East (ICAANE; at Copenhagen and Paris) provided two stimulating experiences in workshops on Islamic archaeology. These meetings resulted in the agreement by the participants that this discipline needs to find "a continuous platform for international meetings in our field." This sentiment was voiced by Dr. Claus-Peter Haase, Director of the Museum for Islamic Art in Berlin, who organized a Symposium on the Archaeology of the Islamic Periods held in Berlin on November 16–18. This forum presented an amazing range of important, recent discoveries in Islamic archaeology. A more important reason for this gathering was to discuss the future of this quickly expanding field of research.

As continuing association with ICAANE seems difficult, the symposium noted that a critical level in numbers and vigor of exchange seems to warrant the foundation of a separate organization. Alastair Northedge summarized this situation, which led to informal discussion throughout the symposium. Claus drew together a preliminary "steering committee," composed of himself, Jeremy Johns, Alan Walmsley, and myself to discuss a new organization, tentatively entitled the Association of Islamic Archaeologists. The aim is, as Claus put it, an institu-

tion which may offer a "better coherency of studies and presentations … and interchange with the colleagues in the Near and Middle East." This symposium had, of necessity, a restricted number of international participants and all were aware of a need for more inclusive future deliberations. This may be effectively achieved through the Internet; several proposals were entertained on accomplishing this, but with no immediate conclusion.

The initial description of this field as the Archaeology of Islamic Periods reflected some concern with misinterpretation of the idea of "Islamic Archaeology." Following the lead of Northedge's 1999 formulation, this term should be seen not as religious but cultural; the subject matter encompasses historic cultures under Islamic political hegemonies within which linguistic, material, and religious aspects may be present. While the focus should be on the "central Islamic lands," this field includes regions affected by Islam, whether in the Mediterranean, Asia, or Africa. Likewise, antecedent and parallel cultural traditions must be considered. Finally, the growing field of Ottoman archaeology must be included within Islamic archaeology. There needs to be recognition that the discipline of Islamic Art History is closely interrelated but has distinctive methodologies and theoretical concerns. More importantly, there is a common focus on the relationship with history and allied philological disciplines that must be clearly formulated. In sum, the field of Islamic Archaeology must address fundamental definitions to be recognized as an independent academic discipline. Islamic Archaeology needs to be more than what archaeologists of medieval periods do in Islamic lands.

An Advanced Seminar

At the Oriental Institute, an initiative in Islamic Archaeology was realized in May 2003 by the first of a new series of Advanced Seminars, advocated by Gil J. Stein, Director of the Oriental Institute. This seminar was an effort to explore comparative contextualizations in Islamic archaeology. Under the title of "Changing social identities in the spread of Islam: Archaeological and textual perspectives," an unlikely combination of archaeologists assembled at the Institute.

The participants included Tim Insoll, University of Manchester, on Islamic archaeology in West Africa; Yury Karev, Russian Academy of Sciences, Moscow, on Samarqand in Central Asia; Jodi Magness, University of North Carolina, on Khirbet Abu Suwwana near Jerusalem; Renata Holod, University of Pennsylvania, on Jerba Island in the Mediterranean; Mark Horton, University of Bristol, on Shanga in East Africa; and Tracy Hoffman, with her new doctorate

from NELC, on Ascalon on the Levantine coast. The discussant was Moain Sadeq from the Palestinian Authority, Gaza.

The goal of this seminar was a comparative analysis of different sites and regions, based on archaeological monuments or artifacts, exploring processes of adaptation or adjustment to local cultural complexes. Islam may be seen as a religion, political system, cultural complex, a trinity of inseparable aspects. The introduction of these variable characteristics of Islam, during the contact and afterwards, resulted in changes in identity approached as a sort of "cognitive" archaeology. In each specific case, one may assess the nature of the pre-Islamic regional tradition, the resulting plurality of cultures as a "multi-cultural" society, and finally a resultant normative condition as a regional or cosmopolitan culture.

Alternative archaeologies may be defined as a search for new contexts. Thus, for Insoll, definition of this field is found in the explicit archaeology of religion, and he attempts to make the case that material culture may be seen consistently through cultic or spiritual influences of this alternative archaeology. Islamic archaeology is practiced as an historical archaeology providing vital evidence for the development of society and economy in Islamic contexts. Each project, whatever its intended goals, produces informative associations which may be applied to relevant textual sources. The intention was not the reduction to a sort of essentialism but regional comparisons exploring Islamic archaeology from different disciplinary perspectives.

MIDDLE EGYPTIAN TEXT EDITIONS FOR ONLINE RESEARCH

Janet H. Johnson

METEOR (Middle Egyptian Text Editions for Online Research) is the acronym given to the project funded as part of a Mellon Foundation grant for Less Commonly Taught Languages. It is preparing an annotated, interactive, electronic Readingbook for Middle Egyptian, the classic stage of the ancient Egyptian language. The Readingbook includes a corpus of texts representing the numerous genres represented in Middle Egyptian and appropriate for students beginning their study of that language and the hieroglyphic script. Students are able to access any section of each text, sentence by sentence, in hieroglyphs, and practice reading the hieroglyphs and transliterating and translating the text. A click of a button brings help with reading signs, understanding grammar, or finding vocabulary. In addition, there are extensive linked informational sidebars and graphics. The sidebars include brief explanations or descriptions of topics mentioned in the texts and supplementary chronological, geographical, historical, and cultural information. The graphics include digital maps and images illustrating Egypt, the areas where individual texts were discovered, items mentioned in the texts, and, to the extent possible, the actual individuals mentioned in the texts, thereby helping the student to place the individual texts in their social, cultural, religious, political, historical, and geographical contexts.

During the academic year 2002/2003, data entry of the transliteration, translation, lexical, and grammatical analyses of the eleven Middle Egyptian texts being entered in Chicago was almost completed. This data entry was done by graduate students working from full transliterations, translations, and grammatical analyses prepared by Johnson. As noted last year, Sandy Schloen, our programmer, has designed an elegant method for entering, stacking, and otherwise manipulating the hieroglyphs, and the hieroglyphs for these texts have been entered and linked to the transliteration and translation. This year, graduate students began checking all the data entry that has been done in Chicago. Students with at least one year of study of Middle Egyptian (including Vanessa Davies, Rod Edwards, and Jackie Jay) worked through the "front-end" of every text, looking for errors, including typos, incorrect links, and the like. More advanced graduate students (including Josh Trampier and Malayna Williams) checked the "back-end" of every text for similar problems. Harold Hays, a doctoral candidate, checked the grammatical analysis of each text for accuracy and consistency. He also worked very closely with Schloen to resolve data entry or retrieval problems as they arose. Michael Berger, who handles all the administrative duties for this project, continued to supervise and coordinate the graduate students when they moved from checking data entry to preparing the "cultural links" providing background and supplemental information for the users. Most of the sign list, which not only gives the identification and common phonetic uses of each sign but also a schematic to help students learn how to draw the sign, was entered this year; links to the hieroglyphs in individual texts will be added when the schematics for drawing the signs are completed.

Schloen, with occasional assistance from Lec Maj, the Computer Research Assistant for the Division of Humanities, is making progress on moving METEOR's text files, which are in XML format, to a more stable "back-end." Tamino, an XML-based database, is being used to store, validate, and index the textual data, offering user-level security and greater flexibility for data entry, querying, linking, and analysis. Conversion of a sample text to the Tamino format has been successfully completed. The process has been established for converting the remaining texts. The possibility of improving and expanding the Readingbook's user interface using the Java environment, with its cross-platform capabilities, improved font handling, and front-end tool set, is also being explored.

The first extensive "classroom" testing of the Readingbook took place this year. During Autumn Quarter, Johnson taught the second year course in Middle Egyptian. That course is designed to expose students to as many genres of Middle Egyptian texts as possible. Each of the texts we read this year was available in the Readingbook. We did not use the Readingbook in the classroom, but all students were encouraged to access the program from home or from the Computer Lab in the Oriental Institute. Most did so regularly and passed along problems that they noted. When, toward the end of the quarter, an electronic "glitch" made it difficult to access one particular text in the Readingbook, the students complained that they felt very lost. In reality, they did very well on that text, so one did not have to worry that they were depending on the Readingbook to "do" their homework for them. The testing continued in the Winter Quarter in Johnson's hieratic class (hieratic is a more cursive script developed from the hieroglyphs); about half of the texts that were studied are included in the Readingbook. During Spring Quarter, she taught the third quarter of the first year course in the Middle Egyptian and again concentrated on texts that were available in the Readingbook. All year long, students were encouraged to pass along information about typos, incorrect links, incomplete information, and the like, and to indicate additional (types of) information they would like to see included. Their corrections have been incorporated, as have several of their suggestions.

Johnson, Schloen, and Berger gave a brief presentation of the project, its purpose and its current status, at a meeting held at Northwestern University in November 2002. This meeting was held to discuss programs funded under the Mellon Foundation's general umbrella of "Cost-Effective Uses of Technology in Teaching." This presentation emphasized, as had the original proposal to Mellon, that the Readingbook is not a stand-alone teaching tool for learning Middle Egyptian. Rather, the Readingbook serves as an excellent, reliable resource to supplement both formal classroom instruction and individual efforts to learn this fascinating, but difficult, language (and script). The presentation also noted that the "shell" which Schloen has developed is very flexible and can be used with any language, not merely Middle Egyptian. It is especially useful for any language for which the student must learn a new script as well as new grammar and vocabulary. The Readingbook may eventually be published as a CD-ROM or DVD, but it is currently being delivered over the Internet using the World Wide Web.

NIPPUR AND IRAQ AT TIME OF WAR

McGuire Gibson

In the summer of 2002, with the Iraq War looming, our attention turned sharply toward Iraq, the fate of its people, and the probable looting of museums and ancient sites. Nippur, as one of the most important and largest sites in Iraq, would be a likely target of looting, although it has been spared throughout the period of the embargo, during which dozens of other sites have been systematically ruined by illicit diggers.

As the market value of Mesopotamian antiquities rose steadily during the past fifteen years, the pace of looting increased to fill the demand. Although initially powerless to stop the wrecking of site after site, the Iraqi State Board of Antiquities was able to obtain emergency funding in the late 1990s and carried out salvage operations at more than twenty-five sites. Chief among these were Umma, Umm al-Aqarib, and neighboring mounds to the southeast of Nippur. The excavation teams had to work through the summers because they knew that if they left the sites the looters would return. By hiring as many as thirteen guards for each tell, they were able to keep the looters away. The day the war started on March 20, however, the looters came back and drove off the guards. Between 200 and 300 men would work every day on each site, brought out in the mornings and taken home each evening on trucks hired for the purpose. At Umma, they even set up a little camp. While we did not know this was happening until much later, we assumed that it was.

As far back as January 2003, I became involved with other archaeologists in trying to make America aware of the importance of Iraq as Mesopotamia, the birthplace of civilization. The Archaeological Institute of America put out a call for archaeologists to give to the Pentagon as much information as possible on the location of sites and standing monuments. I furnished the locations of more than 5,000 sites so that they might be avoided. This much information was easily assembled because we, at the Oriental Institute, have been working with students for years entering the locations that Thorkild Jacobsen, Robert McC. Adams, and other archeologists have put on settlement maps of Iraq since the 1930s into computer format. Using Remote Sensing, or Geographical Information Systems (GIS) technology, these students can give much more precise coordinates than could be done in traditional mapping procedures. At the request of the White House, we compiled a prioritized list of more than 100 sites that are better known, such as Nineveh, Babylon, and Ur of the Chaldees. We also included other sites that were of great significance not for any tourist value, but for the archaeological record. Throughout, we always em-

Statues from the site of Hatra showing failed attempt by looters to remove head, Iraq National Museum

Artifact holding and preparators' room after partial clean-up. Iraq National Museum

phasized the central importance of the Iraq National Museum in Baghdad and the Museum in Mosul. In more than one message to various officials, I also stressed the importance of the National Archive and Library in Baghdad. On two occasions, I was assured that the Pentagon was aware of the importance of these buildings and that they would be secured.

When American troops entered Baghdad and were reported to be at the Ministry of Information on Tuesday, April 8, I assumed that the next reports would be of the saving of the Iraq Museum. I started e-mailing my contacts in the army about this. On April 10, Thursday, when nothing was being reported, I phoned the *New York Times* and the *Chicago Tribune* and asked that they send their reporters to see if the Iraq National Museum was secure.

The world was informed by reporters on April 12 that the Iraq National Museum in Baghdad had been entered by looters on Thursday, April 10, unhindered by U.S. troops nearby. The looters were of two kinds. The first group seems to have been professional, armed and equipped with tools to open safes, doors, and cabinets. This group knew something about the routine of the museum, where storeroom keys would be kept, where important groups of items would be stored. They opened three out of the five storerooms and took thousands of artifacts. They also took forty important objects from the public galleries. They would have gotten much more except that the museum staff had disassembled the display cases and removed all portable objects to a secure storage facility. They had to leave large items and objects mounted on the walls. Thus, all of the Assyrian reliefs, similar to the ones in the Oriental Institute Museum, were left on display, but sandbags were laid out in front of them, and some items were wrapped in foam sheets. The most famous of the forty stolen items were the Warka Vase and the Warka Head. But an important cast copper figure, known as the Bassetki statue, was also lost. This statue weighs more than 300 pounds and seems to have been the object that was bumped down the marble stairs from the second floor gallery to the ground floor, breaking each step as it went down.

Following on the heels of the purposeful looters, crowds of more casual looters went into the Museum and into the wing that houses the State Board of Antiquities. They broke into each of the 120 offices, making huge holes in the wooden doors. They dragged out all of the office machines, computers, tables, chairs, and most of the desks. They seem not to have been very much interested in file cabinets, but they took out the papers and records, strewing them around the offices and all along the halls. The photographic archives of all the work done by Iraqi and foreign scholars since 1923 were trampled and scattered, with negatives badly damaged by dirt and abrasion. In addition, all personnel files, payroll information, and accounting records were thrown around, and the safe containing one month's salary for all employees was drilled, opened, and emptied.

In the museum, the casual looters were probably the ones who broke the glass in empty cases and tried to yank out of the wall smaller pieces of stone and copper decorations from Sumerian temples. They were probably also the people who ransacked the offices of the museum staff, throwing site catalogues, object catalogues, and other records onto the floor, stealing any equipment that would move and wrecking what was too big. They threw around chemicals in the conservation laboratories, scattered equipment, tore up books, and damaged objects that were in process of being conserved. In the storerooms, it was most likely the casual looters who took objects off shelves at random, while leaving others. They seem not to have wanted to steal pots, but they did take the time to smash hundreds of them on the floor.

Luckily, when the professional looters entered the storerooms, the electricity was off. They did not have enough light to work through the collections carefully. There were little piles of ash in the storerooms, evidence of fires made with insulating or packing materials to give them light.

Our associates in Iraq related what they witnessed: Dr. Jabber Khalil, the President of the State Board of Antiquities and Dr. Donny George, the Director General for Research, along with one guard and Muhsin, a man who lived at the rear of the museum, and Muhsin's son, were the only people left in the museum on the morning of Tuesday, April 8. At 11:00 A.M., they saw fedayeen fighters jump over the wall into the Museum grounds, and witnessed the beginning of a battle between them and the U.S. Army. Dr. Jabber decided that they should evacuate the building and come back in a few hours when the fighting had stopped. The only people left on the museum grounds were Muhsin and his son, who retreated to their house.

Iron door to basement storage and protective block wall penetrated by looters between April 10 and 11. Iraq National Museum

When Dr. Jabber and Dr. Donny tried to return that afternoon, they found the Tigris bridges blocked by U.S. troops and were not allowed to proceed. They were still unable to get back to the museum complex until Sunday, April 13, after they knew from a BBC broadcast that the Museum had been undergoing looting since Thursday. They appealed to the Marine commander at the Palestine Hotel to do something. On the previous day, museum personnel who live near the museum arrived to drive off the remaining looters and block the doors. But mobs still threatened to come in until Thursday, April 24, when U.S. Army tanks finally arrived to guard the museum.

The devastation that greeted returning museum employees was reflected in the news reports showing their reaction to empty cases, broken displays, and damaged sculptures in some of the rooms. Many had not been in the museum exhibition halls when they were disassembled, so the employees thought that most objects had been taken from the public galleries by the looters. They also found out fairly soon that three of the storerooms had been entered. The early publicized number of 170,000 objects stolen was a misinformed but not unrealistic figure. A reporter had asked the museum staff, "How many objects are in the Museum?" A person familiar with the collection answered 170,000. This figure did not reflect, however, the fact that registration numbers often include groups of objects. So, 170,000 registration numbers represent many more objects in the museum collection.

Another group of missing objects is not reflected in the registration numbers. The Antiquities Board had as many as fifty ongoing digs. In the week leading up to the war, the Iraqi excavators brought their finds and field catalogues to Baghdad to be accepted by the museum. These objects were laid out and inspected, but the process of entering them into Iraq Museum records was not completed. The objects were put in steel trunks and deposited in a storeroom, one of the three that were opened by looters. These trunks were forced open, the objects dumped out. Looters took what they wanted and smashed many objects.

As a result of the numbering system and the unprocessed objects brought to the museum just before the war, when museum staff go through their painstaking inventory of the burglarized storerooms, they have to check more than one set of records. By June 30, the official tally of known missing items reported by the museum staff (working with a team of U.S. Customs inspectors) had reached 12,000, and there was still much checking to be done. In mid-June, news reports across the world began to downplay the losses in the museum, stating that only thirty-three pieces had been taken. This was as gross a distortion of fact as the initial figure of 170,000.

It was known by then that many of the formerly displayed objects were safe in a very secure, secret storeroom off-site. It also became public knowledge that some of the most vulnerable items, such as the treasures from the Queens' tombs of Nimrud in Assyria and much of the gold from Ur, as well as a famous copper head of an Akkadian king were also safe. The gold items and the head had been put in the deep vaults of the Central Bank in 1991, before the first Gulf War, and had been left there for secure storage. During the current war, this bank was hit by a bomb and debris partially filled the stairs to the vault, so there was still a lot of worry about the fate of those objects. Almost immediately after I had heard about the looting of the museum, I began to send e-mails to the Pentagon and to the White House asking that the Central Bank be secured, as I had known about the gold in the vaults as early as 1992. We then saw on TV vivid pictures of people looting the Central Bank and burning Iraqi money (which they later regretted since it was still usable). It took more than a week before the bank was secure. Some men did get down to the level of the vaults and tried to open one of them with a grenade launcher. The blast killed one of them and it may also have triggered an accidental or planned flooding of the basements of the bank. Only after pumping out 50 feet of water could the vaults be opened, in

Major storeroom of the Iraq National Museum, partially cleaned, notice gaps on shelfs and broken pottery on floor, May 2003

the presence of museum officials, and the still sealed crates identified. Later, the crates were transferred to the museum, where they were unpacked and the objects cleaned and examined for damage.

The losses from the museum in Baghdad were not as catastrophic as they might have been, but they were still major. In the long run, the ransacking of the offices and the loss of valuable records may prove to be even more devastating. Assessing this kind of damage will take a long time. (For more information on the museum looting and attempts to recover stolen objects, see report on the Iraq Museum Project.)

While the world's eyes were focused on the museum in Baghdad, looters were destroying sites, especially in the south, ancient Sumer. The day the war started, hundreds of men went to Umma and drove off the thirteen guards that the Antiquities department had left to protect that site. Nearby sites that had also been the subject of rescue operations in the past few years were hit once again, with looters driving off the posted guards. We now know of at least thirty sites in the south, large and small, that have been or are being dug illegally. Each day, the loss of artifacts from these sites probably outnumbers the losses from the looting of the museum in Baghdad. The looters are quite brazen, greeting the U.S. military with smiles. They pretend that they have been working only a few days, but it is clear from the extent of destruction that the work has been going on for weeks.

I saw the damage firsthand by U.S. helicopter on May 21, when I accompanied Ambassador Piero Cordone, the Occupation Authority's man now in charge of the Iraqi Ministry of Culture. I had given the military a list of eleven sites that I thought had been or were likely to be looted because they are very important, well-known sites. Most had been excavated in the past by for-

Figure 6. U.S. armed forces survey condition of damage at Nippur, May 2003

eign or Iraqi expeditions. Included in my list were Nippur, Umm al-Hafriyat, and Adab, all three of which have been excavated by University of Chicago teams. I led expeditions at the first two, and Edgar James Banks dug at Adab in 1903. I had driven to Nippur on May 16 and had seen holes that had been dug as recently as a week before. We met with the guards and the local shaykh. The guards said that sixteen men came and were better armed than they, so they were powerless to stop the looting. I thought that by paying the guards more, and by engaging the shaykh and his entire group, the site would be safe. The day we visited by helicopter, there were no new holes. But in June, a few weeks after my return to Chicago, I received an e-mail message from someone who had been at Nippur and said that there more than a hundred new holes.

We took off from Nippur and flew over Umm al-Hafriyat, a site to the east where I had excavated in 1977. Circling over the site, we could see that the tell looked like a waffle, full of recently dug holes, but no one was working at the time. On the way south to Adab, I could see two more small sites riddled, but not being worked that day. Adab itself was a revelation. Here, as we circled, we could count between 250 and 300 men digging all over the mound. The damage was unbelievable. Clearly this digging has been going on for years, and Adab's tablets, seals, and other objects must have been flooding into the international antiquities market for some time. We then flew south over Tell Shmid, where fifty men were digging. Then, on to Umma where probably 300 men were busily destroying the parts of the site that had been excavated carefully only a few weeks ago by the Iraqi Department of Antiquities. Here, we landed and the military escort shot into the air, scattering the looters. We walked over the site, taking pictures of the ragged pits and tunnels sunk into the rooms already exposed by the archaeologists. As we took off, I could see the tell that is the ancient city of Zabalam in the distance. Though too far off to make a count, it was clear that men were destroying that site as well. The same was true at

Umm al-Aqarib, another site that had been excavated until recently by the Department of Antiquities.

Over the site of Girsu, I could see that recent digging had occurred, but no one was working at the time. At Tell al-Hiba, the site of ancient Lagash, there appeared to be no damage at all.

From here, we turned west, passing over four sites that showed recent digging. Bad Tibira was one of those. The helicopter touched down at Ur, near the area of houses that has been in part reconstructed. We walked past the tombs of the Ur III kings (ca. 2150 B.C.) and over to the ziggurat, where the son of the guard had set up a little stall to sell bottled water and souvenirs to tourists. Since the site of Ur is occupied by the U.S. military, his only tourists were soldiers and journalists. Interestingly, we were told by a solider that the commander of the nearby Tallil air base was sending Military Police to check our identity. Apparently, we had no prior clearance to land at Ur. As we went back to the helicopter, six Humvees arrived at the ziggurat ready to take care of the intruders. However, we were already in the air before we could be arrested. Apparently, one group of the U.S. military doesn't communicate with the other.

From Ur, we made our way to Larsa and confirmed that it also had huge robber holes dug into it. Again, no one was working that day. Then, we circled Uruk for several minutes, checking that there was no digging there. The guards at Uruk are part of a tribe that has worked with the Germans since the 1920s, and they keep the site intact. We were supposed to stop at Uruk, but we were getting very tired and some of the group were feeling a bit ill because of the fumes from the engine and the heat. Besides, I wanted to make sure that we stopped at Isin, where we already had dramatic testimony from a German archaeologist who had visited the site a few days before. When we landed, the 250 or so diggers came running, very pleased to see us. They began

Site of Nippur, beginning of destruction by looters, July 1, 2003

Members of U.S. armed forces viewing destroyed site of Isin, May 21, 2003

showing us objects that they had found that day. After they were rounded up into a group, they were told that it is forbidden to dig. They left, helped along by a few shots over their heads. One young man, who had come out with a tractor and trailer as a taxi for local villagers, wanted us to pay for his fares since his clients had taken off by foot. I know from a reporter's account that the very next day they were back working, talking about the helicopter visit.

From Isin, we flew back to Baghdad, exhausted and convinced that something urgently had to be done to protect the sites. The stealing of objects is a big loss, but the destruction of archaeological context is devastating. Objects left in their original findspots gain much greater value than they have on their own. It is only from context that we can learn about the real function of objects, the role they played in an institution, and the inter-relations of items that might not appear to be connected at all. A clay tablet with cuneiform inscription is a valuable source of information, but when it is found in a room with dozens of other tablets and other objects, we can begin to reconstruct what went on in that room, the connection between the tablets and the people appearing in the texts, and we can begin to see how specific officials did their jobs. Without such connections only guesses can be made.

There is a U.S. plan to guard sites, but the process is painfully slow. The real key is to strengthen the Antiquities organization, get its representatives functioning all over the country, bring the guards back on sites and back them up with force until it is clear to the Iraqi public that the U.S. occupying power is serious about this issue. It might seem silly to some to worry about antiquities sites when fighting is still going on. But it is no sillier to guard antiquities sites than it is to guard oil wells. In the future, when oil is not so important because it has been replaced by some other fuel, or when it is finally depleted, the country of Iraq will still have an economic base in agriculture, minerals, and tourism based on its cultural heritage. The Iraqi diggers are not thinking of the future, but only about feeding their families. Even the agents who come from

Baghdad each week to collect objects and pay the diggers are just doing a job. The dealers in Baghdad, and especially those in Europe, America, and the Far East, are looking for this year's profits, though they have a gloss of education, of artistic appreciation, and a rationale for the evil they do. The collectors are often from the finest old families and do not like to be compared to drug users, but that is exactly, in my opinion, whom they do resemble. They are abetted by some of the finest museums in the world, which, though they do not buy antiquities with shady provenances, will show objects on loan from Mr. X or Mr. Y. And, unfortunately, some of our colleagues in art history and cuneiform studies authenticate, read, analyze, and write catalogue entries for stolen items. Everyone involved at this level knows that the entire traffic of such objects is illegal and that the voracious appetite of collectors for antiquities is destroying archaeology, but very few ever say a word in public. U.S. Customs tries to halt some of the flow of objects, but the process is very slow. The passage of the Iraqi Heritage Protection Act may finally put some teeth into the law enforcement in the U.S. trade. That would help because our country is now the leading consumer of illegal antiquities. However, until some brave prosecutor indicts one of the collectors, there is little hope for antiquities located around the world, not just in Iraq.

If the situation in Iraq begins to stabilize a bit, we have some hope of returning to work there. For years, we and other archaeologists will be engaged in assessing the damage to sites and running salvage operations. I do not envy the people who try to resume work at Isin or Umma. They will spend most of their time trying to distinguish between robber holes and ancient dirt. I hope that Nippur is not destroyed, but even a hundred holes in what was an un-looted site until the U.S. occupation should not have been allowed to happen. We can only hope there will be better times.

INDIVIDUAL RESEARCH

Richard Beal

Richard Beal spent most of the past year reference checking and copy editing the early entries for the second fascicle of the S volume of the Chicago Hittite Dictionary. He also found some time to work on the word *da-* "to take."

Last year, Beal's article "The Hurrian Dynasty and the Double Names of Hittite Kings," appeared in *Anatolia Antica: Studia in Memoria di Fiorella Imparati* (Eothen 11; Florence, 2002), pp. 55–71. Beal argues that the kings of the Hittite New Kingdom did not form a new Hurrian dynasty but were actually direct descendants of the kings of the Old Kingdom. Thus the long noticed phenomenon of kings having both a "Hittite" and a Hurrian name cannot be accounted for as a Hurrian personal name and a Hittite throne name. Rather, as kings of Hittites and Hurrians, Hatti and Kizzuwatna/Syria, the kings had, perhaps from time of birth, perhaps from the time of accession, both an Anatolian and a Hurrian name.

Another article published is "Gleanings from Hittite Oracle Questions on Religion, Society, Psychology and Decision Making," in *Silva Anatolica: Anatolian Studies Presented to Maciej Popko on the Occasion of His 65th Birthday*, edited by P. Taracha (Warsaw, 2002). This article studies a considerable number of texts in which the Hittites asked the gods a series of yes or no questions on such topics as the reasons for plagues, whether dreams and unsolicited omens really were messages, where the king should spend the winter, the leadership of campaigns, the routes of campaigns, etc. The questions reveal Hittite preoccupations and worries. The Hittites could now discover and categorize new gods. New or foreign cult practices could be established. The Hittites did not live in abject fear of the gods but were often like employees everywhere, sometimes quite negligent, hoping their divine bosses would never notice or care, only fixing things, apologizing, and perhaps paying a fine when the boss grew angry. "Fertility" was not the major obsession for the Hittites that it is for modern scholars. Finally, the gods did not choose one campaign route or leader, but instead ruled out certain options while leaving other options from which the king could choose.

The articles "Le strutture militari ittite i attacco e di difensa" and "I reparti e le armi dell'esercito ittita," appeared in the exhibition catalogue *La Battaglia di Qadesh*, edited by M. C. Guidotti and F. Pecchioli Daddi (Florence).

Beal spent his vacation in the Louvre in Paris and the British Museum in London helping his wife, JoAnn Scurlock, collate Neo-Assyrian and Neo-Babylonian medical texts for her books on Mesopotamian medicine. Most evenings and weekends were dedicated to aiding in proofreading and reference checking her book on ancient Mesopotamian medical diagnostics and prognostics, written with medical professor Burton Andersen.

Robert D. Biggs

Robert D. Biggs spent part of July 2002 studying cuneiform omen texts in the British Museum, London. In November, he presented a paper, "The Human Body and Sexuality in the Babylonian Medical Texts," at the Colloque international "Médecine et médecins au Proche-Orient ancien," in Lyon, France. In connection with his long-standing study of Babylonian medicine, he has been invited to serve on the Editorial Board of the Babylonisch-assyrische Medizin series in Berlin which will continue the work of the late Professor Franz Köcher. He has spent a considerable amount of time in 2003 involved with activities related to the looting of the Iraq Museum, including, at the invitation of the United States Department of State, participating in an international meeting at Interpol headquarters in Lyon, France.

John A. Brinkman

John A. Brinkman visited the British Museum in August 2002 to work on early Neo-Babylonian legal texts. In December 2002 and again in May 2003, he spent a week in the University Museum, Philadelphia, editing Middle Babylonian texts from Nippur and beginning to read through the archeological records documenting the early Nippur expedition (1889–1900) that excavated most of these tablets. Brinkman continued to prepare Neo-Assyrian texts from Khorsabad for publication, concentrating this year on what survives of the inscriptions on the back of the Oriental Institute Museum reliefs before these are closed off from public view in the next few months. He wrote an article on Middle Babylonian family names derived from occupational titles (e.g., Carpenter, Smith, Fisher), a practice that seems to have begun several centuries earlier than generally recognized; and, while preparing a short note on the little-known sixteenth-century Babylonian king Peshgaldaramash for the *Reallexikon der Assyriologie*, he managed to track down several unpublished texts dating from this king's reign. Work on the Middle Babylonian prosopographical database progressed steadily, with about 1,500 additional texts scanned and added to the listings.

Peter F. Dorman

Peter F. Dorman traveled to Cairo during the winter to initiate research at the Egyptian Museum on the final stages of his next volume for the Egyptian Expedition series of the Metropolitan Museum, provisionally entitled *Excavations on the Hillside of Sheikh Abd el Qurna*. On the same journey, he was also able to visit Chicago House for ten days to visit the ongoing fieldwork at the small temple of Amun at Medinet Habu. Dorman also assisted in coordinating arrangements for the publication of the first epigraphic volume from that monument, which will be devoted to the innermost chapels decorated by Hatshepsut and Thutmose III. He focused his efforts primarily on the nature of the programmatic alterations in decoration undertaken within those chapels by Thutmose after the death of his coregent.

Two publications appeared this year: *Faces in Clay*, published as volume 52 of the Münchner Ägyptologische Studien series, and an article concerning an Old Kingdom stone block in the Oriental Institute's Museum that has never been placed on exhibit, "The Biographical Inscription of Ptahshepses from Saqqara: A Newly Identified Fragment," in the *Journal of Egyptian Archaeology* 88 (2002).

Last winter, Dorman served on one of the archaeological review panels for the National Endowment for the Humanities, and, in the spring, delivered a lecture at the Kimbell Museum in Fort Worth entitled "Resurrection and Decline: The Fragile Nature of the Egyptian Eternal," at an inaugural symposium of the exhibit "The Quest for Immortality."

Dorman also secured funding for the Oriental Institute's Phase 4 of the Advanced Papyrological Information System (APIS), a cooperative project involving a number of universities and museums; our own participation is devoted to the online cataloguing of ancient texts on papyri (and other materials) in the collection of the Oriental Institute Museum and Regenstein Library. The annual APIS meeting of consortium members was hosted by Chicago in September of 2003.

Walter Farber

Walter Farber's research and teaching this year again covered many different fields, from an advanced seminar on problems of Akkadian grammar to articles on the use of some Sumerian cultic hymns, the scribal education in Babylonia, some Middle Assyrian administrative texts, and an interesting inscribed magical figurine in the Oriental Institute Museum.

Much of his free time was spent editing (for private publication) a manuscript of memoirs written by Wilhelm Schmid, his great-grandfather. As a classicist, Schmid was famous in his time and is still well remembered for his monumental *Geschichte der Griechischen Literatur* (History of Greek Literature), which he wrote and published as an emeritus between 1929 and 1948. He also took an active part in the musical life of his time, being a personal friend of Hugo Wolf and Anton Bruckner. His memoirs offer a fascinating glimpse into a world of academia, music, and private life, which, though long gone, has some surprising similarities to our own time and reflects many problems the Humanities are still facing today.

McGuire Gibson

McGuire Gibson has been extremely busy in the past year. He has made dozens of appearances on television, been engaged in many more interviews on radio in the U.S. and abroad, and has been quoted in newspapers and magazines all over the world. All this media activity was related to his involvement in trying to save the remains of ancient Mesopotamia. Gibson was invited to a UNESCO conference in Paris on the Iraq Crisis and a follow-up conference at the British Museum in late April. He participated in a UNESCO fact-finding delegation that visited Baghdad in May, but he was already in the country as a member of a team of archaeologists sent by the National Geographic Society. At the end of that mission, Gibson spoke at a meeting entitled *Archaeology in No-Man's Land* in Bonn, Germany. In early June, he also spoke at a New York University-sponsored conference on *The Certainty of Uncertainty: Preserving Art and Culture in the 21st Century*. In Chicago, he gave a Marbury Lecture at the Piper-Rudnik law firm in a teleconference that reached twelve offices of the firm across the country. Also, during the year he addressed the Monday Class and other groups, usually on the question of the impending war or its results.

He has also been deeply involved in re-establishing the American Association for Research in Baghdad, a not-for-profit academic consortium of universities and museums that was nearly established in Iraq in 1990. It is hoped that the organization can set up a research center in Iraq in the very near future to encourage joint Iraqi-U.S. projects, foster exchanges of scholars on all levels, and otherwise strengthen working relationships between the academic communities of both countries.

Besides his continuing direction of Nippur and Hamoukar, he still maintains a major research commitment to the Diyala Objects Project and the Oriental Institute-Argonne Modeling Project. This year, Gibson joined the Advisory Board of the Chicago Humanities Festival. He continues to serve on the executive committee and the Board of Directors of the Council of American Overseas Research Centers. Gibson is also on the board of the American Institute for Yemeni Studies.

Stephen P. Harvey

Stephen P. Harvey joined the Oriental Institute and the Department of Near Eastern Languages and Civilizations as Assistant Professor of Egyptian Archaeology in January 2003, coming to the University of Chicago from the University of Memphis, where he served as Assistant Director of the Institute of Egyptian Art and Archaeology and Assistant Professor in the Department of Art.

Harvey conducted a season of fieldwork at Abydos, southern Egypt from May to July 2002, and, on July 12, he presented the results of his most recent work in London as an invited speaker at the British Museum International Symposium. He spent the autumn in New York City writing, analyzing the results of fieldwork, and preparing for the move to Chicago. His presentations on his research at Abydos included lectures for Columbia University's Seminar on the Ancient Near East on October 9, 2002, and for the Society for the Study of Egyptian Antiquities 28th Annual Symposium on Ancient Egypt held in the Royal Ontario Museum, Toronto, on November 9, 2002. On December 6, 2002, he gave a lecture to the Egyptological Seminar of New York, held in the Metropolitan Museum. On January 22, 2003, he presented his recent discoveries at Abydos to a public audience in an Oriental Institute Members Lecture in Breasted Hall. In April, he attended the Annual Meeting of the American Research Center in Egypt, representing the Oriental Institute on behalf of Janet H. Johnson at its Board of Governors meeting. In May 2003, Harvey gave an illustrated lecture entitled "The Status of the Artist in Ancient Egypt" to the Arts Club of Chicago, discussing evidence for the recognition of individual ancient artist's social and artistic identities. In June 2004 he will lecture on his Abydos work at the Musée du Louvre in Paris, France.

From October 12 to 26, 2002, Harvey traveled to Egypt as Study Leader on a joint Archaeological Institute of America/Field Museum tour entitled "Egypt Revisited," where he had the pleasure of sharing lecturing duties with T. G. H. James, retired Keeper of Egyptian Antiquities of the British Museum. In the past year, Harvey appeared on the introductory video to the international traveling exhibition of Egyptian funerary art entitled "Quest for Immortality," as well as in the first of a three-part BBC/Lion Television series on the New Kingdom entitled "Egypt's Golden Empire," which aired in Chicago on Channel 11 in 2003. While still at the University of Memphis, Harvey developed the concept for a collaboration with Chicago-based photographer Barbara Kasten, entitled "Reflections of Egypt," for which he wrote an accompanying interpretive essay. The exhibition, held in the Art Museum of the University of Memphis from November 16, 2002 to January 18, 2003, displayed Kasten's large-scale visions of selected objects from the Institute of Egyptian Art and Archaeology's collection of Egyptian art.

During the Winter Quarter, Harvey taught a combined undergraduate/graduate survey of Egyptian art and architecture, as well as a graduate seminar on the archaeology of New Kingdom cult places, a subject closely related to his own research. In the Spring Quarter, Harvey had hoped to return to Abydos with students to continue excavation of the monuments of King Ahmose and his family, but the expedition was delayed due to political events in the Middle East. Instead, Harvey remained in Chicago, conducting research and teaching a one-on-one reading course on ancient Egyptian warfare. This spring, with the tremendous assistance of Oriental Institute students Jason Ur, Carrie Hritz, and Jesse Casana, he also began to explore applications of satellite imagery to the archaeological landscape of the Abydos region. With their help and support, Harvey acquired CORONA, ASTER, and LANDSAT imagery and began to analyze these for potential research applications.

This spring, Harvey corrected proofs for an article entitled "Interpreting Punt: Geographic, Cultural and Artistic Landscapes," in *Encounters with Ancient Egypt: Mysterious Lands*, edited by David O'Connor and Stephen Quirke (The Institute of Archaeology, University College London, forthcoming September 2003). An article entitled "New Evidence at Abydos for Ahmose's Funerary Cult" was submitted to the *Egyptian Archaeology* for publication in the upcoming issue.

Harry A. Hoffner, Jr.

The following publications by **Harry A. Hoffner, Jr.** appeared in the period July 1, 2002 to June 30, 2003: "Daily Life among the Hittites," in *Life and Culture in the Ancient Near East*, edited by R. Averbeck, M. W. Chavalas, and D. B. Weisberg, pp. 95–120 (Bethesda: CDL Press, 2003); "The Disabled and Infirm in Hittite Society," in *Eretz-Israel* 27 (Hayim and Miriam Tadmor Volume), edited by I. Ephal, A. Ben-Tor, and P. Machinist, pp. 84*–90* (Jerusalem: Israel Exploration Society, 2003); "Theodicy in Hittite Texts," in *Theodicy in the World of the Bible*, edited by A. Laato and J. C. de Moor, pp. 90–107 (Leiden: Brill, 2003).

During that same period the following were submitted for publication or still await publication from much earlier submission: "A Grammatical Profile of the Middle Hittite Mašrat Texts," in *la-a-ma-an-te-et na-ak-ki-i: Studia Anatolica in Memoriam Erich Neu Scripta*, edited by C. Rüster, J. Catsanicos, and R. Lebrun (Louvain-la-Neuve: Peeters); "Hittite ara- 'companion' in quasi-adjectival use," in *Nouvelles Assyriologiques Brèves et Utilitaires* 2003 No. 1; "On a Hittite Lexicographic Project," Review of *Hittite Etymological Dictionary*, Vol. 5: *Words beginning with L. Indices to* Volumes 1–5, by J. Puhvel (Trends in Linguistics, Documentation 18; Berlin, 2001); Review of *Corpus of Hieroglyphic Luwian Inscriptions*, by J. David Hawkins; Review of *An Akkadian Handbook*, edited by Douglas B. Miller and R. Mark Shipp; Review of *Systematische Bibliographie der Hethitologie 1915–1995*, by Vl. Soucek and Jana Siegelová; Review of *The Kingdom of the Hittites*, by T. Bryce; Review of *Religions of Asia Minor*, by Maciej Popko; Review of *Ethnoarchaeology of Anatolia. Rural Socio-Economy in the Bronze and Iron Ages*, by Jak Yakar.

Hoffner took three important trips during the year for academic purposes. In September 2002, he flew to Turkey and spent eleven days there, where he spoke at the International Congress of Hittitology (Sept. 2–6) on the meaning of the Hittite modal particle *a-as-ma*. The manuscript of which lecture is in the hands of the editor for publication in the journal *Die Sprache*. He flew back to the United States on September 11th! In February and March of 2003, he taught in Costa Rica for one month, and, at the end, he and his wife toured some of the lovely countryside and rain forests of Costa Rica. From April 3–5, he flew together with Theo van den Hout to Los Angeles to attend the world premiere of the new film *The Hittites*, produced and directed by Tolga Örnek, in which he and Theo, together with other Hittitologists, appear as scholarly commentators.

Most of Hoffner's research during the year was spent on preparation of the lectures given in Corum and Costa Rica, on revising CHD articles together with Theo van den Hout, and on finishing the manuscript of a new grammar of Hittite being written with Craig Melchert.

Despite his busy schedule, Hoffner was also active in guiding University of Chicago graduate students in their dissertation research. He was on the dissertation committee of Mary Bachvarova who submitted and successfully defended her dissertation, and of Robert Hawley whose dissertation on Ugaritic Epistolography was successfully defended on May 16, 2003. Both of these students were awarded Honors for their dissertations, and both now have academic positions.

Off and on during the year, together with Theo van den Hout, he consulted with and advised Sandra Schloen in technical matters relating to publishing Chicago Hittite Dictionary volumes online as the "eCHD."

Thomas A. Holland

Thomas A. Holland continued to intermittently work with the Oriental Institute's Publications Office to help prepare the manuscripts for the final publication of the two forthcoming Oriental Institute Publications (OIP) volumes on the archaeological and landscape research studies done by Holland and Tony J. Wilkinson. This research focuses on Tell es-Sweyhat, located in the northeastern sector of the Tabqa Dam area in the upper Euphrates Valley in Syria. Work has progressed well on Wilkinson's introductory volume to Sweyhat, *Tell es-Sweyhat, Syria,* Volume 1: *Settlement and Land Use on the Margin of the Euphrates River and in the Upper Lake Tabqa Area.* Two of this year's work-study students, Lindsay DeCarlo and Katie Johnson, completed the computer scanning of the artwork and the bibliography for the Sweyhat landscape volume. Clemens Reichel, Research Associate, is updating and completing a valuable contribution to Wilkinson's landscape volume, Appendix B. "Gazetteer of Sites in the Upper Tabqa Dam Area." At present, Thomas Urban is editing the volume and Leslie Schramer is formatting it. Wilkinson will soon receive page proofs for his final approval and both Holland and Urban will approve the manuscript for final publication, which we estimate will be towards the end of this calendar year.

The Publications Office also made a good start on the production of Holland's Sweyhat text and plate volumes, entitled *Tell es-Sweyhat, Syria,* Volume 2: *Archaeology of the Bronze Age, Hellenistic, and Roman Remains at an Ancient Town on the Euphrates River.* Lindsay DeCarlo and Alexandra R. Witsell completed the scanning of the 340 photographic and line illustrations and page layout of the plate volume is well underway. One of the new work-study graduate students continues to scan the Sweyhat text illustrations. The Publications Office continues to review the final textual matter for good usage, grammar, punctuation, as well as a thorough check of the extensive bibliographical entries for this volume, which the Publications Office estimates will be ready for press during the early part of 2004.

Holland, personally and on behalf of the Publications Office, wishes to thank everyone who worked so hard during 2002/2003 to help bring the results of our academic endeavors at Tell es-Sweyhat closer to final publication. Wilkinson, Reichel, and Holland worked on the additions and corrections that were necessary for the printing of final excavation reports in the OIP series. Urban did a marvelous job in organizing and assisting all of the work-study graduate students who have greatly contributed to the forthcoming publication of the Sweyhat volumes: Leslie Schramer, Katie Johnson, Lindsay DeCarlo, and Alexandra R. Witsell; Urban also began the tedious job of computer formatting Wilkinson's volume so that initial page proofs will be available for Wilkinson before he leaves Chicago for his new position at the University of Edinburgh. The staff of the Publications Office has again this year done an excellent job in preparing Oriental Institute research.

Janet H. Johnson

Janet H. Johnson spent much of her time during the past year working on the Demotic Dictionary Project (see separate report) and on the annotated Middle Egyptian Text Editions for Online Research project (see separate report). She continued to serve on the Board of Governors and the Editorial Board for the American Research Center in Egypt. Johnson has recently been appointed a member of the Fulbright-Hays National Screening Committee for Egypt for the years 2003–2005. In the University, she served as a member of the Council of the University Senate and as chairman of the Technology Oversight Committee of the Division of the Humanities, through which she keeps the Oriental Institute informed of technological changes in the most closely related part of the University.

Johnson also collaborated with Thomas Dousa and François Gaudard, senior graduate students in the Department of Near Eastern Languages and Civilizations and staff of the Demotic Dictionary Project, on the publication of a Demotic temple inventory, including an analysis of the items included in the inventory. This publication will include the parallels to such an inventory, and the potential functions such an inventory served. The text was written in the town of Soknopaiu Nesos (also known as Dime) in the Fayum near the end of the first century or the beginning of the second century of the modern era, when Egypt was part of the Roman Empire. It is now housed in the collections of the Berlin Museum. The article will appear in a festschrift for a European colleague.

W. Raymond Johnson

W. Raymond Johnson completed his twenty-fourth year working for the Epigraphic Survey in Luxor and his sixth season as Field Director. Recent publications include "The Luxor Temple wall fragment project," co-authored with Conservator Hiroko Kariya, in *Egyptian Archaeology: The Bulletin of the Egypt Exploration Society* (Spring 2003); and "A Composite Statue of Amenhotep III in the Cairo Museum," co-authored with Peter Lacovara, published in *Egyptian Museum Collections Around the World: Studies for the Centennial of the Egyptian Museum*, edited by Mamdouh Eldamaty and Mai Trad (Cairo: American University in Cairo Press, 2002).

Ray gave two gallery talks this summer, one at the opening of the Epigraphic Survey's Lost Egypt photography show at the Oriental Institute Museum on July 10, and another at The Field Museum of Natural History's British Museum Eternal Egypt show on July 24. In New York on June 11, he gave a presentation, "Recent Preservation Work in the Luxor Temple Blockyard," to the World Monuments Fund, who sponsored the work. As a result of the presentation, the World Monuments Fund gave the Epigraphic Survey a new two year, $95,000 matching grant for expanded conservation, documentation, and reconstruction work in the precinct.

Ray was recently invited to join the Visiting Committee of the Metropolitan Museum of Art Egyptian Department, and he attended his first meeting in June. This summer he was promoted to Research Associate (Associate Professor) at the Oriental Institute. He is currently updating and revising his Ph.D. dissertation, "An Asiatic Battle Scene of Tutankhamun from Thebes: A Late Amarna Antecedent of the Ramesside Battle Narrative Tradition," for publication, and is desperately trying to think of a shorter, catchier title for it!

Charles E. Jones

Circumstances prevented a number of delegates, including **Charles E. Jones**, from attending the organizational meeting of *The First International Conference on the Ancient Cultural Relations Between Iran and West Asia* in Teheran in June 2002, but the organization of the conference proceeded. At the time of writing, all are awaiting visas and tickets and fully expecting to attend the conference in Teheran in August 2003. In November, Jones chaired a second annual session at the Society of Biblical Literature (SBL) meeting in Toronto. This annual session, jointly sponsored by the SBL's office of Research and Development, seeks to provide a forum for the presentation of imaginative projects integrating technology in the development of tools for the study of the ancient Near East. The session showcased (among other things) a presentation of the electronically published version of the Chicago Hittite Dictionary (eCHD) by Sandra Schloen. These sessions have been very successful and will continue in November 2003 at the annual meeting in Atlanta. Jones has been appointed to the editorial bard of ARTA: Achaemenid Researches on Texts and Archaeology [http://www.achemenet.com/ressources/enligne/arta/arta.htm]. He has several articles in preparation for publication in collaboration with Matthew Stolper and Wouter Henkelman. An article written with Matthew W. Stolper, "Hallock, Richard T.," appeared in the spring in *Encyclopaedia Iranica*.

Work continues — very slowly — on the Persepolis Fortification Tablets projects. The Persepolis component of the XSTAR project, thanks to Gene Gragg and Sandra Schloen, is nearly ready for a semi-public presentation. This electronic form of publication promises to be an extraordinarily powerful research environment — and the technical and editorial issues involved present very interesting challenges.

The war in Iraq has been the overwhelming event of the past year for many of us. As a central place for communications on the ancient world, the Oriental Institute has been particularly burdened by the crisis. The volume of e-mail handled by Jones, for instance, more than tripled from the normal flow of amount three hundred e-mails per day, to between a thousand and fifteen-hundred e-mails per day in April and May. Jones has been closely involved in the development of the Institute's response to the cultural property crisis in Iraq. His participation focuses around three activities:

(1) Development of a Preliminary bibliography of books documenting the contents of the Iraq Museum, the National Library and Archives, and the Manuscript collection of the Ministry of Religious Endowments — all in Baghdad — as well as of Other Damaged or Destroyed Collections in Baghdad or Elsewhere in Iraq including Mosul, Basrah, Suleimaniyeh, etc. This bibliography is published online as a part of the Institute's Iraq Museum Database Project: [http://www-oi.uchicago.edu/OI/IRAQ/iraq_bibliography.html]. The version online at time of writing is the 25th — including 220 titles — and indexes more than twelve-thousand Iraq Museum numbers.

(2) Organizer and moderator of IraqCrisis: A moderated list for communicating substantive information on cultural property damaged, destroyed, or lost from libraries and museums in Iraq during and after the war in April 2003, and on the worldwide response to the crisis [https://listhost.uchicago.edu/mailman/listinfo/iraqcrisis].

(3) Member of the Middle East Librarians Association Committee on Iraqi Libraries [http://www-oi.uchicago.edu/OI/IRAQ/mela/melairaq.html]. The MELA Executive Board convened the Committee on Iraqi Libraries to coordinate the organization's response to the damage and destruction suffered by libraries in Iraq during and after the war in March and April 2003. The committee is envisioned to be a small task force of MELA members who have firsthand knowledge of, experience, or strong interest in matters related to libraries in Iraq, and who will be able to field questions, play the role of contact, and suggest ways to assist in rebuilding efforts. The web presence of the committee is an important clearinghouse for data relating to the destroyed and damaged libraries of Iraq. At the time of writing it appears that the situation in Iraq will remain as a major focus of Jones's attention for the foreseeable future.

Walter E. Kaegi

Cambridge University Press published **Walter E. Kaegi**'s book H*eraclius Emperor of Byzantium*, which he began investigating many years ago and which he began writing in 1996/97. He also published two lengthy (8,000 words each) articles on "Byzantine Civilization" and "Byzantine Empire" in the second edition of the *New Catholic Encyclopaedia* (Gale). Kadmus Press, Damascus, Syria, published, in book form, the Arabic translation of his 1992 book *Byzantium and the Early Islamic Conquests* translation by Nicola Ziyada (Damascus: Kadmus Press, 2002). He wrote a new Foreword to this Arabic Translation, on p. 35, by agreement with Cambridge University Press. He published an article in a multi-contributor volume in Sardinia, Italy: "Society and Institutions in Byzantine Africa," in *Ai confini dell'impero. Storia, arte e archeologia della Sardegna bizantina* (Cagliari, Sardinia, Italy: M & T Sardegna, 2002), pp. 15–28. He published two articles "Commentary," *Ancient World* 33 (2002), pp. 37–44 [on three papers in panel by John Shean, Michael Meckler, Joel Walker, in "Trends in the Study of Late Antiquity" of Association of Ancient Historians at American Historical Association Annual Meeting, 7 January 2000]; "Robert Lee Wolff Remembered," *Byzantinische Forschungen* 26 (2002), pp. 299–311. Kaegi published his entry on Oriental Institute-related activities in *The Oriental Institute 2001/2002 Annual Report*, edited by Gil J. Stein, pp. 109–10. He published the following book reviews in hard copy form: Review of *Aristocratic Violence and Holy War*, by M. Bonner, *Journal of Near Eastern Studies* 61 (2002), pp. 293–95; Review of *Church and Society in Byzantium under the Comneni*, by M. Angold, *Journal of Near Eastern Studies* 61 (2002), p. 293; Review of *War and Society in the Ancient and Mediterranean Worlds, Asia, the Mediterranean, Europe and Mesoamerica*, by K. Raaflaub and N. Rosenstein, *Phoenix* 56 (2002), pp. 180–82; and Review of *Byzantine Wars*, by John Haldon, *Speculum* 78 (2003), pp. 189–90. He published one review online: Review of *The Development of the Komnenian Army*, by J. Birkenmeier, *De Re Militari* (2003), http://www.deremilitari.org/review17.htm.

Kaegi presented the following papers and public lectures: "Pilgrimage to Jerusalem," Oriental Institute, June 28, 2002, lecture to visiting University of Notre Dame students under Prof. Robert Haak; "Late Antiquity," Seminar Presentation to the National Endowment for the Humanities Summer Seminar on Islamic States, University of Chicago, Biological Sciences Research Building, July 2, 2002. He served as Chair, Session, Byzantine Studies Conference, Ohio State University, Sunday, October 6, 2002. He twice delivered the following lecture: "The Riddle of Constans II in Italy," University of Bologna, Sede Ravenna, March 12, 2003, and University of Bologna, Bologna campus, March 27, 2003. He also spoke on "Byzantine Sardinia Threatened: Its Changing Situation in the Seventh Century," Oristano, Sardinia, Italy, Convegno sui Bizantini in Sardegna: Forme e caratteri della presenza bizantina nel Mediterraneo occidentale: la Sardegna (secoli VI–XI), March 22, 2003. Other papers included "On Writing the Biography of Heraclius," in Historiography Workshop (workshop on biography), May 16, 2003, Social Sciences 224, University of Chicago; and "Byzantium and Early Muslim Penetrations of Anatolia," University of Erfurt, Germany, June 6–8, 2003, International Workshop on "The Encounter of Oriental Christianity with Islam in the 7th and 8th centuries."

Carol Meyer

Much of **Carol Meyer**'s time went into finishing a major article for *Journal of the American Research Center in Egypt*. It is a study of ancient gold mining, ore reduction, and refining at Bir Umm Fawakhir in the Eastern Desert, Egypt, and the eastern Mediterranean in the fifth to sixth century Byzantine period and the roots of the technologies as far back as the second millennium B.C. As a collaborative publication between an archaeologist (Meyer), a mining engineer (Bryan Earl, retired), a geologist (Mohamed Omar of the Egyptian Geological Survey and Mining Authority), and a physicist (Robert Smither of Argonne National Laboratory), the paper required some translation between segments. Bryan Earl is now trying to achieve a micro-smelt with a crushed ore sample from the modern gold mines at Wadi el-Sid, about 5 km southwest of Bir Umm Fawakhir. The Wadi el-Sid mines are modern, but they were worked in antiquity as well, and Earl is trying to test and clarify Agatharcides' less-than-clear second century B.C. smelting instructions. In November, Meyer traveled to Phoenix, Tucson, and Berkeley to present a lecture on Bir Umm Fawakhir to the local chapters of the Archaeological Institute of America (AIA) and the American Research Center in Egypt (ARCE). She also got an ARCE/National Endowment for the Humanities grant to travel to Cairo in the winter of 2003/2004 to write parts of the final reports on the Bir Umm Fawakhir 1996, 1997, 1999, and 2001 seasons. Specifically, she plans to incorporate unpublished material in the Egyptian Geological Survey library and to field-check the final maps and plans. Finally, much of her "free" time in May was given over to revamping her 1977 files and computer records of stone artifacts in the Iraq National Museum. In all, records of about 400 items, about half unpublished and none on display, and 232 drawings of unpublished small finds were reformatted, updated, expanded, and/or scanned and stored on two CDs for Clemens Reichel's Iraq Museum database.

Alice Mouton

From January 2003 until December 2003 **Alice Mouton** has been working as a Research Associate for the Chicago Hittite Dictionary Project. She is financed by the Lavoisier Grant provided by the French Ministry of Foreign Affairs.

Mouton has written several articles for the Hittite Dictionary, primarily on words starting with *ta-*. She has also transcribed the Hittite texts from Kuşaklı (Hittite city of Šarišša) for the Chicago Hittite Dictionary Project files.

On a private note, Alice Mouton has finished and submitted her dissertation and expects the defense of her Ph.D. to take place in Paris (École Pratique des Hautes Études) and Leiden University in the near future. She also took part in a congress on Anatolian Religion in Bonn in February 2003 and wrote two articles, which will be published in *Zeitschrift für Assyriologie* and *Journal of Ancient Near Eastern Religion*.

Clemens D. Reichel

For **Clemens D. Reichel**, 2002/2003 was a more than a busy year; it turned out to have many unanticipated twists and turns. During this time, he continued work on the Diyala Project (see separate report) as its project coordinator. Between November and April, he worked for the museum on the re-installation (object selection, labels, and panels) of the Daily Life section in the

Mesopotamian Gallery. By mid-April of 2003, following the looting of the Iraq Museum, Reichel found himself in charge of coordinating the efforts to build the Iraq Museum Project database to document losses and to help in the recovery of stolen items (see separate report). During the summer of 2002, Reichel continued his work on the clay sealings from Tell Hamoukar (see separate report). His results were summarized in a paper "Seals and Sealings at Hamoukar — New Insights into Administrative Complexity in Syria during the Fourth Millennium B.C.," delivered at the annual meeting of the American Schools of Oriental Research in Toronto. He also gave numerous other lectures on the Diyala Project and the Iraq Museum Project at the Oriental Institute and elsewhere, including lectures before the Visiting Committee of the Oriental Institute in February 2003 and before the Visiting Committee of the Humanities Division in May 2003.

The following article and book chapters written by Reichel have appeared in 2002/2003: "Administrative Complexity in Syria during the Fourth Millennium B.C.: The Seals and Sealings from Tell Hamoukar," in *Akkadica* 123 (2002); "A Modern Crime and an Ancient Mystery: The Seal of Bilalama," in *Festschrift für Burkhart Kienast zu seinem 70. (Geburtstage dargebracht von Freunden, Schülern und Kollegen)*, edited by Gebhard J. Selz (Alter Orient und Altes Testament 274); "Sealing Practice," in *Cuneiform Texts from the Ur III Period*, Volume 2: *Drehem Administrative Documents from the Reign of Amar-Suena*, by Markus Hilgert (Oriental Institute Publications 121; Chicago: The Oriental Institute, 2003).

Erica Reiner

After the end of the academic year, June 26–28, 2002, **Erica Reiner** attended the three day "Workshop on Babylonian Astronomy" held at Brown University in honor of Asger Aaboe. Aaboe is emeritus historian of science at Yale University and was the teacher and mentor of most American historians of Babylonian science, though, alas, not hers, even though she often profited from his learning and advice. At that workshop, Reiner presented a paper on "Stars and Planets: Reflections on Stellar Omens in Enuma Anu Enlil," based on the group of celestial omens she had been working on. From Providence, Reiner continued on to the Netherlands where she attended the Rencontre Assyriologique Internationale in Leiden, at which, together with Miguel Civil and Fumi Karahashi, she represented the Oriental Institute.

At Christmas 2002, she finally received the first copies of her book, *An Adventure of Great Dimension: The Launching of the Chicago Assyrian Dictionary*, on which she had been working for several years. After finishing that project, she returned to the task of publishing a further volume of Babylonian planetary omens, now ready to be submitted to Brill.

Off and on, Reiner performed various tasks for the CAD (reference checking, proofreading, and writing a few words for the final volume). At the April annual meeting of the American Oriental Society in Nashville, she read a paper on "The Four Winds" illustrated with slides. At the annual dinner, she was honored to receive the Society's "Medal of Merit."

Reiner is pleased to report the publication of *La antigua Mesopotamia*, the Spanish translation of A. L. Oppenheim's *Ancient Mesopotamia*, by the publishing house Gredos in Madrid, Spain, for which she wrote a new preface. The translation, by Ignacio Marquez Rowe, is based on the revised edition that she completed in 1977.

Robert K. Ritner

Throughout the past year, **Robert K. Ritner** has served as the formal academic consultant for The Field Museum Exhibit "Eternal Egypt," on display in Chicago from April 25 until August 12, 2003. As content advisor, his duties included regular meetings with Field Museum staff to provide advice and text copy on matters of labels, wall plaques, translations, graphics, timelines, floor plans, case design, lighting, interactive displays, recorded tours, in-house and outreach lectures, staff training, adult education and gift-shop reproductions. Particularly successful innovations for the Chicago installation include three "talking stelae," replicas which play Ritner's recorded introductions and translations while precisely synchronized lights illuminate the relevant text and images. For public relations, Ritner conducted a series of live interviews for television (NBC, CBS, WGN), radio (WBEZ, WHPK) and the print media (Chicago Tribune, The Sun Times, Copley News, North Shore Magazine, Oak Park Journal, Northwestern University Medill School of Journalism, Cachette Magazine).

Ritner lectured extensively for public and professional symposia. On August 14, Ritner spoke at the National Gallery of Art on "Egyptian Magic: Its Use in Temple Ritual, State Practices, and Private Funerary Tradition" in conjunction with "Ancient Egypt: The Quest for Immortality," an exhibit for which he recorded an audio tour. Thereafter, he attended the Eighth International Congress for Demotic Studies in Würzburg, Germany, where he chaired a panel and delivered a grammatical lecture on "Some Problematic Bipartite Nominal Predicates in Demotic" (August 30). On December 7, he discussed "Libya in Egypt: The Culture Wars of the Third Intermediate Period" for the Egypt Exploration Organization of Southern California. For The University of Chicago Women's Board, he analyzed "Reading Egyptian Art: Script and Representation in Ancient Egypt" on January 15. In association with the exhibit "Eternal Egypt," Ritner lectured on "Eternity Held Captive: the Social and Religious Context of Egyptian Art," delivered at The Field Museum on April 24, 26, 27, and 30. Further exhibit lectures were given May 1 (for the Breasted Society), 15 (Field Ambassadors), and 21 (Field Associates and Cultural Collections Committee), and June 9 (Egyptian Consulate and Egyptian Tourist Authority). Concurrently, Ritner lectured for the Kimbell Art Museum in Fort Worth ("Magic in Ancient Egyptian Religion and Funerary Practices" on May 3) and The University of Chicago Alumni Association ("An Introduction to Egyptian Artistic Representation as Exemplified by the British Museum Exhibition 'Eternal Egypt'" on May 17). On June 27, he providing the keynote lecture for the first Egyptological congress in Greece, speaking in Rhodes on "An Eternal Curse upon the Reader of These Lines (with Apologies to M. Puig)."

Ritner's publications for the year include The Context of Scripture, Volume 3 (W. W. Hallo and K. L. Younger, eds.; Leiden); "Third Intermediate Period Antecedents of Demotic Legal Terminology," in *Acts of the Seventh International Conference of Demotic Studies*, edited by K. Ryholt (Copenhagen); "Des preuves de l'existence d'une nécromancie dans l'Égypte ancienne," in *La magie en Egypte: à la recherche d'une définition*, edited by Y. Koenig (Paris: Musée du Louvre); and "Ecstatic Episode from 'The Report of Wenamon' (col. 1/34–43)" in *Prophecy from the Ancient Near East*, by M. Nissinen (Atlanta). In August, Ritner was interviewed regarding Egyptian dentistry by the New York (Science) Times, with the remarks printed as "Q & A: Teeth and Millstones" (August 6). His article on "The 'Breathing Permit of Hôr' among the Joseph Smith Papyri" appeared in the July issue of *Journal of Near Eastern Studies*. Now in press, *The Literature of Ancient Egypt* (third edition, edited by W. K. Simpson) has been announced for September. In addition to University and Oriental Institute committee duties, Ritner taught a full complement of courses, including the popular "Introduction to Religion and Magic in Ancient Egypt." He will be on leave in the fall, having been invited to serve as visiting professor in Egyptology in the Department of Asian and Middle Eastern Studies, the University of Pennsylvania, and as Egyptologist in Residence in the University of Pennsylvania Museum.

Martha T. Roth

Martha T. Roth continues to devote most of her scholarly energies to the Assyrian Dictionary project (see separate report). During the 2002/2003 academic year, she delivered lectures at Yale University (on prostitution in Mesopotamia) and the University of Connecticut Law School (on Babylonian law). Her published papers this year included "Deborah, Rebekah's Nurse," *Eretz-Israel* (Hayim and Miriam Tadmor Volume) 27 (2003), and "Hammurabi's Wronged Man," *Journal of the American Oriental Society* 122 (2002).

Oğuz Soysal

In 2002/2003 **Oğuz Soysal** continued his work on the Chicago Hittite Dictionary Project. He has spent most of his time writing articles on words beginning with *ta-*.

Aside from this, his research activities have continued to focus on Hittite culture/history and Hattian language. The following articles were published between 2002 and 2003: "Zur Herkunft eines gemeinsamen Wortes in Altanatolien: parninka/i-," in *Silva Anatolica. Anatolian Studies Presented to Maciej Popko on the Occasion of His 65th Birthday*, edited by P. Taracha, pp. 315–37 (Warsaw, 2002); "Einige vermißte, übersehene oder verkannte hattische Fragmente," *Anatolia Antica: Studia in Memoria di Fiorella Imparati* 2, edited by St. de Martino and F. Pecchioli Daddi, pp. 753–81 (Eothen 11; Florence, 2002); "Ortak Bir Eski Anadolu Kelimesi parninka/i-'nin Kökeni Hakkında," *Archivum Anatolicum* 5 (2002), pp. 171–91 (in Turkish); "Corrections to readings of Konya-Seal Inscription (1997.12.1)," *Nouvelles Assyriologiques Brèves et Utilitaires* No. 3 (2002) p. 67; with Rukiye Akdoğan, "Yayınlanmamış Boğazköy AnAr fragmanlarından değişik içerikli metinler," *Anadolu Medeniyetleri Müzesi* 2002 Yıllığı (2003), pp. 172–95 (in Turkish); "Kantuzzili in Siegelinschriften," *Bibliotheca Orientalis* 60 (2003), pp. 41–56; "Zu einer Lesung und Bedeutung," *Nouvelles Assyriologiques Brèves et Utilitaires* Nr. 1 (2003), pp. 17–18.

As one of the philological results of Soysal's Hattian research, the Hattian origin of a common Ancient Anatolian word *parninka/i-* (borrowed also into Hittite and Luwian), designating a certain trouble for the human body, has been determined. Having spent the whole summer of 2002 in Chicago, Soysal also had time to study two Hittite seals with hieroglyphic Luwian inscriptions. One of them originated in the Sivas region and is deposited in the Sivas Museum; another one is in the Konya Museum. He dedicated a long article to Sivas and related seals, which appeared in *Bibliotheca Orientalis* 60. Also, a brief notice on the Konya seal is published in *Nouvelles Assyriologiques Brèves et Utilitaires* Nr. 3 2002. The latter object is a uniquely shaped silver Hittite seal and belonged to a person named Šarkuili, the charioteer (a very common profession noted on Hittite seals). The owner of the Sivas-Seal, however, is a very special personality. His name is Kantuzzili and he bears the title "the great lance man," the highest ranking official in the Hittite court. Furthermore, in April 2003, Soysal published, with his Turkish colleague R. Akdoğan, six unpublished Boğazköy tablets from Ankara Museum that appeared in the *Annual of the Ankara Museum* 2002 (pp. 172–95). The article deals with some Hittite, Akkadian, and Hattian fragments. R. Akdoğan made the text copies, and Soysal provided philological comments.

After eight years of intensive work, the *Hattischer Wortschatz in hethitischer Textüberlieferung* is now in the final stage before its publication. In mid-April, Soysal received from Europe a very positively written recommendation letter for publication of his work, and since then he has focused on the final formatting of the book. Tom Urban, very kindly, took over this complicated job and is now preparing a PDF-generated camera-ready version of the book. It is expected that the book will come out in early 2004.

Emily Teeter

Emily Teeter's research continues to be devoted to the publication of artifacts from the Oriental Institute's 1926–33 excavation at Medinet Habu. This year she can report that, thanks to the hard work of the publications office, the first volume on scarabs, scaraboids, seals, and seal impressions, dedicated to the late Joan Rosenberg, has finally appeared. She is now finalizing the text for the next volume on baked clay figurines. Teeter hopes to submit it to the publications committee early next year. Another publication that has taken long to see the light of day, *Ancient Egypt: Treasures from the Collection of the Oriental Institute*, funded by the generosity of the University of Chicago Women's Board, is presently with the printer in China. It is the first of what is envisioned as a multi-volume series on noteworthy artifacts in our museum.

Other publications include two entries for *The World Book Encyclopedia* and a brief note on an artifact in *News & Notes* 178, Summer 2003. She extensively rewrote and edited a children's book *Hieroglyphs*, with Karen Price Hossell. Reviews appeared in the *Journal of Near Eastern Studies* and the online journal *AfricaNet*.

Lectures include a discussion of Egyptian religion at the National Gallery, Washington, D.C., in conjunction with the exhibit, "Quest for Immortality"; a lecture at the St. Louis Art Museum; an Oriental Institute Members Lecture on the Breasted 1905–07 expedition; a similar lecture at the University of Washington co-sponsored by the Seattle chapter of the American Research Center in Egypt; and a presentation on new acquisitions to the Classical Arts Society at the Art Institute of Chicago. In January, Teeter was invited to assess the Egyptian collection of the Chrysler Museum in Norfolk, Virginia, for possible reinstallation, and she also trained their docents. Here in Chicago, she taught "Hieroglyphs By Mail" (assisted by Hratch Papazian), in elementary, intermediate, and advanced levels.

Theo van den Hout

In the past year, **Theo van den Hout** taught two winter classes: Elementary Hittite 2 (an anthology of Hittite texts), and Carian, Pisidic, and Sidetic. Carian represents the latest branch on the Anatolian tree of Indo-European languages. Its state of decipherment is now such that one can be confident that it is a distant relative of Hittite. However, more inscriptions are needed to gain better insight into the language. Even less material is available for the study of Pisidic and Sidetic, but still their Anatolian character seems fairly certain and the three languages together made a very stimulating class. In the spring, he taught a class on Hittite Prayers, concentrating on compositions of King Muršili II. The class tried to use the prayers to determine some of the traits typical of the Hittite script and language of Muršili's days towards the close of the fourteenth century B.C.

Van den Hout's research time was taken up almost completely by the Chicago Hittite Dictionary (CHD) (see the separate report). In addition, he submitted a translation with notes of the two main so-called Plague Prayers of Muršili II for a volume of *Ancient Near Eastern Texts* in translation and edited by Mark Chavalas. He also submitted an article on a combined Lydian and Lycian topic for the festschrift of a colleague and two reviews. He wrote several articles for the *Reallexikon der Assyriologie*: Pala (the area north east of the Hittite capital in the Pontic mountains, home of the Anatolian Palaic language), Palast, Pfand, and Pferd.

Publications released were: "Self, Soul and Portrait in Hieroglyphic Luwian," in Silva Anatolica. Anatolian Studies Presented to Maciej Popko on the Occasion of His 65th Birthday, edited by P. Taracha, pp. 171–86 (Warsaw, 2002); "Another View of Hittite Literature," in *Anatolia Antica. Studi in Memoria di Fiorella Imparati*, edited by St. de Martino and F. Pecchioli Daddi, pp. 857–78 (Eothen 11; Florence, 2002); "Another Middle Hittite Oracle Fragment," *Nouvelles Assyriologiques Brèves et Utilitaires* (2002), p. 44; and "De affaire Tarhunmija. Brieven van een Hettitische hofschrijver," in *Zij Schreven Geschiedenis. Historische Documenten uit het Oude Nabije Oosten (2500–100 v. Chr.)*, edited by R. J. Demarée and K. R. Veenhof, pp. 145–53 (Leuven). The following article was electronically published: "Miles of Clay: Information Management in the Ancient Near Eastern Hittite Empire," at http://www.fathom.com/story/story.jhtml?story_id=190247›http://www.fathom.com/story/story.jhtml?story_id=190247. Also, the second issue of the *Journal of Ancient Near Eastern Religions* was released.

On the latter topic of the character of the Hittite tablet collections and information management during the Hittite Empire, van den Hout presented several papers: at the V. International Congress of Hittitology, Çorum, Turkey, September 5; during the Humanities Open House, University of Chicago, October 26; at the symposium Digital Genres: Semiotic Technologies This Side of the Millennium, University of Chicago, May 30; and in German at the Ludwig-Maximilians Universität München, June 16. He spoke about "Kingship and Political Structure in Hittite Anatolia (1650–1180 B.C.)," in the Organizations and State Building Workshop, Department of Political Sciences, University of Chicago, April 14.

Finally, he was very pleased with the appointment as "Correspondent" member of the Royal Dutch Academy of Arts and Sciences.

Donald Whitcomb

While this last year did not appear to be an optimal time for fieldwork, **Donald Whitcomb** seemed to travel more than usual to various meetings. He attended the Seminar for Arabian Studies in London in July. Then in the fall, he gave a lecture at the first symposium of Shah Nematollah Vali sufi order in San José. In November, he went to Ann Arbor for a conference on

Communities and Commodities: Western India and the Indian Ocean (11th–15th Centuries); his talk was on the Sheikh's house at Quseir al-Qadim. Directly after that, he flew to Berlin, where he presented a paper on "Methodological difference in archaeology and history: the example of Qusayr/Egypt."

Back in Chicago, Don chaired a panel on Architecture and Society at *Middle East History and Theory Conference* and presented a paper at the workshop on "Archaeology and History" at the *Oriental Institute Workshop on Landscape Archaeology*. Finally, the major activity of the spring was organizing the first Advanced Seminar at the Oriental Institute, entitled *Changing Social Identity with the Spread of Islam: Texts and Archaeology*. This seminar provided a fascinating comparative perspective on this growing discipline, one which will have more fieldwork in the near future (see separate report, *Islamic Archaeology*).

Don gave two lectures for the 2002 National Endowment for the Humanities (NEH) seminar on *Early Islamic States*, one on the Dome of the Rock and the other on the trade of Aqaba. The latter subject was also presented at the MacDonald Institute of Archaeology in Cambridge University. Another lecture was given to the Cardiff Archaeology Research Seminar, advertised as "Quseidr al-Qadm," apparently a Welsh spelling of the archaeological site. These two venues were facilitated by visits to serve as examiner for the viva (dissertation defense) of two Islamic archaeologists, Alison Gascoigne and Andrew Petersen. Closer to home, Tracy Hoffman successfully defended her thesis and became the Oriental Institute's first Ph.D. in Islamic Archaeology. Following in her footsteps, Katherine Strange Burke and Choukri Heddouchi (both of the Department of Near Eastern Languages and Civilizations) and Ian Straughn (Anthropology) presented successful proposals for dissertation research in the same field of studies.

The opening of the new Persian Gallery in the Oriental Institute Museum provided a fine attraction for an international group of journalists. This group was visiting the United States, and Chicago, as part of the Silk Road Project, and it was a privilege to assist the museum office in guiding them through this hall. This same gallery provided the backdrop for an Oriental Institute conference on ancient Iran, in which Don gave a paper called "Mythology and Heritage: The Meanings of Persepolis."

Tony J. Wilkinson

As the world now seems to be engaged in a continuous cycle of wars, it is inevitable that the Oriental Institute's programs of fieldwork in the Near East will become ever more vulnerable to changes or cancellations than before. Despite the constant rumor of a war with Iraq, **Tony J. Wilkinson** managed to sneak in some brief spells of fieldwork in Turkey and Iran (in September/October 2002) and Yemen (in early 2003) before major conflict in Iraq took place during the spring of 2003. The seriousness of the war and its aftermath was made painfully obvious during a brief damage assessment trip he made to Iraq between May 8 and 17, 2003. The team, which included McGuire Gibson and Mark Altaweel of the Oriental Institute, was part of a larger group sponsored by the National Geographic Society which had as its primary objective the assessment of damage to archaeological sites as a result of the recent war. In contrast to the Baghdad of the 1980s, which was a vigorous and thriving city, in May 2003 we found that the sprawling metropolis was punctuated by burning or bombed out public buildings and ringed by numerous battlefields. Mosul, in the north of the country, on the other hand, was in a much better state with less damage and a commercial life well on the way to recovery. Nevertheless, the Assyrian capitals of Nimrud and Nineveh, as well as the Mosul Museum, had suffered significantly from looting. Although this was not as severe as in the south of Iraq where McGuire Gibson found that numerous sites bore the evidence of extensive plunder pits, the looting and damage to northern sites still represents a cause for considerable concern. During this visit we therefore placed emphasis not only on pinpointing where damage had occurred but also on suggesting where it was crucial for guards to be placed.

Because the war in Iraq and its aftermath resulted in a massive media blitz, the busy teaching spell of the spring quarter was made even more hectic than normal. Wilkinson, like other members of the Oriental Institute associated with Mesopotamian Archaeology, was involved in numerous TV and radio interviews. As a result of this he received the supreme accolade of modern life: his first hate mail!

With the award of a $1.2 million grant from the National Science Foundation, the autumn of 2002 and 2003 witnessed a new phase in the development of the program of modeling ancient settlement systems. This award, which commenced in August 2002 for a five year term, will enable a team from the Oriental Institute, together with colleagues from the Department of Anthropology and the DIS division at the Argonne National Laboratory, to model the development of Bronze Age Mesopotamian cities and to determine how such cities might have developed in the face of a capricious physical and economic environment. The Oriental Institute team, comprises Tony Wilkinson and McGuire Gibson as senior principal investigators — in conjunction with David Schloen, Chris Woods, John Sanders, and Magnus Widell, a Modeling Ancient Settlement Systems (MASS) post-doctoral fellow, plus several graduate students. The research will mainly be concerned with assembling input data for the model, namely information on the agricultural production, families, and social relationships of third and second millennium B.C. communities. In addition, the Oriental Institute team will be bringing together information on the settlement landscape as it developed through the third and second millennium B.C. in both northern and southern Mesopotamia (see separate report, *CAMEL*).

This new spell of modeling activity is inevitably resulting in a flurry of conferences, workshops and meetings. In addition to the normal round of conferences and invited lectures, Wilkinson participated in a meeting on October 19, 2002, at George Mason University to present a paper entitled "Modeling complex settlement systems in the ancient Near East" and was also the co-organizer of a Workshop (with Nick Kouchoukos of the Department of Anthropology) on Landscape Archaeology in Greater Mesopotamia and Iran. This meeting brought in participants from many parts of the U.S. and featured splendid state of the art papers on remote sensing, Geographic Information Systems (GIS), and satellite imagery by a number of senior graduate students from the Oriental Institute and the Department of Near Eastern Languages and Civilizations, as well as the Department of Anthropology. In addition, Wilkinson took the opportunity to organize a special session on the Landscapes of Nineveh at the Rencontre Assyriologique Internationale in London in July 2003. Papers in this session by Eleanor Barbanes, Jason Ur, Mark Altaweel, Tony Wilkinson, and Julian Reade discussed landscapes of settlement, irrigation systems, ancient roads, and the Assyrian economy.

Last but not least, the book *Archaeological Landscapes of the Near East* is now in its production stages and is due to be published by the University of Arizona Press in November 2003, and a monograph on the archaeology of the Upper Lake Tabqa area (with a contribution by Clemens Reichel) will appear in the series Oriental Institute Publications (124).

After eleven productive and stimulating years at the Oriental Institute, Wilkinson is now preparing for a move to the University of Edinburgh, U.K., where he will take up a position teaching Near Eastern archaeology. Within the constraints of a new working environment, he will however be making several visits a year to Chicago in order to continue his involvement with various research and academic commitments.

Karen L. Wilson

Most of **Karen L. Wilson**'s time was devoted to directing the museum activities described in the museum section of this report. She also contributed an essay entitled "Excavations in the Diyala Region" and catalogue entries for Oriental Institute objects to the exhibition catalogue *Art of the First Cities: The Third Millennium B.C. from the Mediterranean to the Indus*, published by the Metropolitan Museum. Karen also served on the Cultural Directors Marketing Task Force and on the advisory board for the Center for the Presentation of Science, both at the University of Chicago.

Christopher E. Woods

Christopher E. Woods spent this year preparing his book on the Sumerian verbal prefixes and finalizing several articles: "On the Euphrates," submitted to *Zeitschrift für Assyriologie*; "Akkadian and Eblaite" (with John Huehnergard) for the *Cambridge Encyclopedia of the World's Ancient Languages*; and a revision and an expansion of an earlier paper, "The Sun-God Tablet Revisited," which was submitted to the *Journal of Cuneiform Studies*. Two further articles are in progress, one concerned with the Warka Vase and its relationship to Sumerian literary themes and glyptic, and the other with the god Utu and conceptions of Mesopotamian cosmic geography. Both will be submitted this fall and will appear as festschrift articles. Additionally, Woods has begun work on the 18th and final volume of *Materials for the Sumerian Lexicon* (MSL). He has also collaborated with David Schloen, McGuire Gibson, and Tony Wilkinson on the Modeling Ancient Settlement Systems (MASS) project.

Woods presented a paper at the 213th meeting of the American Oriental Society entitled, "The element *-re* and the organization of Erim-huš." This is part of a longer project on Sumerian demonstratives, which he hopes to finish this year. In October, Woods gave the inaugural address before the Oriental Institute's Breasted Society, "Sumerian Writing: Some Problems Relating to Origins, Nature, and Development."

K. Aslıhan Yener

During 2002, **K. Aslıhan Yener** directed the eighth season of the broadly based Amuq Valley Regional Projects (AVRP) in Antakya, Turkey. This included directing the final pre-excavation seasons of work at Tell Atchana (ancient Alalakh). The previously excavated materials from Sir Leonard Woolley's dig were studied at the Hatay Archaeological Museum. Yener's work in the Amuq is published in "Tell Atchana," *The Oriental Institute 2001/2002 Annual Report*, edited by Gil J. Stein, pp. 13–19 (Chicago: The Oriental Institute, 2002); and with T. Harrison and H. Pamir, "University of Chicago, Oriental Institute 2000 Yili Hatay Aççana, Ta'yinat Höyükleri ve Samandağı Yüzey Araştırmaları," in *XIX Araştırma Sonuçları Toplantısı*, pp. 289–302 (Ankara: Ministry of Culture, 2002).

Honors, grants, and awards during 2002 included the Institute of Aegean Prehistory Grant and the American Schools for Oriental Research Grant; and also service in the University of Chicago Senate and several search committees. As faculty advisor on conceptualizing the reinstallation of the Syro-Anatolia East Galleries of the Museum, Yener helped in the selection of artifacts.

Yener was invited to give lectures on the following topics: "The Oriental Institute Amuq Valley Regional Projects, the 2001 Surveys at Atchana," Meetings of the International Symposium of Excavations, Surveys, and Archaeometry, May, Ankara, Turkey; "Amik Ovası ve Aççana Höyük Çalışmaları," Symposium at the Mustafa Kemal University in Antakya; "The Amuq Valley Regional Projects: Tell Atchana (Ancient Alalakh) 2000–2002," Amuq session at the American Schools of Oriental Research Meetings, Toronto; "Reactivating Tell Atchana, Ancient Alalakh," Seminar for Aegean Prehistory, Institute of Fine Arts, New York; "The Oriental Institute Amuq Valley Regional Projects, the 2001 Surveys at Atchana," Workshop on the Orontes, Durham, U.K.; "Excavations at Tell Atchana (Ancient Alalakh): Past and Present," Canadian Society for Mesopotamian Studies, Toronto, Canada.

Courses taught were Art and Archaeology of Anatolia I, which covered the sequences from the Neolithic through the end of the Early Bronze Age; Anatolia II, which covered the sequences through the end of the Iron Age; and Method and Theory in Near Eastern Archaeology, Reading Course.

This year saw the furnishing of the archeometallurgy laboratory in the basement of the Oriental Institute, Room 36, with new equipment. The lab purchased a desiccation cabinet, a Buehler multiple sample preparation armature, and supplies for processing hundreds of polished cross sections. Work published stemming from metallurgical research includes the following chapters and articles: "Introduction. The Analyses of Metalliferous Residues, Crucible Fragments, Experimental Smelts, and Ores from Kestel Tin Mine and the Tin Processing Site of Göltepe, Turkey," in *Mining and Metal Production Through the Ages*, edited by P. Craddock, pp. 123–35 (London: British Museum Occasional Publications, 2003); "Swords, Armor, and Figurines: A Metalliferous View from the Central Taurus," in *Across the Anatolian Plateau: Readings in the Archaeology of Ancient Turkey*, edited by David C. Hopkins, pp. 35–42 (Annual of the American Schools of Oriental Research 57; Boston: American Schools of Oriental Research, 2002); with A. B. Adriaens, H. Earl, and H. Özbal, "Characterisation of Early Anatolian Bronze by Electron Probe Microanalysis and Alloying Simulation," *International Mining and Minerals* 2 (2002): 35–39; with A. B. Adriaens, H. Earl, and H. Özbal, "Tin Bronze Metallurgy in Transformation: Analytical Investigation of Crucible Fragments from Tell al-Judaidah, Amuq (Turkey) Dating to Circa 3000–2900 BC," in *Archaeometry 98 Proceedings of the 31st Symposium Budapest, April 26–May 3 1998* (2002), edited by Erzsebet Jerem and Katalin T. Biro, pp. 273–77 (BAR International Series 1043/2; Oxford: Archaeopress).

RESEARCH SUPPORT

COMPUTER LABORATORY

John C. Sanders

Thanks to the generous support of the University's Networking Services and Information Technologies (NSIT) department, visitors to the Institute's Research Archives can now paraphrase Shakespeare's famous line "to wire, or not to wire, that is the question" whenever they wish to connect to the Internet from the Library. In May 2003, the Research Archives had wireless networking equipment installed, making most of the second floor of the Institute "wireless capable." During the fall of 2003, we hope to expand our wireless coverage into the basement, including the Archaeology Lab, the LaSalle Banks Education Center, and perhaps the museum registration and the object storage areas as well.

Continuing in this infrastructure vein, between December 2002 and March 2003 most computers in the Institute (well over one hundred) were switched from a regime of "hard" to "soft" Internet Protocol (IP) addresses without too many headaches and with no interruption to network traffic throughout the building. This was a behind-the-scenes, technical adjustment, and most faculty and staff never knew anything changed at all. Let me take this opportunity to thank NSIT's Martin Moses and Loren Wilson for their assistance in this transition to the use of Dynamic Host Control Protocol (DHCP) throughout the Institute.

The third infrastructure change which occurred this past year had been in a discussion phase for a longer period of time than either of the above changes. I am referring to moving the Institute's entire website from our own in-house web server to an NSIT-supported server. Originating with discussions in the fall of 2000, the agreement with NSIT to host the Oriental Institute website was signed in March 2003, and I started to transfer over 33,000 files (4.9 gigabytes of data) to the new website in April. Two months of periodic testing has corrected small errors and operational differences in the two hosting computers. I expect to permanently switch the Institute's website to the new server by late summer or early fall 2003. You will have to wait until next year's *Annual Report*, however, for details on the final days of the transition.

Laboratory Projects

"Lost Treasures from Iraq" Website

Following the looting of the Iraq Museum in April 2003, the Computer Laboratory joined with several Institute faculty and staff to form what became known as the Iraq Museum Project (see separate report). It was agreed among the members that the Oriental Institute should take the lead in assisting law enforcement authorities worldwide by providing them with relevant information and photographs regarding artifacts known to have been in the collections of the Iraq Museum at the time of the looting.

Electronic Publications

In conjunction with Tom Urban, Oriental Institute Publications Office, Professor Janet Johnson finished work on two additional Adobe Portable Document Format (PDF) files, the letters aleph, and B from the Chicago Demotic Dictionary, and these documents are now available on the Institute's website.

Professor Norman Golb's article, "The De Rossi Collection of Hebrew Manuscripts at the Biblioteca Palatina and Its Importance for Jewish History," was published on the Institute's website as an Adobe Acrobat Portable Document Format (PDF) document in August 2002. In March 2003, additional information was made available on our website with the publication of Professor Golb's article, "Further Evidence Concerning Judah b. Soloman and the 'Tower of Las Metamis' Mentioned In Ms de Rossi 1105."

Professor John Brinkman's Mesopotamian Directory, his yearly updated listing of names, addresses, and contact information for Mesopotamian scholars and students worldwide, switched from print to electronic publication via the Oriental Institute's website in February 2003.

The Epigraphic Survey has made additional Chicago House Bulletins: Bulletin X, No. 1 (September 15, 1999); Bulletin XI, No. 1 (October 1999–April 2000); and Bulletin XII, No. 1 (October 2000–April 2001) available on the Institute's website.

The Chicago Hittite Dictionary (CHD) Project wrote a progress report on the electronic version of the CHD in September 2002, available on our website, describing the multi-stage process of converting the printed dictionary files into XML documents. The electronic version, or eCHD, is a part of the Institute's XML System for Textual and Archaeological Research (XSTAR) database system being developed by Professor David Schloen and his wife, Sandra.

Work on the 1980 Oriental Institute publication *Ptolemais Cyrenaica*, by David Nasgowitz, for the Photographic Archives section of the Oriental Institute website has been temporarily put on hold while John Larson, the Institute's Museum Archivist, and his staff, track down some pesky references and cross-check photograph and negative numbers. Work on the project should resume during the 2003 calendar year.

Museum Education's Online Teacher Resource Center

In September 2002, a completely redesigned Teacher Resource Center was unveiled in the Museum Education section of the Oriental Institute's website. Teacher Services and Family Projects Coordinator Wendy Ennes, along with Nitzan Mekel-Bobrov, Department of Near Eastern Languages and Civilizations (NELC) student volunteer/programmer, worked many long hours with teachers and educators to develop this content-rich resource. A detailed description of the Teacher Resource Center is available in the Museum Education section of this *Annual Report*.

Laboratory Equipment / Institute Resources

Three of the four Macintosh computers in the Laboratory were upgraded to System X in August 2003 (10.2.6 by June 2003), and several programs, such as Photoshop, were upgraded so as to run natively under System X. Users' responses to the operating system change on these Macintosh computers has been mixed ("takes getting used to…"; "Where's the Chooser?"), but most adapted to the changes quickly and everyone appreciates that System X is a much more stable operating system than System 9 or earlier versions.

In December 2002, two new computer systems were purchased to improve the high-end capabilities of the Computer Laboratory:

1. 2.4 MHz Dell Optiplex with 1 GB RAM, 80 GB hard disk, DVD-ROM/CD-RW, and a 19" monitor, running Windows 2000, and

2. 1 GHz Macintosh eMac, G4 processor with 768 MB RAM, 80 GB harddisk, DVR-R/CD-RW drive, and a 17" flat display, running both Systems X and 9.2

Both of the above computers were equipped with new Microtek ScanMaker X12 scanners, capable of true 1200 dpi resolution.

I want to acknowledge a generous gift by Bruce Beyer Williams to the Computer Laboratory: a 2 GB Jaz drive complete with accessories and cables. It provides a backup unit to the Lab's existing 1 GB Jaz drive, and provides us with the means to write data to an ever-widening range of media. Thank you, Bruce, a longtime friend of the Institute in general and the Computer Laboratory in particular.

World-Wide Website

For further information concerning several of the above mentioned research projects, the Institute's World-Wide Web (WWW) database, and other Electronic Resources in general, refer to the What's New page on the Oriental Institute's website, at (URLs are case-sensitive):

> http://www-oi.uchicago.edu/OI/INFO/OI_WWW_New.html

The homepage for the Oriental Institute website is at:

> http://www-oi.uchicago.edu

See the Electronic Resources section of this *Annual Report* for the complete URL to each of the website resources mentioned in this article.

ELECTRONIC RESOURCES

Charles E. Jones and John C. Sanders

Oriental Institute World-Wide Web Database
New and Developing Resources In 2002/2003

Several Oriental Institute units and projects either updated existing pages or became a new presence on the Institute's website during the past year (Note: URLs are case-sensitive).

ABZU: Guide to Resources for the Study of the Ancient Near East Available on the Internet

> http://www.etana.org/abzu

ETANA: Electronic Tools and Ancient Near Eastern Archives — Core Texts

> A substantial selection of digitized titles from the collections of the Research Archives have been added to the ETANA Core Texts this year. For more information on the development of this tool, see the Research Archives section in this *Annual Report*.
> http://www.etana.org/coretexts.shtml

Research Archives: Research Archives Catalogue Online

Web version of the Research Archives Catalogue. Approximately ten thousand new records have been added this year. For more information on the development of this tool, see the Research Archives section in this *Annual Report*.

http://oilib.uchicago.edu/oilibcat.html

Research Archives: Acquisitions Lists of the Research Archives

Two Acquisitions lists have appeared this year. For more information on the development of this tool, see the Research Archives section in this *Annual Report*.

Acquisitions — November-December 2001
http://www-oi.uchicago.edu/OI/DEPT/RA/RABooks.2001.11-12.html

Acquisitions — January-February 2002
http://www-oi.uchicago.edu/OI/DEPT/RA/RABooks.2002.01-02.html

IRAQCRISIS

A moderated list for communicating substantive information on cultural property damaged, destroyed, or lost from libraries and museums in Iraq during and after the war in April 2003, and on the worldwide response to the crisis. A component of the Oriental Institute's response to the cultural heritage crisis in the aftermath of the war in Iraq, this list provides a moderated forum for the distribution of information. At the time of writing, 548 e-mail addresses are subscribed worldwide. For more information on the development of this tool, see the Research Archives section in this *Annual Report*.

https://listhost.uchicago.edu/mailman/listinfo/iraqcrisis

The Middle East Librarians Association Committee on Iraqi Libraries

The Oriental Institute Research Archives has been hosting the web presence of The Middle East Librarians Association Committee on Iraqi Libraries since shortly after the outbreak of the war in spring 2003. For more information on the development of this tool, see the Research Archives section in this *Annual Report*.

http://www-oi.uchicago.edu/OI/IRAQ/mela/melairaq.html

And note in particular the following documents:

Iraqi Library Stamps
http://www-oi.uchicago.edu/OI/IRAQ/mela/LibraryStamps/LibraryStamps.htm

Pictures of Damaged Libraries in Iraq
http://www-oi.uchicago.edu/OI/IRAQ/mela/LibraryPix/LibraryPix.htm

Archaeology: "Lost Treasures from Iraq" Website

Information and photographs regarding artifacts known to have been in the collections of the Iraq Museum at the time of the looting. For more information on the development of this tool, see the Iraq Museum Project and Computer Laboratory sections in this *Annual Report*.

http://www-oi.uchicago.edu/ OI/IRAQ/iraq.html

Museum Education: Teacher Resource Center

Online teacher resources for high school curriculum in ancient Near Eastern studies. For more information on the development of this tool, see the Museum Education / Computer Laboratory sections in this *Annual Report*.

> http://www-oi.uchicago.edu/OI/MUS/ED/TRC/trc_home.html

Archaeology: Epigraphic Survey

Chicago House Bulletins from 1999 to 2001:

> http://www-oi.uchicago.edu/OI/PROJ/EPI/CHB/CHB12-1.html
> http://www-oi.uchicago.edu/OI/PROJ/EPI/CHB/CHB11-1.html
> http://www-oi.uchicago.edu/OI/PROJ/EPI/CHB/CHB10-1.html

Philology: Chicago Demotic Dictionary

Two new letters, B and *aleph*, have been added, bringing the full dictionary entries to eleven letters of the Demotic alphabet. For more information on the development of this tool, see the Demotic Dictionary / Publications Office / Computer Laboratory sections in this *Annual Report*

> http://www-oi.uchicago.edu/OI/DEPT/PUB/SRC/CDD/CDD_B.pdf
> http://www-oi.uchicago.edu/OI/DEPT/PUB/SRC/CDD/CDD_3.pdf

and the entire Dictionary at:

> http://www-oi.uchicago.edu/OI/DEPT/PUB/SRC/CDD/CDD.html

Philology: The Dead Sea Scrolls and Other Hebrew Manuscripts Project — Norman Golb

The De Rossi Collection of Hebrew Manuscripts at the Biblioteca Palatina and Its Importance for Jewish History

> http://www-oi.uchicago.edu/ OI/PROJ/SCR/PARMA/Parma.pdf
> http://www-oi.uchicago.edu/OI/PROJ/SCR/PARMA/Methamis.pdf

Philology: Individual Scholarship — John A. Brinkman

Names, addresses, and contact information for Mesopotamian scholars and students worldwide.

> http://www-oi.uchicago.edu/OI/DEPT/PUB/SRC/CDD/CDD.html

Philology: Chicago Hittite Dictionary

A progress report on the electronic version of the CHD.

> http://www-oi.uchicago.edu/OI/PROJ/HIT/eCHD/eCHDWeb.htm

PUBLICATIONS OFFICE

Thomas A. Holland

The staff of the Publications Office for this year consisted of Thomas Holland and Thomas Urban in the Editorial Office. Curtis Myers worked in the Sales Office until the end of February, when the distribution of titles published by the Oriental Institute was outsourced. We were also fortunate to have the assistance of graduate students Katherine Strange Burke, Lindsay DeCarlo, Thomas Dousa, Harold Hays, Katie Johnson, Munira Khayyat, Adam Miglio, Leslie Schramer, and Alexandra Witsell. Catherine Dueñas, Volunteer Coordinator, and Emily Napolitano, Assistant to the Director of the Epigraphic Survey, continued to assist on a number of projects. Rebecca Laharia, Membership Director, and Debora Donato, Development Director, were a pleasure to work with, each helping to promote the sales of Oriental Institute titles. Carla Hosein, Financial Manager, effectively handled all the paperwork and time cards necessary to employ the students. Jean Grant, Photographer, and John Larson, Archivist, provided invaluable assistance as always. Charles E. Jones, Head, Research Archives, loaned the Editorial Office a much-needed computer during summer 2002 when we found ourselves with more workers than computers. John Sanders, Head, Computer Laboratory, kept our computers online and web pages up-to-date.

At the end of the fiscal year, the Publications Office inaugurated a special bookcase in the Suq for displaying all of our titles in print, except for the oversized volumes. We are very grateful to Denise Browning, Suq Manager, and Gil Stein, Director, for their help in accomplishing this project.

Aside from the production of the Oriental Institute's serial monographs, we continued preparing *News & Notes* and the *Annual Report* for press. The experimental electronic distribution of two titles (see below) has gone quite well, judging by the consistent number of "hits" to their web pages.

Sales

As of April 1, 2003, volumes published by the Oriental Institute began to be distributed by the David Brown Book Company (DBBC) in the U.S. and Oxbow Books in Great Britain.

TABLE OF SALES

Series	OI July–Dec. 2002	OI Jan.–July 2003	OI Total July 2002–July 2003	DBBC/Oxbow April–June 2003	Grand Total
OIP*	$23,856	**$29,120	$52,976	$4,265	$57,241
ES	$1,290	$260	$1,550	$1,124	$2,674
CAD	$17,659	$1,868	$19,527	$2,174	$21,701
CHD	$5,572	$447	$6,019	$609	$6,628
OINE	$184	$176	$360	$164	$524
Total	$48,561	$31,871	$80,432	$8,336	$88,768

Key: OIP = Oriental Institute Publications (OIP), Studies in Ancient Oriental Civilization (SAOC), Assyriological Studies (AS), Oriental Institute Communications (OIC); ES = Epigraphic Survey volumes OIP 112 and OIP 116; CAD = Chicago Assyrian Dictionary; CHD = Chicago Hittite Dictionary; OINE = Oriental Institute Nubian Expedition (OINE).

*Includes sales of volumes in AS, OIC, OIP, and SAOC series.

**Includes $22,721 earned from the 2003 remainder sale.

Volumes Distributed Online

1. *Thus Wrote 'Onchsheshonqy: An Introductory Grammar of Demotic.* J. H. Johnson. Third edition. SAOC 45.
   http://www-oi.uchicago.edu/OI/DEPT/PUB/SRC/SAOC/45/SAOC45.html

2. *Demotic Dictionary of the Oriental Institute of the University of Chicago* (Introduction, ₃, Y, B, F, L, R, H, Ḥ, K, Ṭ, Ḏ, and Problematic Readings). J. H. Johnson, editor.
   www-oi.uchicago.edu/OI/DEPT/PUB/SRC/CDD/CDD.html

Volumes Printed

1. *Cuneiform Texts from the Ur III Period in the Oriental Institute,* Volume 2: *Drehem Administrative Documents from the Reign of Amar-Suena.* M. Hilgert. OIP 121

2. *Scarabs, Scaraboids, Seals, and Seal Impressions from Medinet Habu.* E. Teeter. OIP 118

Volumes in Preparation

1. *Ancient Egypt: Treasures from the Collection of the Oriental Institute, University of Chicago.* E. Teeter. Oriental Institute Museum Publications (OIMP) 23

2. *Catalog of Demotic Texts in the Brooklyn Museum of Art.* G. R. Hughes

3. *Excavations at the Prehistoric Mound of Chogha Bonut, Khuzestan, Iran, Seasons of 1976/1977, 1977/1978 and 1996.* A. Alizadeh. OIP 120

4. *Neo-Babylonian Texts of the Oriental Institute Collection.* D. Weisberg

5. *Taxes, Tax-Payers, and Tax-Receipts in Early Ptolemaic Thebes.* B. P. Muhs

6. *Tell es-Sweyhat, Syria,* Volume 1: *Settlement and Land Use on the Margin of the Euphrates River and in the Upper Lake Tabqa Area.* T. J. Wilkinson

7. *Tell es-Sweyhat, Syria,* Volume 2: *Archaeology of the Bronze Age, Hellenistic, and Roman Remains at an Ancient Town on the Euphrates River.* T. A. Holland

8. *Temple of Khonsu,* Volume 3: *Graffiti from the Khonsu Temple Roof at Karnak.* H. Jacquet-Gordon

Manuscripts Accepted for Publication

1. *Megiddo,* Volume 3: *Final Report of the Oriental Institute Stratum VI Excavations.* T. P. Harrison

2. *Origins of State Organizations in Prehistoric Fars, Southern Iran.* A. Alizadeh

3. *Nippur,* Volume 5: *Area WF Sounding at Nippur and the Early Dynastic to Akkadian Transition.* A. McMahon

RESEARCH ARCHIVES

Charles E. Jones

Introduction

For all of us with an interest in the ancient Near East, the affairs of the modern Middle East have loomed large during the past year. In a region where delicate and dangerous political situations are routine, this year has been extraordinary by any accounting. Hardly a country from the Mediterranean to the Indus has not been challenged by the geopolitical climate. The world's press has focused on the region in ways never before experienced in history and hardly predictable as recently as a decade ago. Global communications networks enable virtually all inhabitants of the planet to recognize pictures of the streets of Baghdad, Jerusalem, Kabul — and even such unlikely places as Umm Qasr.

Likewise, the tragic effect of the war and postwar events on cultural institutions — museums, libraries, archives, archaeological sites — have focused the world's attention on the historical depth of the cultures of the region, the "Cradle of Civilization." The losses suffered in the Iraq Museum in Baghdad and at archaeological sites (about which much more appears in other contributions within this *Annual Report*) have overshadowed the equal or greater damage to institutions such as the National Library and Archives and the Library of the Ministry of Religious Endowments. Best estimates at the time of writing are that the National Library has lost not only its building and equipment, but also all copies of its catalogues and about half of its circa 1.2 million volumes. The Ministry of Religious Endowments has lost about half of its manuscripts and ninety percent of its printed books. Comparable losses have also taken their toll on the Iraqi Center for Manuscripts and the Mustansiriya University Library — all in Baghdad [http://www-oi.uchicago.edu/OI/IRAQ/mela/LibraryPix/LibraryPix.htm]; the Central Public Library, Central University Library, and the Islamic Library in Basra; and the Central Public Library, Central University Library, and the Library of the Museum in Mosul. It will take years — probably decades — to recover from the losses to all such institutions in Iraq.

The national collections of Iraq, as they existed until recently, have their origins in colonial institutions established under British rule in the period after the First World War. The documentation of the establishment of the Iraq Museum is rich and interesting — much of it is available online in the archives of the papers of Gertrude Bell [http://www.gerty.ncl.ac.uk/home/index.htm]. It is not clear, at present, how much of this kind of documentary material survives in collections in Iraq. As early twentieth-century institutions, they are approximately the same age as the Oriental Institute; the relationships between the Institute and the Iraqi partners have developed in parallel for eight decades. In many ways, we are partner institutions engaged in the struggle to understand antiquity and the origins of society and civilization. Objects excavated under the aegis of Oriental Institute expeditions, and the records associated with them, are in the collections and custody of museums and archives in Iraq. Other records and photographs associated with these projects are in the collections of the Oriental Institute. Published assessments of these projects are in libraries in Iraq and Chicago and the world. These publications collectively become the cumulative record of our understanding of the ancient world and the measure and means by which our knowledge is continuously reassessed. No collection exists in isolation. Damage to one institution is damage to all institutions and to the collective heritage of mankind.

The damage suffered by these institutions in Iraq in the past half-year should remind us of the fragility of the infrastructure of scholarship and should instruct us to redouble our efforts to preserve, maintain, and offer access to the resources in our custody. In such efforts, libraries and archives need to lead the way.

Global Resources Hosted at the Research Archives

For more than a decade, the staff of the Research Archives has been working to offer global access to its own collections and to develop tools that will increase communication among those interested in the ancient Near East.

ANE – ANENews: Ten years ago this summer, in early July 1993, the Ancient Near East (ANE) list was opened to the public. Intended to provide a medium for discussion among scholars and students actively engaged in research and study of the ancient Near East from the Indus to the Nile, and from the beginnings of human habitation to the rise of Islam, it has admirably fulfilled its mission. The discussion list allows scholars and students to ask and answer questions publicly; to quickly gain a feel for the opinions of peers; to distribute drafts of articles to a wide but focused audience; to comment on issues of concern in the news media; and to instantly send out announcements of jobs, conferences, and changes of address or status. It also provides a forum for the occasional angry argument, and a soapbox for polemic and lament. At present, about eighteen hundred addresses are subscribed. Among the suite of lists focusing on ancient topics, ANE is one of the oldest and heaviest trafficked — clear indications that it provides a useful service. Those interested can direct their browsers to the ANE pages at:

https://listhost.uchicago.edu/mailman/listinfo/ane

and

https://listhost.uchicago.edu/mailman/listinfo/anenews

IraqCrisis: In April 2003, in response to increased traffic on the subject of the war in Iraq on ANE and other lists, and in response to the widespread need for a forum to communicate substantive information on cultural property damaged, destroyed, or lost from libraries and museums in Iraq during and after the war, we established a new list, distributed under careful moderation. IraqCrisis has a subscribership of about six hundred souls — mostly professionals in the museum, library, cultural heritage, and university communities. It is a part of the Oriental Institute's formal response to the crisis in Iraq. Those interested can direct their browsers to the IraqCrisis pages at:

https://listhost.uchicago.edu/mailman/listinfo/iraqcrisis

ETANA — Core Texts: For two years, the Research Archives has been in partnership with a number of sister institutions in the development of ETANA (Electronic Tools and Ancient Near Eastern Archives), operating under a grant from Andrew W. Mellon Foundation. During the past year more than sixty volumes from the collections of the Research Archives have been scanned, processed and added to the ETANA Core Texts collection, available publicly and free of charge on the web. A full listing of these volumes is available at:

http://www.etana.org/coretexts.shtml

Many of these books were chosen because their condition in libraries is poor, mostly due to heavy use. An enormously useful side product of the project is the production of hardbound, acid-free duplicate readers' copies of each of the volumes selected, which can now be placed on the shelves for those who wish to use them in that format. While they are indexed "locally" at the website of ETANA (URL cited above), records for each of the volumes also now appear in

Abzu [http://www.etana.org/abzu/] (the rebuilding of which I discussed in last year's report). Even more significantly, partner institutions have taken on the burden of producing formal MARC records for each volume, linked to the web-accessible version of the volumes, so that anyone working at a University (or other networked) library worldwide can have immediate access to these publications. This project is an important early step in the collaborative production and access to the published record of the ancient Near East.

Iraq Bibliography: In the weeks following the looting and destruction of institutions in Iraq, members of the Research Archives staff began to collect references to published works documenting the contents of the museums, libraries, and other collections in Iraq. In collaboration with the Oriental Institute Iraq Working Group, and with the Middle East Librarians Association Committee on Iraqi Libraries (see below), we produced the bibliography of the basic publications. This bibliography is available online at:

http://www-oi.uchicago.edu/OI/IRAQ/iraq_bibliography.html

The most recent version includes some 220 volumes and an index of 12,423 Iraq Museum (IM) numbers for published objects in the collections of the Iraq Museum. [Note however, that many published objects — especially well known objects — will appear repeatedly in the published record. Therefore, this number does not indicate the number of discrete objects included in the publications listed here.] In addition, many of these volumes include publications of objects in the collections of the Iraq Museum that either did not have IM numbers assigned at the time of publication, or for which the IM numbers are not indicated in the publication. As news of the actual extent of loss and damage to these collections has emerged, we have shifted our focus to concentrate on particular classes of objects. This emerging bibliography is an important baseline assessment of the secondary documentations of the collections in question, and we expect to develop and augment it in the next few months.

Middle East Librarians Association Committee on Iraqi Libraries: In a parallel effort, a committee has been established to coordinate the response of librarians in North America to the crisis in Iraq. I joined this committee at the outset and have been an active participant. Among the efforts the Research Archives and the Oriental Institute have contributed is the Web presence of the committee, which you can find at:

http://www-oi.uchicago.edu/OI/IRAQ/mela/melairaq.html

The first assessment of the library situation in postwar Iraq, written by Nabil al-Tikriti, a graduate student in the Department of Near Eastern Languages and Civilizations at the University of Chicago, was published by the Committee on its website. Other useful documentation published there includes:

- Iraqi Library Stamps. The aim of this project is to collect images (scanned photographs or photocopies) of library stamps and other ownership marks used by various libraries and manuscript collections in Iraq and make these images available on the Internet.

- Pictures of Damaged Libraries in Iraq. The photographs presented here document damage to libraries in Iraq during and after the war in April 2003. Most of them are provided by Nabil al-Tikriti. They were taken during his trip to Baghdad on May 25-31, 2003. They accompany his report: Iraq Manuscript Collections, Archives, & Libraries: Situation Report, dated June 8, 2003. The remaining photographs were taken by McGuire Gibson, Professor of Mesopotamian Archaeology, the Oriental Institute, University of Chicago. He was a member of the UNESCO team that visited Baghdad in May 2003.

The Online Catalogue and Acquisitions Lists: During the past year we have added about ten thousand records to the online catalogue. The total number of records stands at 121,741. The Catalogue is available online at:

http://oilib.uchicago.edu/oilibcat.html

The online catalogue records are used by about seven hundred users worldwide each day.

During the past year we have produced two Acquisitions lists:

Acquisitions - November–December 2001.

Acquisitions - January–February 2002.

Information on how to read them online and how to subscribe to the mailing list is available at:

http://www-oi.uchicago.edu/OI/DEPT/RA/RABooks.html

We currently have 460 subscribers to the mailing list.

Current Acquisitions

Following are the acquisitions statistics for the past year:

	May 2002–April 2003	*Total*
Monographs and Series	744	26,372
Journals	253	10,707
Total Books	997	37,079

This year's acquisitions statistics remain consistent with the publication trends of the past few years in ancient Near Eastern studies, and with the acquisitions policies of the Research Archives. We continue to be committed to acquiring all the basic published resources for the study of the ancient Near East.

Staff

The staff of the Research Archives has always been drawn from the talented and accomplished pool of University of Chicago students. During the past year, I have been fortunate to have the help of three excellent assistants. Kathy Wagner has held down the Wednesday evening shift for another year. In the autumn, we welcomed the addition of Eudora Bernsen, first-year student in Archaeology, and Foy Scalff, first-year student in Egyptology. Eudora shouldered much of the cataloging burden while Foy focuses on a number of special projects. These three assistants have made an excellent team, and together we have accomplished a great deal this year.

Acknowledgments

As always, the Research Archives is indebted to a large community of supporters. The partnership for more than a decade between the Research Archives and the Computer Laboratory is of inestimable value. John Sanders and I communicate with one another on a continuous basis on every conceivable matter. This partnership goes far beyond the usual ties among colleagues. Likewise, relationships between the Research Archives and the Museum, particularly the Museum Archives and Registration Departments and the Education Department and the Publications Office are of fundamental importance for the smooth operation of the library. I gratefully acknowledge the support and friendship of the members of those units of the Oriental Institute. As always, the Journal of Near Eastern Studies has provided and maintained exchange subscriptions in support of the library. In addition, Robert D. Biggs, its editor, has offered us a steady stream of donations of books and journals, old and new, from his own library and on behalf of the Journal of Near Eastern Studies.

TABLET COLLECTION

Walter Farber

More than a year after the conversion of our former Tablet Room to a faculty office, staff and files of the Tablet Collection finally moved into a new, permanent Students' Room again in June 2003. During its first two weeks, it has already provided quiet and well-lit working space for one visiting Assyriologist. We hope the new location on the third floor will become a favorite working space for visiting scholars researching small objects (not necessarily only cuneiform tablets), as well as a productive center for the ongoing activities of the Tablet Collection itself. I am grateful for the flexibility of the visitors who had to work in changing, and never ideal, spaces during the time of our displacement, and bid a heartfelt "welcome!" to all future users of this new facility.

Overleaf. Male Figure. Gypsum. Sin Temple IX, Khafajah, Iraq. Early Dynastic Period (ca. 2500 B.C.).
Excavated by the Oriental Institute, 1933/34. OIM A12440

MUSEUM

Karen L. Wilson

During the past year, most of the museum staff's attention has been focused on the installation of the new Edgar and Deborah Jannotta Mesopotamian Gallery, including the Robert and Linda Braidwood Prehistory Exhibit and the Yelda Khorsabad Court. It has been exciting and deeply satisfying to see it all coming together into what promises to be a stunning whole, thanks to the creative energies of everyone involved.

At the very beginning of the year, Dianne Hanau-Strain of Hanau-Strain Associates was hired to be in charge of graphic design for the gallery. Dianne came to the Institute two afternoons a week to meet with the Mesopotamian Gallery Installation Committee — McGuire Gibson, myself, and Exhibit Designer Joe Scott, who was just recently replaced by Installation Coordinator Markus Dohner. Together we worked on case layouts, image selection, and graphic design. The completion of the Prehistory Exhibit proved to us that we had made the right choice in Dianne — her graphics really give both context and life to chipped stone tools 150,000 years old. As of this writing, that section of the gallery plus the entire Chronology section, Khorsabad Court, and Seals and Sealing Practices exhibit have been installed by Gallery Preparator Erik Lindahl and Mount Maker Beal Stafford. Work is about to get underway on constructing buildups and making mounts for the Daily Life section, the graphics for which are at the production house, and

Markus is embarking upon case layouts for Writing and Intellectual Life. McGuire Gibson and Tony Wilkinson have completed text and image selection for the Introduction to Mesopotamia section, Head of Museum Education Carole Krucoff is leading the team that is developing the Visitor Orientation Center, and my last writing task is to complete Cities, Palaces, and Temples. Clemens Reichel, Research Associate and Project Coordinator for the Diyala Project, and NELC graduate student Jonathan Tenney (who is also assistant curator of the tablet collection) contributed greatly to the content of the gallery. Clemens took on responsibility for the Daily Life section and Jonathan combed the tablet collection for items for Writing and Intellectual Life and wrote lively text copy. I wish to thank them both for their dedication to this work and willingness to be goaded by our deadlines.

Evelien Dewulf joined the museum staff in February as Administrative Assistant for Reinstallation. We have kept her busy with a broad range of reinstallation tasks including helping the conservators make cylinder seal

Erik Lindahl, Beal Stafford, and Laura D'Alessandro installing a statue from Khorsabad in the Mesopotamian Gallery

Vicki Parry and Vanessa Muros filling in the gap between two Khorsabad reliefs

impressions, scheduling meetings, formatting, mounting, and cropping labels, and most importantly, scanning and touching up images for both the Mesopotamian Gallery and the East Wing Galleries for use in publicity, exhibition, and fund-raising presentations.

On March 17, the East Wing Installation Committee met for the first time to begin planning for the next phase of the installation. That committee now consists of Theo van den Hout, David Schloen, K. Aslıhan Yener, Gabrielle Novacek, Markus, Dianne, and myself.

We are grateful that our indefatigable colleague at the University News Office, William Harms, returned to Chicago after a year in Washington, D.C., with the National Science Foundation. Bill has again made sure that the Institute received prominent media coverage and used the events in Iraq to focus media attention, in part, on the opening of our new Mesopotamian Gallery. On Sunday, April 27, the Institute was featured on the front page of the Arts and Entertainment section of the *Chicago Tribune*, which also contained a full-page spread by art critic Alan Artner highlighting Mesopotamian treasures from the collection. In March, Bill arranged for a media availability day to spark initial interest in the new gallery, and he has been busily writing all the press materials for the gallery press kit and circulating them to the appropriate individuals for comment.

All this activity kept Senior Curator and Registrar Raymond D. Tindel extremely busy. Ray and the others in Registration handled nearly 19,000 objects over the course of the year. The transit area of storage, where items are brought to be considered as exhibition material, now has well over 6,000 objects on its shelves. These include some 2,600 items to be used in the Mesopotamian Gallery, over 1,100 in preparation for the Syrian-Anatolian exhibit, and 358 in preparation for the Megiddo exhibit.

Ray and his staff also have added more than 4,000 objects to the registered collections in the last year, including nearly 1,000 classical sherds, over 1,200 Nippur tablet casts, approximately

500 Persepolis arrowheads, and over 500 sherds collected by Robert McCormick Adams on his Warka Survey in 1967. Ray also continues his transition to a new, more modern database system, which will be able to incorporate digital images that are being taken by a digital camera acquired with funds from an Institute of Museum and Library Services (IMLS) Conservation Project Support Grant.

Use of the collection for research was also heavy this past year. For her dissertation, Near Eastern Languages and Civilizations (NELC) graduate student Gabrielle Novacek is going through nearly 300 boxes of material from the site of Khirbet Kerak in Israel, excavated in the early 1950s by Pinhas Delougaz. Gabrielle is also working as a part-time Student Curator selecting objects for the Albert and Cissy Haas Megiddo Gallery. Other users of the collection included Ali Hussain of Loyola University, who looked at thirty-one Arabic manuscripts as part of his research into early Arabic epigraphy. John Landgraf came from Minneapolis to study pot-throwing techniques at Megiddo and handled 158 ceramic pieces. Tom Hefter spent several months in Registration cataloguing 165 Arabic manuscripts for a project called the American Committee for South Asian Manuscripts, and William Hafford of the University of Pennsylvania studied thirty-six Nippur weights. NELC graduate student Catherine Chou is currently studying 127 Nippur tablets and tablet casts for a reading course she is taking with Walter Farber, and Donald Whitcomb used 328 Islamic sherds from Bob Adams' excavations at Jundi Shapur for a class. Markus Hilgert visited from the University of Jena and examined 263 Ur III cuneiform tablets in preparation for his next publication. (You can see from these precise numbers what careful records Ray maintains about the movement of the objects in his care — a precision of which we are deeply appreciative).

Thanks to the efforts of Head of the Conservation Laboratory Laura D'Alessandro, the museum was again awarded an IMLS Conservation Project Support Grant (the museum's fourteenth since 1987). The funds were used to purchase twenty additional state-of-the-art storage cabinets — this time for some 1,500 Egyptian artifacts and pottery, mostly from the late periods. Thanks to this grant, those pieces have been unpacked and photographed and are once again accessible for study.

In December, Muriel Newman, a longtime friend of the Institute, donated twenty-four Near Eastern seals (stamp seals, cylinder seals, and scarabs) that she had purchased in Beirut in 1964. The museum lent six of its best Mesopotamian objects to the Metropolitan Museum of Art for its "Art of the First Cities: The Third Millennium B.C. from the Mediterranean to the Indus" exhibit, which opened in early May and will run until August. The pieces will be back in Chicago and in place in the gallery in time for our own first event related to the opening.

All of this was made possible by a wonderful group of assistants and volunteers, namely Aimee Drolet, Leon Drolet, Mary Grimshaw, Masako Matsumoto, Toni Smith, and Jim Sopranos. We say good-bye regretfully to Registrar's Assistant and NELC graduate student Joey Corbett, who has left for a year of research in Egypt and Jordan, but we welcome with great enthusiasm his successor, Dennis Campbell, also a NELC graduate student.

In February, Head of Security Margaret Schröeder took part in this year's National Conference on Cultural Property Protection: "Best Practices For 2003 and Beyond," sponsored by the Smithsonian Institution. The Conference announced its intention to have a representative from a university museum appointed to its board, and Margaret — as well as all the other attendees from university museums — immediately applied. Several weeks later, Margaret was informed that she had been selected. She and her fellow appointee for this year, who is from the National Archives of Canada, are only the second and third women ever appointed to this board, which is about thirty years old. Congratulations to Margaret! It's not only a great step for her professionally, it's also wonderful to have the Oriental Institute represented on the board of the National Conference on Cultural Property Protection. Margaret attended the board meeting to plan the 2004 conference in Washington, D.C., in June. The working title for the conference is "People Are Security's Prime Concern." At that conference, Margaret will be heading two different sessions (and speaking at least a bit at each of these), and possibly speaking at a third session, which will focus on recent thefts and looting in Iraq.

With over 2,600 objects being installed in the new Mesopotamian Gallery, the conservators had their hands full over the year. In September, Contract Conservator Vicki Parry left to accept a position in the Greek and Roman conservation laboratory at the Metropolitan Museum in New York and was replaced by Getty Intern Alison Whyte when her fellowship year ended. Laura, Assistant Conservator Vanessa Muros, and Alison alternated their time between the Yelda Khorsabad Court and the lab. In the Court, they worked to make the display visually attractive by covering the steel frames with an acrylic modeling paste containing sand to imitate the texture and color of the original stone. They also conserved the faces of the reliefs, removing old, deteriorated patches of restoration and replacing them with more visually attractive and more conservationally sound materials. In the lab, they treated more than 500 pieces.

Vicki Parry, Laura D'Alessandro, and Alison Whyte reattaching a fragment of Khorsabad relief

In July, the conservators held a half day workshop for area objects conservators (and one paper conservator) on the Assyrian relief conservation project. In March, Laura flew to Washington, D.C., to serve on the awards panel for IMLS Conservation Project Support grants. The same month, the conservators met with members of the Museum Education Department and representatives from the Chicago Board of Education to plan a series of science workshops for Chicago public school teachers. In April, the lab hosted a visit by Nancy Micklewright, a Program Officer of the Getty Grant Program, who came to assess the first four years of the Institute's Getty-funded conservation internship program. Both Vanessa and Laura attended conferences in June. Vanessa traveled to Arlington, Virginia, for the American Institute for Conservation annual meeting, and Laura attended the Fifth World Archaeological Congress in Washington, D.C.

In May, Laura began preparing for the conservators' September/October activities, when the Assyrian relief project will begin its final phase and the remaining Assyrian reliefs will be installed in the East Wing of the Museum. This included scheduling the riggers and framers and ordering conservation supplies.

Museum Archivist John A. Larson hosted a number of visiting scholars over the year. They included Norma Franklin, from Tel Aviv University, who examined materials in the Megiddo Archive for her dissertation; Jeffrey Abt of Wayne State University, who continues to write on the career of James Henry Breasted; and Ann Gunter, curator at the Sackler Gallery, Smithsonian Institution, who is interested in the work of Ernst Herzfeld at Persepolis.

In June, John began pulling together the primary field records and secondary source materials on the sites of Khirbet Kerak (Beit Yerah) and Nahal Tabor in Israel for Gabrielle Novacek's dissertation research.

John is pleased to report that the Archives have received several new acquisitions. A. Dale Northrup of Douglas, Michigan, donated two original nineteenth-century photographs of Egypt. One is a picture of the obelisk of Senwesret I at Heliopolis, number 120 by Maison Bonfils; the other, by an unknown photographer, records a "Baptism of Pharaoh" scene at the Temple of Kom Ombo, in which Ptolemy XII, the father of Cleopatra the Great, is shown between the gods Thoth and Horus. We thank Mr. Northrup for his generosity. In April, Professor Robert D. Biggs presented the Archives with a copy of the program for "A Night in Egypt," the Oriental Institute benefit that took place on October 8, 1985. On May 13, he donated a copy of the program for the memorial service for Klaus Baer (May 16, 1987) and the newspaper obituary of Charles F. Nims from the *Chicago Tribune* of November 22, 1988. We thank Bob for his thoughtful support of the Archives.

Hazel Cramer, Peggy Grant, Patricia Hume, Sandra Jacobsohn, Lillian Schwartz, and Carole Yoshida continued working with John as Oriental Institute Archives Volunteers throughout fiscal year 2002/2003. In February, James P. Baughman joined as a new volunteer in the Archives; he has begun to research and write biographical sketches of selected former Oriental Institute personnel for a planned "Oriental Institute Biographies" section on our website. This year, Hazel continued working on materials from the Oriental Institute Publications Office. Peggy Grant has transcribed the handwritten letter/reports of Edgar James Banks from the University of Chicago's 1903–1905 expedition to the site of Bismaya in Iraq, and Hazel has begun the process of proofreading. Pat continues her long-term project based on the Papers of Helene Kantor. Sandy checked-in the Epigraphic Survey negatives and photographs from the past two field seasons and prepared them for long-term storage. Lillian is working on the metadata for the photographs from the microfiche publication of Carl Kraeling's work at Ptolemais in Libya, so that the images and their descriptions can be posted on the Oriental Institute website. Carole continues with the task of re-mounting and re-labeling the 35 mm transparencies in the Slide Library. We are grateful for the generous contributions of time by these volunteers in support of the ongoing functions of the Archives.

Museum Office Manager Carla Hosein took on a new position in the Oriental Institute administrative office in July 2002. Since then, John has been assisted by student assistants Carrie Hritz and Justine Warren, who have had the responsibility for preparing the necessary paperwork and handling all the other details that are involved in processing the requests that we re-

The obelisk of Senwesret I at Heliopolis, number 120 by Maison Bonfils

ceive for photographic image materials and reproduction permissions — a total of 134 transactions during fiscal year 2002/2003.

Photographer Jean Grant has been kept busy photographing Mesopotamian objects to be used for publicity related to the new gallery or to be lent to the Metropolitan Museum and with printing for the photograph order program. She is bemoaning the fact that, with the advent of digital photography, many of the supplies she needs are becoming difficult, or impossible, to find. Good black and white photographic paper is difficult to find or non-existent and 5×7 sheets (preferred by those writing Ph.D. dissertations) have to be trimmed down from 8×10 inch paper. RC (resin-coated) papers are now more plentiful than fiber-based paper, which is archival in quality. All papers now contain less silver, which is necessary for obtaining rich black when printing.

Jean spent many weeks photographing Oriental Institute Egyptian treasures for Emily Teeter. She says it was like finding them all over again because of the attention given them by those in conservation. Jean is again grateful to have had Irene Glasner volunteer for the Photo Lab. She notes that Irene, whether spotting slides from the volunteer collections or printing, is game. Unfortunately, volunteer Pam Ames broke her ankle this year, but we are happy to report that she is slowly on the mend.

By the time you read this, the Mesopotamian Gallery will have opened, and we will have embarked on the East Wing Galleries in earnest. As we move into a busy and productive new year, I would like to thank the entire museum staff, as well as our many dedicated volunteers, for their continued support and good humor. Without their team work, none of our past or future accomplishments would have been or would be possible.

MUSEUM EDUCATION PROGRAM

Carole Krucoff

Service to the University of Chicago community and outreach programs in partnership with sister institutions on campus were major emphases for Museum Education this past year. These programs, along with many other educational services for adults, youth, and families, attracted 7,258 participants, a 14% increase over last year. Much of this increase is directly related to the user-friendly redesign of the Education pages on the Oriental Institute website, which has made information on all of our educational services more accessible to the large numbers of people who visit the Oriental Institute site. The many other ways that computer technology is helping us to expand our audience, diversify our public programs, and broaden our educational services to the community's schools are visible throughout this report. Support from the Lloyd A. Fry Foundation, the Polk Bros. Foundation, and the Regents Park/University of Chicago Fine Arts Partnership is enabling us to enter the virtual realm and also to continue our efforts to develop and present innovative educational experiences in the galleries of the museum.

Outreach to the University Community

Museum Education has always wanted to expand our audience of visitors from the University community, especially the student population that often graduates without ever having viewed the museum's world-renowned collection. But, since University of Chicago students have great demands on their time, finding the right programmatic format to attract and serve them has been a challenge. This changed last year when Maria Krasinski joined the Education staff as Programs

The Oriental Institute of the University of Chicago
What's New Announcements Public Programs Website Information & Statistics Copyrights & Permissions Comments Website Navigational Aid

Museum Education

Adult Education
Family Programs
Sunday Films
Tours
Outreach
Teacher Resource Center
Curriculum Guides
Loan Materials
Kids' Corner
Volunteering
More Resources
Annual Reports

Where to find us

Redesigned Museum Education homepage on the Oriental Institute website makes programs and services more accessible to all who visit us on the Internet

Assistant. A recent University of Chicago graduate, Maria was especially alert to student needs and interests, and her contacts in the undergraduate and graduate community allowed her to survey students for input on programs that would appeal to them. She learned that drop-by open houses held on a weeknight early in the academic quarter would work well. Events that featured food and fun as well as educational programming would be most attractive. She also knew from her own student days that blanketing the campus with flyers about events might be the best way to publicize them.

The outcome of Maria's research was "Can You Dig It? The Real Indiana Jones," and "A Taste of Ancient Egypt," two highly successful open houses that attracted hundreds of students from departments throughout the University. Most had never visited the Oriental Institute and were fascinated by the galleries and intrigued by the graduate student archaeologists, linguists, and historians who volunteered to present informal demonstrations of their work. The graduate students who generously donated their time to these programs included Francois Gaudard, Carrie Hritz, Jackie Jay, Leslie Schramer, Josh Trampier, and Alexandra Witsell. The student visitors also enjoyed the free auditorium programs. "Can You Dig it? offered a free film showing of "Raiders of the Lost Ark." Research Associate Emily Teeter gave an introductory lecture on ancient Egyptian art for "A Taste of Ancient Egypt." Middle-eastern style treats were served at each event and all who attended were given a one-year complimentary membership to the Oriental Institute. They also added their names to our newly created e-mail list, which allows us to contact them all immediately with information on upcoming events.

E-mail was the format used to inform students about our last evening event of the year. The Museum Education and Membership Offices invited all our new and longtime student members to take part in preview tours of the Mesopotamian Gallery led by graduate student Mark Altaweel and Laura D'Alessandro, Head of the Oriental Institute Conservation Laboratory. After the tours, Education and Membership staff hosted a dinner and roundtable discussion to learn what kinds of educational programs related to the new gallery would appeal to the students and what activities would inspire them to renew the complimentary memberships they had received this year. The information we received is helping us develop a full calendar of student activities for next year.

Collaboration on Campus

While the Student Open Houses were presented by Oriental Institute departments, we also joined forces with the University's College Programming Office to take part in its annual "Experience Chicago Day," an event that invites newly enrolled students to select and spend a full day at an on-campus cultural institution during Orientation week in September. Forty students, the maximum we could host, selected the Oriental Institute. Thanks to the involvement of many staff members and volunteers, these students received a fascinating introduction to the Oriental Institute's work. Aslıhan Yener, Associate Professor of Archaeology, presented a slide lecture on her recent excavations in Turkey. Karen L. Wilson, Oriental Institute Museum Director, lectured on the history of the Institute. She then led the students on tours behind the scenes, joined by John Larson, Museum Archivist; Maria Krasinski, Education Programs Assistant; Charles E. Jones, Research Archivist and Bibliographer; Vanessa Muros and Alison Whyte, Conservators; Raymond Tindel, Registrar and Senior Curator; and Carole Yoshida, Docent Captain. The students also took docent-led tours of the galleries, and they met with Martha Roth, Professor of Assyriology and Associate Chair of the Undergraduate Program of the Department of Near Eastern Languages and Civilizations. Professor Roth shared ways

Francois Gaudard, Egyptology graduate student, explains his work on the Demotic Dictionary Project during "Can You Dig It," an Oriental Institute open house for University of Chicago students. Photograph by Carole Krucoff

the students could become involved as Oriental Institute volunteers and work study students. Several are now active members of our volunteer program.

Along with outreach to students, collaboration with campus partners this past year has helped us meet our mission to serve the wider community in all its diversity. Alumni, parents, and community residents joined Saturday docents Dorothy Blindt, Lucie Sandel, and Carol Yoshida for special Egyptian and Persian Gallery tours that they created for the University's annual Humanities Day in the fall. We also joined with the Alumni Association Office to present tours during June Reunion. And this year we developed two special events for the Alumni Office — a family program that invited children and parents to tour the Egyptian Gallery and then create headdresses in the style of King Tut, and a special lecture on the work of Chicago House by W. Raymond Johnson, Director of the Epigraphic Survey. Both programs attracted large audiences.

We became part of the campus music scene when we partnered with the Center for Middle Eastern Studies to present a Breasted Hall concert in conjunction with the city of Chicago's celebration of Arab-American Heritage Month in November. Qanun player Hicham Chami of Morocco, voted by *Chicago Magazine* as the city's best exotic instrumentalist, and percussionist Kalyan Pathak from India, drew standing ovations from their large and enthusiastic audience, most of whom were new visitors to the Oriental Institute.

Several long-term campus collaborations also took place during the year. We worked with 6th-grade teachers at the Laboratory Schools Middle School to enhance the 6th-grade ancient studies curriculum using the Oriental Institute's award winning curriculum guides. At the high school level, the

Qanun player Hicham Chami (left) and percussionist Kalyan Pathak (right) drew standing ovations in Breasted Hall during "Sounds of the Orient," a concert co-sponsored by the Center for Middle Eastern Studies. Photograph by Wendy Ennes

Education Department collaborated with Laboratory Schools world studies teacher Diane Puklin and Oriental Institute graduate student Jonathan Tenney, who worked together to develop a 9th-grade unit that used primary sources to focus on trade in the ancient Near East. We are exploring the prospect of piloting this unit in other local high schools during the next school year.

The Smart Museum of Art has long been our programming partner, and this past fall we collaborated once again to present a highly successful Family Day for parents and children in Hyde Park/Kenwood. This year, however, we also came together to create and present a semester-long program of joint guided tours for 6th grade students enrolled in the Chicago Public Schools' Global Studies and International Baccalaureate Programs. The tours, which brought classes to both museums in a single day, introduced students to "Sacred Fragments: Magic, Mystery, and Religion in the Ancient World," a special exhibit of Graeco-Roman and Chinese antiquities at the Smart Museum. This was followed by a visit to concentrate on the same topics in the Oriental Institute's Egyptian Gallery. Staff and docents at both museums worked together to develop the tours and accompanying curriculum materials for this in-depth program that served more than 600 Chicago Public School students during the fall and winter.

The second annual Hyde Park-University of Chicago Arts Fest involved us with many campus partners, as we worked together to plan and present a wide range of activities for this community-wide celebration of the arts during the weekend of the 57th Street Art Fair. Sponsored by the University of Chicago, the Fest featured programming by more than 20 campus and community organizations that were connected throughout the weekend by free trolley service. These trolleys brought hundreds of visitors to the Oriental Institute for free gallery tours, documentary film showings, and a free festival of activities for families. The Chicago Storytelling Guild, back with us for a second year, delighted parents and children with a full afternoon of ancient tales and contemporary stories.

Adult Education

The wide variety of adult education opportunities Museum Education offers each year are part of another major collaboration with a University of Chicago partner. All of our on-campus courses, as well as those we present at the Gleacher Center in the Loop, are done in partnership with the University's Graham School of General of Studies, which works with us on course creation and development of advertising and also joins us in taking registrations. This year, our courses with the Graham School included: Ancient Conquers: The Rise and Fall of the Assyrian Empire, and Mesopotamia: Cradle of Civilization, taught by Mark Altaweel; Archaeology and the Bible, Before the Bible: The Archaeology of Prehistoric Israel and the Levant, and Current Debates in Biblical Archaeology, taught by Aaron Burke; The Ancient Egyptian Coffin Texts, taught by Harold Hays; Science and Archaeology, taught by Nitzan Mekel-Bobrov; A Thousand Gods: The Religion of the Ancient Hittites, taught by Kathleen Mineck; The Literature of Coptic Egypt, taught by Jennifer Westerfeld and Phil Venticinque; and Ancient Egypt and the Bible, Ancient Egypt and Its Neighbors, and Ancient Thebes: City of the Pharaohs, all taught by Frank Yurco.

When the special exhibition entitled *Eternal Egypt: Masterworks of Ancient Art From the British Museum* arrived at The Field Museum this spring, it gave us the opportunity to join with colleagues there to create a unique new adult education course. An Introduction to the Land of Pharaohs, taught by Oriental Institute Archivist John Larson, took advantage of the resources at both museums by providing tours and discussion of the Egyptian Gallery at the Oriental Institute as well as viewings and discussion of the *Eternal Egypt* and *Inside Ancient Egypt* exhibitions at

The Field Museum. This course may serve as a model for future joint programming with The Field Museum and other Chicago cultural institutions.

The role that technology and the computer are playing in our adult education program has been growing steadily over the past several years. Close to one-third of our participants now register online, especially for the classes that we offer via distance learning. One of the most popular of these is Hieroglyphs by Mail, a correspondence course that was taught this year by Oriental Institute Research Associate Emily Teeter with the assistance of Hratch Papazian. Aaron Burke presented his Archaeology and the Bible course as a distance learning opportunity on audio-tape, enhancing the course with discussion via e-mail and with slides that he posted on the Oriental Institute

Adult education instructor Frank Yurco (right) joins one of this students, Dr. Leon Topouzian (left), for a class coffee break this past fall. Photograph by Carole Krucoff

website. Nitzan Mekel-Bobrov taught his Science and Archaeology course completely online, in association with a University of Chicago organization called Chalk, which is a provider of Blackboard, an online course software. All of these distance learning vehicles enabled us to serve students from twenty-five different states and from locales that ranged from Europe to Australia to South America.

In addition to formal courses, other adult education opportunities were available during the year. In the summer of 2002, we presented Exploring the Medieval Middle East: The Cairo Geniza, a field trip to the Spertus Museum in conjunction with the special exhibition *A Gateway to Medieval Mediterranean Life*. This program featured a richly-illustrated slide lecture by Norman Golb, Ludwig Rosenberger Professor in Jewish History and Civilization, on the treasure trove of historic documents discovered in the geniza, a special storeroom in the famed Ben Ezra Synagogue in Cairo, Egypt.

In March 2003, we joined with the Graham School of General Studies to present *Paradise Unearthed: The Rediscovery of Ancient Persia*, a day-long symposium on the history of ancient Iran and the major role played by Oriental Institute archaeologists in the search for the Persian past. Oriental Institute lecturers included Gil Stein, Oriental Institute Director and Professor of Mesopotamian and Anatolian Archaeology, who welcomed participants and introduced the program; Matthew W. Stolper, John A. Wilson Professor of Assyriology, who spoke on "The Achaemenid Persian Empire and Achaemenid Persia"; and Donald Whitcomb, Research Associate and Associate Professor of Islamic and Medieval Archaeology, on "Mythology and History: The Meanings of Persepolis." Guest lecturers included Mark Garrison, Professor of Art History, Trinity University at San Antonio, Texas, who spoke on "Achaemenid Persian Art: New Perspectives from Persepolis," and William M. Sumner, Director Emeritus of the Oriental Institute and Professor Emeritus of Iranian Archaeology, who returned to lecture to the large audience of Oriental Institute members and friends on "Demographic Cycles in the Marv Dasht, Fars Province, Iran, 6000–500 B.C."

Gil Stein, Oriental Institute Director (right), and William M. Sumner (left), Director Emeritus, spend a few moments in quiet conversation over lunch during "Paradise Unearthed," a day-long symposium on ancient Persia which included presentations by both. Photograph by Wendy Ennes

Informal, drop-by programs were also available throughout the year. During the summer, we repeated "Lunchtime in Another Time," a free series of noontime gallery talks for the University community and Hyde Park neighbors. Docents Gabriele Da Silva, Joe Diamond, Kathleen Mineck, and Mari Terman developed and presented these special gallery talks. For this year's program, we were also fortunate to have the assistance of Leigh Goldstein, who came to us from Columbia University in New York to serve as a summer intern. Leigh's writing talents and marketing skills brought the summer program more media attention than it had ever received, including a feature article and weekly coverage in the *Hyde Park Herald,* as well as a visit from WTTW, the local pubic television station.

In September, we celebrated Illinois Archaeology Awareness Month with "Camels to Khartoum," a special lecture by Emily Teeter on the Oriental Institute's historic expedition to Egypt and Sudan in 1905/1906. Informal programming was also available every Sunday year-round, with docent-led gallery tours following each of our free documentary film showings.

Youth and Family Programs

Familiar favorites combined with new programs helped us continue serving children and their families throughout the year. For the sixth straight summer we collaborated with the Lill Street Art Center on the north side to present "Be An Ancient Egyptian Artist," our popular children's day camp that fills to capacity almost as soon as it is announced. We also offered ancient-style art-making sessions at the Institute for all the children attending summer camps at the Hyde Park Art Center.

For the first time we also collaborated on family programming with the Graham School of General Studies, our longtime partner in adult education. The new program — a two-part presentation called "What do Archaeologists Really Do?" — invited parents and children to learn how archaeologists excavate ancient sites, reconstruct ancient artifacts, and how recoveries from ancient tombs can tell us about life long ago. This program was presented by Museum Education's Maria Krasinski and by Carrie Hritz, graduate student in Mesopotamian Archaeology. "Pharaoh's Garden," a spring program also presented by Maria Krasinski, along with docent Rebecca Binkley, offered families a gallery tour to discover the flowers and plants of ancient Egypt. This was followed by a visit to the Oriental Institute's "secret" Middle Eastern-style courtyard garden, and then a workshop to decorate pottery with ancient Egyptian-style floral designs.

In addition to workshops, we offered a full calendar of free family programs in collaboration with city-wide events. For the seventeenth straight season we returned to the 57th Street Children's Bookfair where docents Terri and Bill Gillespie, Rebecca Binkley, and junior docent Kristina Cooper showed hundreds of fair-going children and parents how to create an ancient-Egyptian-style book. We also joined in the city-wide celebration of Chicago Book Month in October by presenting "Tales from Ancient Egypt," a storytelling program featuring master storyteller Judith Heineman. Along with ancient tales, this event included hands-on arts projects, self-guided gallery activities, and the chance to try on reproduction costumes from "King Tut's Closet." Hundreds of family visitors enjoyed this special program, which was co-sponsored by the Regents Park/University of Chicago Fine Arts Partnership.

In winter, we took part in Chicago's first *Winter Delights* series, the city's new initiative to attract the tourist audience during the winter season. "Mummies, Mummies, Mummies!" — our Winter Delights program in January — attracted hundreds of family visitors, due in much good measure to the free advertising we received as part of the city's widespread press and television campaign.

The success of these audience-building programs was evident in May when huge crowds attended the new event we presented on Mother's Day. Called "Happy Mummy's Day," this program featured children's films, hands-on arts, and gallery tours. Long lines also formed at our interactive, touch-screen computer kiosks, which encourage parents and children to explore and learn new concepts about ancient Egypt as they virtually interact with our collection in ways it would be impossible for them to do in the exhibits. These kiosks, developed with the support of the Polk Bros. Foundation, are part of a major and ongoing educational initiative to attract the family audience and enhance the museum's educational experiences for children and parents.

Maria Krasinski, Education Programs Assistant, helps Abby Stein build a pyramid during a family workshop co-sponsored by the Graham School of General Studies. Photograph by Carole Krucoff

Children surround the Oriental Institute touch-screen computer kiosk during Family Day in October 2002. Photograph by Wendy Ennes

Exploring the Cradle of Civilization: A Museum Learning Project for Families

In 1999, the Polk Bros. Foundation awarded the Oriental Institute a major grant to research and implement a comprehensive program of museum learning experiences that would attract and serve families who generally do not visit museums. This generous support, which focused on activities for the Egyptian Gallery, enabled us to install the two highly successful computer kiosks described above, as well brightly colored, family-friendly exhibit labeling for our statute of King Tut. We also produced a rich array of Family Activity cards that direct parents and children to search for, and make discoveries about, specific artifacts and then continue the learning experience with follow-up activities to do at home. Since the spring of 2002, when the cards were first made available to the public, tracking has shown that 6,993 family visitors have used and taken home these handsome and engaging learning materials.

In the fall of 2002, renewed support from the Polk Bros. Foundation enabled us to turn our attention to self-guided family activities for the new Mesopotamian Gallery. Called *Exploring the Cradle of Civilization: A Museum Learning Project for Families*, this new initiative provides funding to develop family-friendly exhibit labeling, a new series of Family Activity Cards, and a wide variety of computer activities for the kiosks that will be housed in the Mesopotamian Gallery.

Development of such a major project requires extensive research, evaluation, and assessment long before the creative work of materials design and the making of computer interactives ever begins. For the previous project on ancient Egypt, we had the assistance of a group of families from the North Kenwood/Oakland Charter School (NK/O) who helped us shape and then test all of our Egyptian Galley activities. This project has the support of ten new NK/O families, as well as Dr. Marvin Hoffman, Founding Director and Director of Instruction of NK/O, who is serving as educational advisor. Jane Dowling and Teresa Vasquez of Wellington Consulting Group in Chicago are the project's evaluation consultants.

The family advisors include: Marsha Brookins and Shomari Crocket (age 6); Joanne Cowart and Ellis (age 8); Gary Foster and Gary, Jr. (age 12) and Gabrielle (age 7); Mosea and Schena Harris, and Mosea (age 7); Tressey and Erik King and Quintin (age 6); Janelle LaVigne and Danielle (age 12); Juanita Mahdi-Smith and Brianna (age 5); Robert Palmer and Sabrina (age 5); Fatou and Mamodou Sow and Abdoulaye (age 6); and Veronia and Michael Thompson and Michael (age 13), Terrance (age 10), and Tyler (age 6). These committed parents and children are working with Wendy Ennes, the Oriental Institute's Teacher Services and

Karen L. Wilson, Oriental Institute Museum Director, previews Mesopotamian Gallery for fascinated children from the North Kenwood/Oakland Charter School. These children and their parents are helping us develop gallery activities for families in a project supported by the Polk Bros. Foundation. Photograph by Wendy Ennes

Family Projects Coordinator, who is supervising the *Exploring the Cradle of Civilization* project. Wendy's research began by polling the families to discover the role that museum visits play in their family life and also determine what they find interesting about Mesopotamia, as well as what more they would like to learn. The families also previewed the new Mesopotamian Gallery with Wendy and Karen Wilson to identify the objects they found intriguing and to suggest the kinds of activities they might enjoy and find meaningful as learning experiences. The results from these sessions will help Wendy shape the next stage of the project, when she begins creating the printed materials and computer interactives for future families to use in the Mesopotamian Gallery. In addition to enhancing our services for families, these new learning experiences will also help expand our family audience since the new grant is providing support to translate all of the printed materials into Spanish.

Teacher Training Services

In the city of Chicago and throughout the nation, major attention is being focused on the role that instructional technology plays in the education of elementary and high school students. Wendy Ennes, Teacher Services and Family Projects Coordinator, stated this clearly in her Summer 2003 *News & Notes* article "Utilizing Computer Technology in Museum Education":

> An evolving emphasis within school districts is how their schools develop, use, and maintain instructional technology. There is nationwide concern about overcoming the digital divide by ensuring that every child is technologically literate by the time he or she finishes eighth grade. This is but one example of the federal investment that the U.S. Department of Education is making in the nation's schools with the "No Child Left Behind Act." With public policy and federal dollars driving the educational technology mission of our schools, the educational mission of our museum cannot lag too far behind in making its curriculum and collection resources available to teachers and students via the World Wide Web.

Thanks to generous support from the Lloyd A. Fry Foundation, Museum Education took its first steps in this direction in 2001 by creating the prototype for a Teacher Resource Center to exist entirely online. The Center, which began by focusing on ancient Egypt, provided background information and selected lesson plans to help local educators enhance their teaching on ancient civilizations. Continued support from the Fry Foundation this past year has enabled Wendy Ennes to expand and refine the online Center in ways that best meet teacher and student needs. A panel of teachers and technology coordinators from the Chicago Public Schools (CPS) assisted her with this project. They included Mary Cobb, Ray Elementary School; Richard Diaz, Field Elementary School; Ingia Jackson, Nettlehorst Elementary School; Lisa Perez, Von Steuben Metro High School; Trish Ronan, Clissold Elementary School; and Hermine Zakas, Drummond Elementary School. Deborah Pitluk from the CPS Department of Instructional Technology also serves on the panel. Nitzan Mekel-Bobrov, a University of Chicago graduate student in biomolecular archaeology who has expertise in computer programming, assisted Wendy with technical support.

Along with background information and resources on ancient Egypt, the redesigned online Teacher Resource Center now includes a wide variety of resources on ancient Mesopotamia. In addition, it provides digitized images as well as information on pertinent artifacts from the museum's Egyptian and Mesopotamian collections. It also offers easily accessible classroom and museum lesson plans and student activities organized around key curriculum areas that teachers must present as part of mandated classroom study on the ancient Near East.

Tamiko Langston and Jim Mitchell of Smyth School examine a reproduction of an ancient Egyptian scarab during an Oriental Institute/Chicago Public School teachers' seminar supported by the Lloyd A. Fry Foundation. Photograph by Wendy Ennes

The lesson plans that appear in the online Teacher Resource Center have been created by the educators who have attended our on-campus professional development seminars for teachers. Over the past five years, the Fry Foundation has provided the Oriental Institute with support to present these seminars, which have provided in-depth training for

Wendy Ennes, Teacher Services and Family Projects Coordinator, at Spotlight on Chicago event for educators. Sponsored by the city's Department of Cultural Affairs, this event allowed us to publicize all our educational resources, including the new online Teacher Resource Center. Photograph by Maria Krasinski

177 teachers who have reached more than 14,000 students. This year's seminar, which took place during the summer, focused on ancient Egypt. Teachers also visited the Spertus Museum to see "A Gateway to Medieval Mediterranean Life," a special exhibition on medieval Egypt, and they took part in a simulated dig in the museum's Artifact Center, where a recreated tell explores ancient Near Eastern history from the earliest eras to the time of the Romans.

The computer will soon be helping us provide professional development for an even broader audience of educators. The teacher advisors who evaluated the online Teacher Resource Center this past year suggested the Center become the springboard for online professional development that would serve the many teachers who cannot attend our on-campus program, but who would benefit greatly from the content and the Illinois State Teacher Recertification credit that our seminars provide. Wendy Ennes is in the process of developing a prototype online professional development lesson on ancient Mesopotamia that will be tested by elementary and high school educators this year.

Wendy's knowledge and skills in computer-based learning also make her ideally suited to serve as our liaison to Chicago Webdocent, a collaboration for online curriculum development between the Chicago Public Schools/University of Chicago Internet Project and several Chicago cultural institutions. Along with the Oriental Institute, these include the Adler Planetarium, the Chicago Historical Society, The Field Museum, the Museum of Science and Industry, and the Newberry Library. Over the past two years, the Oriental Institute has provided digital images of artifacts, primary source materials, and editorial support to help Chicago Webdocent create five online units of study on ancient Egypt and Mesopotamia. Most are designed for use only by the Chicago Public Schools, but one highly interactive unit on preparing an ancient Egyptian mummy for burial can be found by clicking on the "Kids Corner" section of the Oriental Institute Museum Education webpage. Visit this highly engaging learning experience to see an ex-

Volunteer docent Carole Yoshida helps children create ancient Egyptian style books during family event sponsored by the Regents Park/University of Chicago Fine Arts partnership. Volunteers contributed invaluable time and talents to many public programs this past year. Photograph by Wendy Ennes

ample of how the tools and products of computer technology can enhance and enrich classroom and museum learning in new and exciting ways [http://www-oi.uchicago.edu/OI/MUS/ED/kids.html].

Our services for teachers expanded into the realm of the life and physical sciences this year when the Chicago Public Schools invited us to join its highly-regarded Museum Partners in Science program. This program, funded by CPS, asks selected city museums to create professional development seminars for elementary school educators who wish to build their science teaching skills. Our very first Museum Partners in Science seminar, offered in May for twenty educators, focused on archaeology. Aaron Burke, a Ph.D. candidate in Syro-Palestinian Archaeology, introduced the teachers to ways archaeology draws upon both the life and physical sciences to learn about the ancient past. Nitzan Mekel-Bobrov, a graduate student in biomolecular archaeology, focused on how archaeologists interpret history through the study of ancient DNA. Along with lectures and discussion, the program included workshops in the Egyptian and Persian Galleries and an introduction to the Oriental Institute's curriculum materials on science and inventions in ancient Egypt and Mesopotamia.

Other services for teachers this year included our participation in Spotlight on Chicago, an annual resource fair for educators and administrators sponsored by the city's Department of Cultural Affairs. This by-invitation-only event allowed us to share our curriculum materials, classroom resources, and museum visit opportunities with teachers from throughout the metropolitan area. Wendy Ennes used a laptop computer to introduce fascinated educators from the city and suburbs to all the assistance they now can find in the online Teacher Resource Center.

Regents Park/U of C Fine Arts Partnership

Closer to home, generous support from a local foundation is helping us further our associations with the public schools in Hyde Park/Kenwood. This year, the Regents Park/University of Chicago Fine Arts Partnership, funded by the Clinton Companies, awarded a fifth year of support to the Oriental Institute, the Hyde Park Art Center, the Smart Museum of Art, and the University of Chicago Music Department, so that all of us can expand our educational enrichment services for the schoolchildren in our community.

At the heart of our participation in the Regents Park Fine Arts Partnership is our special relationship with five neighborhoods schools — Bret Harte School, Murray Language Academy, the North Kenwood/Oakland Charter School, Ray School, Shoesmith School, and Kenwood Academy. Partnership support allows us to offer these schools a wide range of educational experiences, including guided tours and special study sessions at the museum as well as artists' residences that enable students to recreate ancient arts processes. Support from the Partnership also enables us to serve these schools in an even wider way. This fall, students and families of all Hyde Park/Kenwood's elementary schools were invited to "Tales from Ancient Egypt," our second annual celebration of Chicago Book Month that is described in the Youth and Families section.

Lavie Raven (center) Kenwood Academy social studies teacher, poses in the West Gallery with Carmia Arrington and Darryl Wade, two of his students, in front of a 48 foot mural of the Nile Valley. Raven and his students created the mural as part of "Ancient Egypt: A Hip Hop Perspective," an Oriental Institute/Kenwood project supported by the Regents Park Fine Arts Partnership. Photograph by Jason Smith

Partnership support also helped us host an open house for local teachers and administrators. Presented in collaboration with the Frank Lloyd Wright Preservation Trust and the staff of Robie House, this event took place during Chicago Artists Month in October and featured demonstrations by the artists who provide Oriental Institute residencies for our partner schools.

Our special relationship with Kenwood Academy continued this past year. As we have done for the last four years, we offered the classroom lectures, museum visits, and pottery reconstruction sessions focusing on Roman Egypt giving Kenwood students studying Latin a new perspective on ancient Roman life and times. The Kenwood program that had the most impact this past year was the direct outcome of a major project begun in 2002. That spring, the Oriental Institute offered a series of workshops on ancient Egypt for students in the University of Hip Hop (Healthy Independent People Helping Other People), an after school initiative at Kenwood that is part of a city-wide program created for young people to explore modern urban culture through the arts and music. As a result of the Oriental Institute workshops, the students transformed what they had learned into a vibrantly colored forty-eight foot long mural of the Nile Valley, as well as four smaller murals that explored ancient Egyptian motifs from a contemporary urban perspective.

Support from the Regents Park Partnership enabled the Oriental Institute to bring these extraordinary murals to our museum, where Wendy Ennes, Lavie Raven, Kenwood world history teacher, and our preparators mounted the murals as a special exhibit in the West Gallery. Called "Ancient Egypt: A Hip Hop Perspective," the murals exhibit had a special opening for its student artists and their friends and families and then went on public view. The exhibit was covered widely in the Chicago press and was seen by thousands of visitors, many of them awed schoolchildren, during its six-month run from November to April. The unique collaboration that led to such remarkable student work and the ability to share the work with the public could not have taken place without the support of the Regents Park/University of Chicago Fine Arts Partnership.

Oriental Institute School Affiliates

Generous support and major grant funding has been crucial to development of our wide-ranging services and programs for schools. In 1998, principals of several schools that had been collaborating with us over the years joined together to help create the Oriental Institute/Chicago Public Schools Affiliates Program, a structured system that encourages schools to pay a modest fee for services as grant-funded support comes to an end. We are delighted that, for the fifth year in a row, principals and local school councils have voted to renew the Affiliates program, allowing materials production, museum visits, and outreach services to continue for their schools. We appreciate this reaffirmation of the value schools place on the educational services we offer teachers and students.

Behind the Scenes

Taking stock of all that has been accomplished this past year, I would like to say how much I appreciate the interest, encouragement, and support that Museum Education has received from the Oriental Institute's faculty, staff, and students. Grateful thanks also go to our dedicated Museum Education volunteers; none of our gallery-based public programs, including thematic tours, family programs, and special events for the University community, could have taken place without the time and talents contributed by Debbie Aliber, Jane Belcher, Rebecca Binkley, Dorothy Blindt, Myllicent Buchanan, David Covill, Gabriele Da Silva, Catherine Deans-Barrett, Joe

Museum visitors admire smaller murals created by Kenwood Academy High School students as part of the "Ancient Egypt: A Hip Hop Perspective" project. Photograph by Jason Smith

Diamond, Dario Giacomoni, Bill Gillespie, Terry Gillespie, Anita Greenberg, Bud Haas, Debby Halpern, Ira Hardman, Mary Harter, Lee Herbst, Teresa Hintzke, Elizabeth Lassers, Kathleen Lisle, Michael Lisle, Lo Luong Lo, Masako Matsumoto, Robert McGuiness, Roy Miller, Kathleen Mineck, Donald Payne, Diane Posner, Semra Prescott, Melissa Ratkovich, Patrick Regnery, Stephen Ritzel, Lucie Sandel, Deloris Sanders, Larry Scheff, Joy Schochet, Anne Schumacher, Daila Shefner, Bernadette Strnad, Mari Terman, Karen Terras, and Carole Yoshida. Special thanks to Junior Volunteers Kristina Cooper, Sam Dresson, and John Whitcomb; we couldn't have managed without them at our large events for families.

The commitment, creativity, and vision of the Museum Education staff are what make everything happen. The contributions of Wendy Ennes, Teacher Services and Family Projects Coordinator, are evident throughout this report. Wendy's extraordinary talents as an educator and museum professional make her an invaluable asset to the Oriental Institute.

Maria Krasinski, Education Programs Assistant, shines as developer of University student programming and youth and family workshops. But all would come to a complete standstill without the writing talents, artistic skills, and organizational abilities that make her the quiet but firm command central in our office. Maria is in charge of implementing the registration, confirmation, and financial depositing processes for all reserved adult education, family, and guided tour programs. She also serves as our public relations officer, editor, and graphic design expert. She writes and distributes our quarterly press packets and all individual press releases, and she designs and supervises production of all our educational and marketing materials, including our quarterly calendar of events, which she has given a highly professional new look. All of this belies the frugal nature of the marketing budget with which she works! We are fortunate to have Maria with us.

Two additional people deserve special mention here. In 2003, Catherine Dueñas and Terry Friedman marked their tenth year as the Oriental Institute's Volunteer Coordinators. Under the leadership of these gifted and dedicated women, the Volunteer Program has reached new heights. The program has been resilient in the face of change, has developed new avenues for volunteer service, and has grown in strength and stature to become a model for volunteer programs throughout the city and state. Turn to the Volunteer Program section in this *Annual Report* to see all that Cathy and Terry, and their remarkable corps of volunteers, have accomplished in this tenth anniversary year.

SUQ

Denise Browning

Tribute to the Volunteers: Past and Present

Working as manager of the Suq all of these years, I have had the privilege of working with an amazing group of women. All of them strong, very intelligent, and well educated, independent yet gracious, and full of spunk and humor. They are a major part of the Suq, with most of them donating more than fifteen years of service.

Unfortunately, this year we had to say good-bye to Eleanor Swift, one of the most amazing women I have ever met. Eleanor was involved with the Suq almost since its inception in 1967, when it was nothing more than a small table with a few postcards — most of which were still around when I came ten years later. She loved working in the Suq, where she could handle 100 children at once with ease and understanding, while having the unique ability of being able to melt the most difficult of customers. She was also devoted to the students who worked in the Suq, making sure they had her extra tickets to the Lyric Opera or the Chicago Symphony, believing that an education in the arts outside of the university was also important.

We who had the pleasure of knowing Eleanor Swift will never forget her. I will miss her strength, her logic, her beauty, her humor, but most of all her laughter.

Working in the Suq on Mondays to restock the store beside Eleanor for years was Georgie Maynard. Add strong willed to the above characteristics and you have Georgie. As a young bride, she was off to teach English in Turkey during World War II. Her love of travel never subsided. After her husband's death she and Eleanor would trek off around the world together. They would not embark on elaborate cruises, but instead they took a mail boat up the coast of Iceland. Even just a few years ago, Georgie decided to take a tour of Central Asia. When they arrived, the guide decided to abandon the tour because he felt that the political climate at the time was unsafe for travel. Did that deter Georgie? No! She was in her eighties when she took off on the tour by herself. She was busy organizing the books in the Suq until she died.

Inger Kirsten was a particularly strong woman, yet she always thought to bring flowers from her garden to warm up the Suq. If it was Friday morning, that meant Peggy Kovacs and Leonard Byman. Peggy was always full of fun and must have had one of the best collections of jewelry from years of working in the Suq. Leonard Byman, one of the few men working in the Suq was not to be outdone. Among his many accomplishments was an incredible knowledge of play-wrights.

Some of the women have moved away from Chicago or on to other interests. Tuesday mornings was the regular day for Rochelle Rossin and Charlotte Collier to work together ... what a perfect match! Charlotte with the patience of Job and a true woman of the world brought out the best in Rochelle. Rochelle would make sure that the customer purchased that perfect piece of jewelry to match her outfit.

Wednesday afternoons for years were filled with the laughter of Barbara Watson and Mary Schulman. Barbara, an accomplished artist and jewelry designer, spurred my love of beads by sharing her knowledge and enthusiasm. They both gave me an education in life.

The list continues ... What would the Suq have been without Diana Grodzins, Evelyn Dyba, Kay Ginther, Mardi Trosman, Carol Goldstein, Jane Hildebrand, Maria Ahlstrom, Agnethe Rattenborg, Barbara Frey and Ruth Hyman who have all given many dedicated years to the Suq?

Some of those remarkable women continue to contribute to the Suq: Peggy Grant, Norma van der Meulen, Muriel Brauer, Florence Ovadia, Jane Thain, Patty Dunkel, and Jo Jackson.

What a remarkable group! Those listed, plus all of the others, have added their strengths and talents to make the Suq. Thank you!

With their help we will continue the tradition they have created for the Suq in meeting the challenges of the future. With the completion of the museum's renovations we will have a whole new public to introduce to the wonders of the Suq in very challenging economic times.

VOLUNTEER PROGRAM

Catherine Dueñas and Terry Friedman

Out of turmoil can come understanding and resolve. The war in Iraq and the subsequent looting of the Iraq Museum in Baghdad and other provincial museums has increased public awareness and interest in Mesopotamian art. In light of these recent events, the Oriental Institute Volunteers have a serious responsibility to educate the public about this part of the world with tact and grace. With the opening of the new Edgar and Deborah Jannotta Mesopotamian Gallery rapidly approaching, the value of education about the Near East has never been so timely and important. The goal of our docents has always been to explain ancient Near Eastern cultures as accurately and objectively as possible, while at the same time drawing parallels with our own culture across millennia of time. We have great faith in our docents' ability to serve as goodwill ambassadors between the museum's collection and the community.

Tour Program

Docent-led tours of the permanent galleries (the Joseph and Mary Grimshaw Egyptian Gallery and the Persian Gallery) continue to be in popular demand, keeping museum docents actively engaged and interacting with audiences of all ages. Whether school students, religious groups, community organizations, or senior citizens, the Oriental Institute Museum docents are always ready to share their knowledge and their enthusiasm for the museum's beautiful collection. Throughout the year, many museum docents initiated informal study sessions to collaborate on the development of special interest tour topics to enhance their own knowledge in specific areas of interest pertaining to the collection. These informal gatherings were a dynamic information exchange to help improve tour content as well as interactive touring techniques.

The Docent Captain System, which was instituted decades ago, continues to be a vital link between the museum docents and the administrative staff. Each captain's dedicated supervision over the organization and maintenance of docent staffing for the morning and afternoon tour schedules allow the program to function with efficiency and purpose. Their administrative skills and unwavering support are essential elements in maintaining the tour program's excellence as an enriching educational experience. We are grateful to the captains: Debbie Aliber, Gabriele Da Silva, Joe Diamond, Mary Harter, Teresa Hintzke, Nina Longley, Masako Matsumoto, Roy Miller, Charlotte Noble, Donald Payne, Patrick Regnery, Stephen Ritzel, Lucie Sandel, Deloris Sanders, Larry Scheff, Anne Schumacher, Daila Shefner, Karen Terras, and Carole Yoshida for their patience and cooperation. We salute them for their support and hard work throughout the year.

The monthly docent captains' meetings continue to foster an excellent opportunity for captains to communicate concerns and offer suggestions for improvements within the Volunteer Program as well as throughout the Institute. These meetings provide a venue for an open dialogue between the captains. Within this informal setting, the docents and volunteers are able to share and discuss ideas on various aspects of the Volunteer Program. These observations are helpful for initiating change and improvements within the entire program. This year for the first time in the thirty-six year history of the Volunteer Program, we were honored to have the Oriental Institute Director and the Director of the Museum attend one of these monthly captains' meetings. Gil Stein, the new Oriental Institute Director, addressed the questions and concerns expressed by many of the captains, docents, and volunteers.

We continue to revamp and streamline the reservation and booking procedures for tour reservations, which are now handled exclusively by mail. This process continues to operate efficiently under the supervision of Maria Krasinski, our Education Programs Assistant. With the volume of calls and inquiries concerning museum tours and programs, we have instituted procedures to make the process as systematic and error-free as possible. This format has been very successful, not only in the processing of our tour/reservation/confirmation forms and fee-based program requests, but also in the tracking and compilation of statistical data. We now are able to retrieve important information concerning the number of museum visitors enjoying a docent-led tour and what these numbers represent in terms of geographic distribution, educational level, and age profile. We are pleased to announce that over 7,000 people enjoyed the advantages of a docent-led tour during the past year.

Volunteer Recruitment and Training

With the announcement of the opening of the Edgar and Deborah Jannotta Mesopotamian Gallery and Yelda Khorsabad Court in the fall of 2003, plans were immediately initiated to produce an enticing recruitment brochure aimed at attracting new volunteers to the Oriental Institute's Docent and Volunteer Corps. Several members of the Thursday morning volunteer team began this effort last summer by spearheading a campaign to merge their creative talents and energies into the development of our first recruitment brochure. They worked tirelessly to create a tool that would showcase the Oriental Institute's Volunteer Program to the general public and allow individuals to explore how they might fit into the program. Our thanks to Masako Matsumoto, Charlotte Noble, and Karen Terras for their imagination, creativity, and dedication to the development of this wonderful recruitment brochure. We also want to thank Debby Halpern, Maria Krasinski, and Clemens Reichel for their careful editing and graphic design contributions to this project.

"Open your eyes to the world of the ancient Near East" became the slogan that caught the attention of many eager volunteer recruits. We are pleased to welcome twenty-seven new members into the volunteer corps: Sabat Adil, John Aldrin, Sylwia Aldrin, Jane Arkell, Ann Avouris, James Baughman, Jo Burgess, Stephen Esposito, Ruth Goldman, Tom Hunter, Denis Kelley, Barbara Levin, Kathleen Lisle, Michael Lisle, Mitch Mikalik, Erin Hardacher Morr, David Ray, John Ray, Micah Shender, Sabrina Sholts, Levi Smith, Pierangelo Taschini, Kristine Thompson, Pramerudee Townsend, Robert Wagner, Michael Wasniowski, and Monica Wood.

In preparation for the opening of the Mesopotamian Gallery, a four-part series of training sessions was developed to orient the new, current, and returning volunteers to the new gallery space. We are pleased to announce that the 2003 Training Class was the largest class in recent history, with over ninety participants.

The class gathered weekly for four Saturdays to hear a broad range of topics designed to help familiarize the volunteers with the archaeological, cultural, and historical aspects of the museum's collection. We extend our appreciation to: John Brinkman, Clemens Reichel, Martha Roth, Gil Stein, Jason Ur, Tony Wilkinson, and Karen Wilson for sharing their wealth of knowledge with the docents and volunteers. It was an extraordinary experience for everyone!

We would also like to thank Oriental Institute Museum Director, Karen Wilson, who compiled an informative training manual with supplementary readings for the Mesopotamian Gallery. These materials will be a valuable resource for all the volunteers for years to come.

Volunteer Days

Volunteer Days continue to provide a stimulating environment for Oriental Institute docents and volunteers to explore topics for further research and study. These interactive monthly educational seminars serve as a unique forum where one can broaden one's knowledge of the ancient Near East while enjoying special camaraderie with fellow volunteers, faculty, and staff members at the Institute, as well as with colleagues from other cultural institutions.

This year's programs included a broad spectrum of research, projects, and interests. Our thanks to participating faculty and staff members of the Oriental Institute: Wendy Ennes, McGuire Gibson, Norman Golb, W. Ray Johnson, Charles E. Jones, Carlotta Maher, John Sanders, and Gil Stein. Our thanks to Sara Skelly and Jacqueline Terrassas of the Smart Museum for their informative presentations and involvement in the joint-venture program with the Oriental Institute Docents and Volunteers.

Several of our own docents have enjoyed taking center stage as presenters for the monthly continuing education Volunteer Day programs.

In November, docents Joe Diamond, Kathy Mineck, and Charlotte Noble were the guest speakers for a program that spotlighted Persia. They shared their independent research on Persia during a special three-part program. Each speaker approached the topic from a different perspective, which added so much to our understanding and appreciation of the history, language, and culture of this amazing ancient civilization.

In February, Karen Terras presented her research on "From Prudery to Pornography: Sexuality in New Kingdom Egypt." Her talk gave us a whole new perspective on Egyptian art and

"Spotlight on Persia" brought together three docent presenters for November Volunteer Day. Each docent dealt with a different aspect of ancient Persian culture. From left to right: Joe Diamond, Charlotte Noble, and Kathy Mineck. Photograph by Terry Friedman

sexuality, broadening our appreciation for the interpretation and study of ancient Egyptian culture through the graphic images as well as the more subtle nuances expressed through their art forms.

We hope that these presentations will encourage and inspire other volunteers to pursue independent research and to become presenters at future Volunteer Day programs. Our thanks to everyone for their valuable and substantive contributions to Volunteer Day programming and research.

Collaborations

Volunteers were pleased to have the opportunity to participate in two special collaborative programs this past year, one with The Field Museum and the other with the David and Alfred Smart Museum.

In March and April, The Field Museum welcomed our volunteers to participate in training sessions for the "Eternal Egypt: Masterworks of Ancient Art" exhibit which is on tour from the British Museum. Following a series of training classes, The Field Museum Docents served as exhibit interpreters and facilitators for museum visitors. Our thanks to: Rebecca Binkley, Gabriele Da Silva, Joe Diamond, Robert McGuiness, Roy Miller, Donald Payne, Stephen Ritzel, Lucie Sandel, Larry Scheff, Lillian Schwarz, and Carole Yoshida who took the opportunity to join forces with The Field Museum for this special exhibit.

Tuesday and Thursday afternoon Museum Docents were invited to collaborate with the Smart Museum on a special program that would bring sixth graders to both museums to study artifacts and interpret their meaning. The Smart Museum's exhibit, "Sacred Fragments: Magic, Mystery, and Religion in the Ancient World." served as the springboard for these specialized tours where the volunteers made connections and comparisons between the objects in the Oriental Institute's Egyptian and Persian collections and those on display at the Smart Museum.

Volunteer Voice

The Volunteer Voice (formerly The Docent Digest), the monthly newsletter for the Oriental Institute Docent/Volunteer Program, has been an important means of communication between the faculty, staff, and volunteer corps and the Volunteer Services Coordinators for many years. The monthly mailing had traditionally been sent through the postal service; however, with changing times and faster communications technology, we now are able to deliver The Voice via e-mail. This approach has saved the program hundreds of dollars in duplicating costs as well as ever-increasing postal fees. We would like to thank Thursday Docent Co-captain Masako Matsumoto for this very cost-effective suggestion for the Docent/Volunteer Program.

Book Review

We were also pleased to have Mari Terman share a fascinating book review in the March Volunteer Voice on *Before Writing*, Volume 1: *From Counting to Cuneiform*, by Denise Schmandt-Besserat. Her informative and insightful report helped to prepare the volunteers for the Mesopotamian training sessions.

Docent Library

This year, the Docent Library continued to expand and flourish under the skillful guidance and supervision of Debbie Aliber and Margaret Foorman. Margaret Foorman worked very closely with Debbie this past year in order to prepare to assume the responsibilities of Head Librarian. Aided by the many generous donations and contributions from the faculty, staff, and volunteers, our library's collection has enjoyed many new additions. This year Debbie and Margaret, together with their Library Committee, Patricia Hume, Sandra Jacobsohn, Deloris Sanders, and Daila Shefner, orchestrated an extremely successful booksale on May 3rd. The sale was planned in conjunction with the Mesopotamian Training Sessions to help new and current volunteers supplement their reading materials economically and, at the same time, support the Docent Library Fund.

Field Trip to the Field Museum

June Volunteer Day gave us an opportunity to visit our friends at The Field Museum. Our docents and volunteers were invited by Bob Cantu, the Docent Coordinator at The Field Museum, to see the special exhibit on "Eternal Egypt" and have coffee with The Field Museum Docents. It is always a treat for our volunteers to visit and exchange ideas with the volunteers from another museum. It broadens their perspectives and helps us to evaluate how other museum docents handle their presentations to the public.

Volunteer Recognition and Annual Holiday Luncheon

As a yearly tradition, faculty, staff, and volunteers gather to enjoy a festive holiday celebration for December Volunteer Day. This popular program includes a guest speaker, the introduction of new volunteers, and the volunteer recognition ceremony. The program culminates with a lovely

At December Volunteer Recognition Day, Oriental Institute Director Gil Stein posed with the Volunteer Recognition Award Recipients. Top row, pictured from left to right are: Kitty Picken, Gil Stein, Masako Matsumoto, Nina Longley, Lillian Schwartz, bottom row Joan Friedmann, Peggy Wick, Rita Picken, Larry Scheff, Elizabeth Spiegel, and Anne Schumacher. Photograph by Jean Grant

holiday luncheon at the Quadrangle Club. This year's special event took place on Monday, December 2.

Our guest speaker was Oriental Institute Director, Gil Stein. His presentation, "What Mean These Bones?" was a fascinating topic. We gained a whole new perspective and appreciation for the role of zooarchaeologists and how the study of animal bones can unlock many mysteries about ancient cultures, revealing a great deal about their diet, mobility, religion, settlement patterns, and much more.

Immediately following Dr. Stein's talk, the program continued with the introduction of the new volunteers and the Recognition Awards Ceremony. We were pleased to welcome into the Volunteer Corps: Ann Avouris, Elizabeth Dyer, Charlotte Noble, Kristine Thompson, Kavita Macchar, Katrina Paleski, Melissa Ratkovich, and Monica Wood.

This year twenty-one volunteers were recognized for their distinguished and loyal commitment to the Oriental Institute. Bravo and congratulations to all!

Recognition Award Recipients

5 Years

Janet Kessler   George Morgan

10 Years

Joan Friedmann   Betsy Kremers   Carole Krucoff   Barbara Rollhaus   Anne Schumacher

15 Years

Masako Matsumoto   Dawn Prena   Larry Scheff   Lillian Schwartz   Richard Watson

20 Years

Nina Longley

25 Years

Lilian Cropsey   Kitty Picken   Rita Picken   Mardi Trossman

30 Years

Janet Russell   Elizabeth Spiegel   Peggy Wick

35 Years

Jim Sopranos

We would like to express our gratitude to Gil Stein and the Office of the Director for underwriting the delicious Annual Holiday Luncheon at the Quadrangle Club and to Denise Browning, Suq Manager, for her valuable assistance.

Outreach

The Outreach Program continues to delight and engage audiences of all ages. Outreach has grown in stature and popularity over the past seven years. It continues to generate a loyal following of schools as well as attract new audiences who enjoy this "in-school field trip" alternative. Whether adults, educators, parents, or students, the program receives praise and rave reviews from all of its participants. Even with the reopening of the Egyptian and Persian Galleries, many schools and community groups view an outreach visit as an enhancement to their total museum experience. This year the Outreach Docents took the "show on the road" to more than 300 participants.

"Outreach on the Road Again" at James Hart School in Homewood, Illinois. Docent Anne Schumacher and James Hart teacher Gail Huizinga pose with the students who participated in the dress-up. Photograph Terry Friedman

Randel Tea

The home of President and Mrs. Randel was the location for a special July Volunteer Day program. The docents, faculty, staff, and volunteers of the Oriental Institute were invited to enjoy a beautiful tea reception with President and Mrs. Randel. We thank the Randels for their generous hospitality and for extending such a warm and gracious welcome to everyone.

We also extend our thanks and gratitude to Carlotta Maher and W. Ray Johnson for their unique presentation "Tales from the Crypt: Recent Work and Discoveries of the Epigraphic Survey at Chicago House in Luxor." Their talk highlighted some of the impressive work accomplished by the Epigraphic Survey and its significant contributions towards the preservation of ancient Egypt for future generations of scholars to study.

"Outreach on the Road Again" brought Carole Yoshida to James Hart School as the slide show presenter. Here she posed with students who participated in the ancient Egypt dress-up activity. Photograph by Terry Friedman

Intern

We were delighted this year to have the opportunity to work with Ann Avouris from the University of Chicago. From administrative tasks to assisting on special projects, Ann's energetic spirit and calm demeanor were appreciated by all who worked with her. Throughout the past year her numerous contributions have helped to enhance and support many vital areas of the Volunteer

The Docents and Volunteers get invited to tea at the Randels. Enjoying a lovely afternoon at the President's home are from right to left: W. Ray Johnson, Director of the Epigraphic Survey, Carlotta Maher, Terry Friedman, and Cathy Dueñas

Program's ongoing operation. We are proud to announce that Ann has received an internship to work at the Brooklyn Museum of Fine Arts this summer. Congratulations, Ann!

In Memoriam

We were saddened this past year to lose two devoted friends and supporters of the Oriental Institute: William Boone and Eleanor Swift.

They were extraordinary individuals whose gifts of time, talent, and dedication helped to enrich the Volunteer Program, the Museum, and the Institute in many ways. They will be greatly missed.

Reflection

This year has witnessed an increase in activity in the Volunteer Office, as efforts to recruit new docents were combined with ongoing educational programs in preparation for the opening of the new Mesopotamian Gallery in the fall. Our volunteers, both new and current, have shown their dedication to the museum by attending both Volunteer Day Programs and the additional Mesopotamia training sessions. The continued curiosity, enthusiasm, and unwavering support of the docents and volunteers are the key elements to the program's success and longevity.

We would also like to thank our colleagues in Museum Education for their faithful support throughout this past year: Wendy Ennes, Teachers' Services and Family Project Coordinator, Maria Krasinski, Education Programs Assistant, and Carole Krucoff, Head of Education and Public Programs. In an environment bustling with activity, their calm reassurance, prudent guidance, and good humor provide a congenial and productive work atmosphere.

We gratefully acknowledge the friendship and support of the faculty and staff of the Oriental Institute for their accessibility and involvement with the program. As our teachers and mentors, they continue to motivate and inspire the high level of volunteer involvement throughout many vital areas of the Oriental Institute and the museum. We thank them for continually sharing their wealth of knowledge, sparking our curiosity, and supplying countless resources for the ongoing education of the docents and the volunteers.

The Volunteer Program has continued to thrive and evolve over the past thirty-six years, providing meaningful opportunities for the volunteers to be challenged intellectually as well as to demonstrate their many talents. Throughout its history, the program has gained strength and stature due to its ability to adapt well to change and embrace new challenges.

We await the opening of the Edgar and Deborah Jannotta Mesopotamian Gallery with confidence that our museum's docents and volunteers will bring ancient Mesopotamia to life as they have done so impressively with Egypt and Persia.

Collectively and individually our docents and volunteers are a rare and treasured asset. As the following list demonstrates, our volunteers are vital contributing partners and valued intellectual resources in the Institute's and the museum's ongoing operation. We are proud of all that they have accomplished and look forward to a rewarding future with their help and support.

Advisors to the Volunteer Program

Carlotta Maher   Peggy Grant   Janet Helman

Honorary Volunteers-at-Large

Carol Randel   Elizabeth Sonnenschein

Museum Docents

Debbie Aliber
Ann Avouris
Bernadine Basile
Jane Belcher
Christel Betz**
Rebecca Binkley
Dorothy Blindt**
Myllicent Buchanan
Andrew Buncis
David Covill
Joan Curry
Gabriele Da Silva
Catherine Deans-Barrett
Joe Diamond
Erl Dordal
Sam Dreessen
Margaret Foorman
Joan Friedmann
Dario Giacomoni
Anita Greenberg
Debby Halpern

Ira Hardman
Mary Harter
Janet Helman
Lee Herbst
Teresa Hintzke
Tom Hunter
Henriette Klawans
Elizabeth Lassers
Nina Longley
Lo Luong Lo
Kavita Machhar
Sherif Marcus
Masako Matsumoto
Robert McGuiness**
Roy Miller
Kathy Mineck
Charlotte Noble
Katrina Paleski
Nancy Patterson**
Denise Paul
Carolyn Payer**

Donald Payne**
Kitty Picken
Rita Picken
Semra Prescott
Patrick Regnery
Stephen Ritzel
Lucie Sandel
Deloris Sanders
Larry Scheff
Joy Schocket
Anne Schumacher
Mary Shea**
Daila Shefner
Toni Smith
Bernadette Strnad
Mari Terman
Karen Terras
Claire Thomas
Monica Wood
Carole Yoshida

**We are sorry that the names of these Docents were not included in last year's *Annual Report*. We apologize for this oversight on our part.

Outreach Docents and Volunteers

Bernadine Basilie
Myllicent Buchanan
Janet Calkins
Hazel Cramer
Bill and Terry Gillespie
Debby Halpern
Ira Hardman
Mary Harter
Janet Helman
Lee Herbst

Mary Jo Khuri
Henriette Klawans
Betsy Kremers
Nina Longley
Kavita Machhar
Masako Matsumoto
Robert McGuiness**
Caryl Mikrut
Roy Miller
Kathy Mineck

Nancy Patterson
Stephen Ritzel
Deloris Sanders
Larry Scheff
Anne Schumacher
Karen Terras
Claire Thomas
Carole Yoshida
Agnes Zellner

Suq Docents

Muriel Brauer
Patty Dunkel
Peggy Grant

Neta Rattenborg
Rochelle Rossin
Jane Thain

Norma van der Meulen

Substitute Suq Docents

Janet Helman   Jo Jackson

Suq Jewelry Designer

Norma van der Meulen

Museum Archives Volunteers

James Baughman	Patricia Hume	Levi Smith
Hazel Cramer	Sandra Jacobsohn	Carole Yoshida
Peggy Grant	Lillian Schwartz	

Registrar's Office Volunteers

Aimee Drolet	Masako Matsumoto	Peggy Wick
Leon Drolet	Toni Smith	
Mary Grimshaw	O. J. Sopranos	

Membership Volunteers

Jo Burgess   Gabriele Da Silva   Rita Picken   Mica Shender   Levi Smith

Diyala Project Volunteers

Richard Harter   Betsy Kremers   George Sundell

Hamoukar Project Volunteers

Richard Harter   Betsy Kremers   George Sundell

Iraq Museum Database Project

Karen Terras

Photography Lab Volunteers

Pam Ames   Irene Glasner

Courtyard Volunteers

Terry Gillespie   Bill Gillespie   Robert Herbst

Docent Library

Head Librarians Debbie Aliber / Margaret Foorman

Assistant Librarians

Pat Hume   Sandra Jacobsohn   Deloris Sanders   Daila Shefner

Museum Education and Family Programs Volunteers

Debbie Aliber
Jane Belcher
Rebecca Binkley
Dorothy Blindt
Myllicent Buchanan
David Covill
Gabriele Da Silva
Catherine Deans-Barrett
Joe Diamond
Dario Giacomoni
Bill Gillespie
Terry Gillespie
Anita Greenberg
Bud Haas
Debby Halpern

Ira Hardman
Mary Harter
Lee Herbst
Teresa Hintzke
Elisabeth Lassers
Kathleen Lisle
Michael Lisle
Masako Matsumoto
Robert McGuiness
Roy Miller
Carl Mineck
Kathleen Mineck
Donald Payne
Diane Posner
Semra Prescott

Melissa Ratkovich
Patrick Regnery
Stephen Ritzel
Lucie Sandel
Deloris Sanders
Larry Scheff
Joy Schochet
Anne Schumacher
Daila Shefner
Bernadette Strnad
Mari Terman
Karen Terras
Carole Yoshida

Assistants to Epigraphic Survey and Chicago House

Debbie Doyle   Mary Grimshaw   Carlotta Maher   Crennan Ray   David Ray

Assistants to the Prehistoric Project

Diana Grodzins   Andree Wood

Demotic Dictionary

Anne Nelson

Iranian Prehistoric Project Volunteers

Janet Helman

Volunteers Emeritus

Elizabeth Baum
William A. Boone†
Charlotte Collier
Mary D'Ouville
Bettie Dwinell

Carol Green
Bud Haas
Cissy Haas
Alice James
Dorothy Mozinski

Rochelle Rossin
Janet Russell
Eleanor Swift†
Peggy Wick

†Denotes Deceased

**DEVELOPMENT
AND MEMBERSHIP**

DEVELOPMENT

Debora Donato

Overview

In the fiscal year 2003, the Oriental Institute raised $1,140,995 in non-federal private gifts and grants. The year-end appeal raised $45,650. On behalf of the faculty and staff, I would like to thank our generous donors for their support of the Oriental Institute. An honor roll of donors follows this report.

The East Wing Campaign

Tom Heagy, Chairman of the Visiting Committee, brought together a group from the Executive Committee to help raise money for the installation of the East Wing. The members of the East Wing Committee are Tom Heagy (chair), Carlotta Maher, Roger Nelson, John Rowe, and O. J. Sopranos.

Many of the Visiting Committee have made a commitment to the East Wing Campaign and included are:

Thomas Heagy, Tony Dean, Carlotta Maher, Roger Nelson, Patrick Regnery, John Rowe, O. J. Sopranos, Gretel Braidwood, Alan Brodie, Jean Brown, Marion Cowan, Emily Fine, Margaret Foorman, Isak and Nancy Gerson, Peggy Grant, Howard Haas, Rita Picken, Ray Crennan, Norman and Alice Rubash, Robert Schloerb, Mrs. Maurice Schwartz, and Mary Shea.

Other Fundraising Highlights

The Oriental Institute received generous support from several foundations and corporations. They include LaSalle National Bank, Exelon Corporation, The John Nuveen Company, the Polk Bros. Foundation, the Coleman Foundation, the Lloyd A. Fry Foundation, the C. William and Louise Vatz Foundation, the Luther I. Replogle Foundation, the University of Chicago Women's Board, and the Marilyn M. Simpson Charitable Trust.

Visiting Committee

During the fiscal year 2002/2003, the Visiting Committee met on three occasions. The first meeting was held on October 23, 2002, in the recently reinstalled Khorsabad Court. During the second meeting, February 20, Director Gil Stein introduced the new Development Director, Debora Donato, and Membership Director, Rebecca Laharia. Both gave reports on their respective areas. Clemens Reichel gave a presentation on the Diyala Project. After the formal portion of the meeting ended, dinner was served at the Quadrangle Club. During the June 5th meeting, Abbas Alizadeh presented "Archeological Innovations in Southwest Iran and the Establishment of a Research Center at the National Museum of Iran." Gil Stein and Tom Heagy outlined the East Wing Campaign. Dinner followed at the Quadrangle Club.

Thanks

Bill Harms, University of Chicago News and Information Office, has done a fantastic job for the Oriental Institute this year. The war in Iraq resulted in heightened interest and concern about Mesopotamian history and antiquities. As a result, the Oriental Institute gained considerable press coverage. Bill successfully and skillfully coordinated the resulting media campaign.

Reflecting on the year provides the welcome opportunity to thank all our members and especially the docents and volunteers for their support.

HONOR ROLL OF DONORS

We are pleased to recognize the friends of the Oriental Institute who have given so generously during the period from July 1, 2002 through June 30, 2002. We are most grateful for your support. The Donor Honor Roll is alphabetical by gift level. Gifts received after June 30, 2002 will appear in next year's Annual Report. We have made every effort to verify gift levels and donor names.

Please contact the Development Office at (773) 834-9775 if you wish to make changes in your honor roll listing.

$50,000 and Above

Prof. Robert Z. Aliber and Mrs. Deborah Aliber, Hanover, New Hampshire
Exelon Corporation, Chicago, Illinois
Mr. Thomas C. Heagy and Mrs. Linda H. Heagy, Chicago, Illinois
Dr. Arthur L. Herbst and Mrs. Lee Herbst, Chicago, Illinois
Jewish Communal Fund, New York, New York
Estate of Dorothy Beatrice McCown Mattison, Washington, D.C.
Mr. Joseph Neubauer and Ms. Jeanette Lerman-Neubauer, Philadelphia, Pennsylvania
Polk Bros. Foundation Inc., Chicago, Illinois
Marilyn M. Simpson Charitable Trust, New York, New York
Prof. W. Kelly Simpson, Katonah, New York
C. William and Louise Vatz Foundation, Highland Park, Illinois

$10,000–$49,999

Mr. Alan R. Brodie, Chicago, Illinois
Mr. Eric Colombel and Mrs. Andrea Colombel, New York, New York
The Coleman Foundation, Inc., Chicago, Illinois
Ms. Marion E. Cowan, Evanston, Illinois
Mr. Anthony T. Dean and Mrs. Lawrie C. Dean, Long Grove, Illinois
Max M. and Marjorie S. Fisher Foundation, Inc., Franklin, Michigan
Dr. Marjorie M. Fisher, Bloomfield Hills, Michigan
Mr. James L. Foorman and Mrs. Margaret E. Foorman, Winnetka, Illinois
Lloyd A. Fry Foundation, Chicago, Illinois
Mr. and Mrs. Isak V. Gerson, Chicago, Illinois

$10,000–$49,999 (cont.)

The Institute for Aegean Prehistory, Philadelphia, Pennsylvania
LaSalle National Bank, Chicago, Illinois
Mr. Daniel A. Lindley Jr. and Ms. Lucia Woods Lindley, Evanston, Illinois
Mr. Piers Litherland, Peoples Republic of China
Mrs. Barbara Mertz, Frederick, Maryland
Mr. Roger R. Nelson and Mrs. Marjorie Nelson, Glenview, Illinois
Friends of the Oriental Institute
Mrs. Rita T. Picken, Chicago, Illinois
Mr. Patrick Regnery and Mrs. Deborah K. Regnery, Burr Ridge, Illinois
Luther I. Replogle Foundation, Washington, D.C.
Mr. and Mrs. James T. Rhind, Glenview, Illinois
Mr. John W. Rowe and Mrs. Jeanne Rowe Chicago, Illinois
Mr. Norman J. Rubash and Mrs. Alice E. Rubash, Evanston, Illinois
John Mark Rudkin Charitable Foundation, France
Mr. Mark Rudkin, France
Mr. Robert G. Schloerb and Mrs. Mary W. Schloerb, Chicago, Illinois
Mrs. Maurice Schwartz, Los Angeles, California
Mr. H. Warren Siegel and Mrs. Janet Siegel, San Juan Capistrano, California
Mr. O. J. Sopranos and Mrs. Angeline B. Sopranos, Winnetka, Illinois
Mrs. Roderick S. Webster, Winnetka, Illinois

$5,000–$9,999

Alan R. Brodie Fund, Boston, Massachusetts
Mr. Cameron Brown and Mrs. Jean McGrew Brown, Lake Forest, Illinois
Ms. Deborah Long, Bellevue, Washington
Ms. Jan McDole, Ms. Juli Greenwald, and Dr. E. James Greenwald, Reno, Nevada
Mr. David K. Ray and Mrs. Crennan M. Ray, Santa Fe, New Mexico
Mr. Raymond D. Tindel and Ms. Gretel Braidwood, Chicago, Illinois
Estate of Chester D. Tripp, Chicago, Illinois
World Monuments Fund, New York, New York

$2,500–$4,999

Mr. Peter H. Darrow and Ms. Katharine P. Darrow, Brooklyn, New York
Ms. Aimee Leigh Drolet, Los Angeles, California
Fidelity Investments Charitable Gift Fund, Boston, Massachusetts
Mrs. Emily Huggins Fine, San Francisco, California
Mr. Robert M. Grant and Mrs. Margaret H. Grant, Chicago, Illinois
Mr. Richard Gray and Mrs. Mary L. Gray, Chicago, Illinois
Mr. Albert F. Haas and Mrs. Cissy R. Haas, Chicago, Illinois
Mr. Howard G. Haas and Mrs. Carolyn W. Haas, Glencoe, Illinois
Mr. Collier Hands, Lovell, Maine
Mr. Jonathan Janott, Chicago, Illinois
Mrs. Marjorie H. Buchanan Kiewit, Chestnut Hill, Massachusetts
The Lassalle Fund, Inc., New York, New York
Ms. Nancy Lassalle, New York, New York
Mr. Robert M. Levy and Mrs. Diane Levy, Chicago, Illinois
The New York Community Trust, New York, New York

$2,500–$4,999 (cont.)

Ms. Muriel Kallis Newman, Chicago, Illinois
Mr. Andrew Nourse and Ms. Patty A. Hardy, Woodside, California
Mr. David W. Maher and Mrs. Carlotta Maher, Chicago, Illinois
Nuveen Benevolent Trust, Berkeley, California
The John Nuveen Company, Chicago, Illinois
Dr. Miriam Reitz Baer, Chicago, Illinois
Mr. Charles M. Shea and Mrs. Mary G. Shea, Wilmette, Illinois
St. Lucas Charitable Foundation, Burr Ridge, Illinois
Dr. Francis H. Straus and Mrs. Lorna P. Straus, Chicago, Illinois
Ms. Karen M. Terras, Sawyer, Michigan
Mr. James Q. Whitman and Mrs. Gillian S. Whitman, New Haven, Connecticut

$1,000–$2,499

Alsdorf Foundation, Chicago, Illinois
Mrs. James W. Alsdorf, Chicago, Illinois
Amsted Industries Foundation, Chicago, Illinois
Mr. Ronald R. Baade and Mrs. Marsha Baade, Winnetka, Illinois
Mr. William M. Backs and Ms. Janet Rizner, Evanston, Illinois
Mr. E. M. Bakwin, Chicago, Illinois
Mr. John Batchelor and Mrs. Suzanne Batchelor, Fernandina Beach, Florida
Mr. Douglas Braidwood and Mrs. Patricia Braidwood, Virginia Beach, Virginia
Cameron Brown Foundation, Lake Forest, Illinois
Mr. Joseph Daniel Cain and Ms. Emily Teeter, Chicago, Illinois
The Chicago Community Foundation, Chicago, Illinois
Mr. James E. Conway and Ms. Patricia Conway, Flossmoor, Illinois
DOMAH Fund, Chicago, Illinois
Exxon Mobil Foundation, Irving, Texas
Mrs. Ann B. Fallon, Tucson, Arizona
Feitler Family Fund, Chicago, Illinois
Mr. Robert Feitler and Mrs. Joan E. Feitler, Chicago, Illinois
Dr. Leila M. Foster, Evanston, Illinois
Mr. John W. Fritz II† and Mrs. Marilyn F. Fritz, Kenilworth, Illinois
Mr. Paul J. Gerstley, Santa Monica, California
Mrs. Joseph N. Grimshaw, Wilmette, Illinois
Mr. I. A. Grodzins and Mrs. Diana L. Grodzins, Chicago, Illinois
Mr. Dietrich M. Gross and Mrs. Erika Gross, Wilmette, Illinois
Mrs. Hans G. Güterbock, Chicago, Illinois
Mr. Howard E. Hallengren, New York, New York
Mr. Philip Halpern and Mrs. Deborah G. Halpern, Chicago, Illinois
Mr. and Mrs. William Harms, Alsip, Illinois
Harris Trust and Savings Bank, Chicago, Illinois
Mr. David P. Harris and Mrs. Judith A. Harris, Lake Forest, Illinois
Prof. and Mrs. Albert McHarg Hayes, Chicago, Illinois
Mr. Robert A. Helman and Mrs. Janet W. Helman,, Chicago, Illinois
Dr. David C. Hess and Mrs. Betty S. Hess, Downers Grove, Illinois
Mr. Roger H. Hildebrand and Mrs. Jane B. Hildebrand, Chicago, Illinois
Mr. Marshall M. Holleb and Mrs. Doris B. Holleb, Chicago, Illinois
Mr. Wayne J. Holman III, Glen Ellyn, Illinois
Mr. Peter P. Homans and Mrs. Celia E. Homans, Chicago, Illinois
Howard Haas Associates, Chicago, Illinois
Mr. Roger David Isaacs and Mrs. Joyce R. Isaacs, Glencoe, Illinois

$1,000–$2,499 (cont.)

Mr. Richard Lewis Jasnow, Baltimore, Maryland
Mr. and Mrs. Ellis O. Jones Sr., Somerville, Massachusetts
Mr. Glen A. Khant, Chicago, Illinois
Prof. Anne Draffkorn Kilmer, Tucson, Arizona
Mr. Neil J. King and Ms. Diana Hunt King, Chicago, Illinois
Mr. Jack A. Koefoot, Evanston, Illinois
Mr. Richard Kron and Ms. Deborah A. Bekken, Chicago, Illinois
Mrs. Edward H. Levi†, Chicago, Illinois
MacLean-Fogg Company, Inc., Mundelein, Illinois
Mr. Barry L. MacLean and Mrs. Mary Ann Shirley MacLean, Mettawa, Illinois
Ira and Janina Marks Charitable Trust, Chicago, Illinois
Mrs. Janina Marks, Chicago, Illinois
Mr. John W. McCarter, Jr. and Mrs. Judith McCarter, Northfield, Illinois
Mr. William Brice McDonald, Chicago, Illinois
Merrill Lynch and Co. Foundation, Inc., Princeton, New Jersey
Dr. Carol Meyer, Chicago, Illinois
Ms. Bobbi Newman, Chicago, Illinois
Mr. Donald Oster, United Kingdom
Mr. Dennis G. Pardee and Mrs. Nancy D. Pardee, Des Plaines, Illinois
Pfizer Foundation Inc., Princeton, New Jersey
Philip Morris Companies, Inc., New York, New York
Miss M. Kate Pitcairn, Kempton, Pennsylvania
Mr. Harvey B. Plotnick and Mrs. Elizabeth Plotnick,, Chicago, Illinois
Mr. J. Dwight Prade and Ms. Stephanie G. Prade, St. Louis, Missouri
Mr. Don M. Randel and Mrs. Carol E. Randel, Chicago, Illinois
Dr. Erica Reiner, Chicago, Illinois
Mr. and Mrs. John F. Richards, Wilmette, Illinois
Mr. Robert Ritner and Mrs. Margaret S. Ritner, Houston, Texas
Mr. William J.O. Roberts and Mrs. Ann V. Roberts, Lake Forest, Illinois
The Honorable George P. Shultz, Stanford, California
Mr. John Howell Smith, New York, New York
Ms. Lowri Lee Sprung, San Pedro, California
Mr. Anthony Syrett and Ms. Ann S. Syrett, APO, Military - A.E.
Dr. David M. Terman and Mrs. Mari D. Terman, Wilmette, Illinois
Mr. Thomas G. Urban, Chicago, Illinois
Dr. Donald S. Whitcomb and Dr. Janet H. Johnson, Chicago, Illinois
Ms. Anna M. White, Terre Haute, Indiana
Mr. and Mrs. Kenneth C. Williams, Canada
Dr. Sharukin Yelda and Mrs. Elizabeth Yelda, Chicago, Illinois
Mr. Bahjat Z. Yousif, Roselle, Illinois

$500–$999

Dr. Thomas G. Akers and Dr. Ann B. Akers, New Orleans, Louisiana
The Honorable and Mrs. James E. Akins, Washington, D.C.
Miss Janice V. Bacchi, Encinitas, California
Mr. Anthony J. Barrett and Ms. Marguerite Kelly, Harpswell, Maine
BP Foundation, Inc., Chicago, Illinois
Mr. Malcolm K. Brachman, Dallas, Texas
Calvanese Family Foundation, Oak Brook, Illinois
Mr. and Mrs. Dennis A. Calvanese, Oak Brook, Illinois
Mr. and Mrs. Robert O. Delaney, Winnetka, Illinois

$500–$999 (cont.)

Mr. Irving L. Diamond and Ms. Dorothy J. Speidel, Wilmette, Illinois
Dr. Erl Dordal, Chicago, Illinois
Ms. Andrea M. Dudek, Orland Park, Illinois
Drs. Martin J. Fee and Janis D. Fee, North Tustin, California
Mr. Wolfgang Frye, Tempe, Arizona
Mr. James J. Glasser and Mrs. Louise Glasser, Lake Forest, Illinois
Mr. and Mrs. Robert Dunn Glick, Chicago, Illinois
Ms. Jane Davis Haight, Napa, California
Ms. Lorena M. Holshoy, North Canton, Ohio
Mr. Michael L. Keiser and Mrs. Rosalind C. Keiser, Chicago, Illinois
Mr. H. David Kirby and Mrs. Faye Taylor Kirby, West Linn, Oregon
Dr. John M. Livingood and Mrs. Amy Livingood, Bethesda, Maryland
Mr. Stephen G. Mican, Rockford, Illinois
Ms. Vivian B. Morales, Miami, Florida
Morgan Stanley Dean Witter, Jenkintown, Pennsylvania
Mr. Richard M. Morrow and Mrs. Janet Morrow, Glenview, Illinois
Mr. Anthony John Mourek and Dr. Karole Schafer Mourek, Riverside, Illinois
Ms. Holly J. Mulvey, Evanston, Illinois
Mr. Douglas G. Murray, Santa Barbara, California
Ms. Mary Jane Myers, Los Angeles, California
National Philanthropic Trust DAF, Jenkintown, Pennsylvania
Dr. Harlan R. Peterjohn, Bay Village, Ohio
Petty Foundation, Inc., Littleton, Colorado
Mr. William D. Petty, Littleton, Colorado
Mr. A. V. Pogaryan and Ms. Chilton Watrous, Turkey
Mr. and Mrs. F. Garland Russell Jr., Columbia, Missouri
Mr. Patrick G. Ryan and Mrs. Shirley Ann Ryan, Winnetka, Illinois
Mr. Charles N. Secchia, Grand Rapids, Michigan
Dr. Henry D. Slosser, Altadena, California
Dr. Clyde Curry Smith and Mrs. Ellen Marie Smith, River Falls, Wisconsin
Ms. Toni Sandor Smith, Chicago, Illinois
State Farm Companies Foundation, Bloomington, Illinois
Ms. Linda Stringer, Garland, Texas
Mrs. Eleanor Ransom Swift†, Chicago, Illinois
Mr. Landon Thomas, Lincolnville Beach, Maine
United Way/Crusade of Mercy, Chicago, Illinois
Mr. Robert Wagner and Mrs. Rose Wagner, Chicago, Illinois
Mr. LeRoy Weber Jr., Rio Vista, California
Mr. Charles Mack Wills Jr., East Palatka, Florida
Ms. Lee Hanle Younge, Big Flats, New York

$250–$499

Mr. and Mrs. Stanley N. Allan, Chicago, Illinois
Dr. Donald H. Amidei, Park Ridge, Illinois
Mr. Roger Atkinson, Riverside, California
Ayco Charitable Foundation, Clifton Park, New York
Dr. and Mrs. Robert M. Ball, Amarillo, Texas
Mrs. Guity Nashat Becker, Chicago, Illinois
Dr. Barbara Bell, Cambridge, Massachusetts
Dr. Sidney J. Blair and Ms. LaMoyne C. Blair, Oak Park, Illinois
Ms. Laurie A. Boche, North Saint Paul, Minnesota

$250–$499 (cont.)

Mr. Leo N. Bradley and Mrs. Patricia Q. Bradley, Golden, Colorado
Mr. O. John Brahos, Wilmette, Illinois
Brown University, Providence, Rhode Island
Mr. and Mrs. Charles E. Bryan, Baltimore, Maryland
Mr. Bruce P. Burbage, Nokomis, Florida
Mr. Charles N. Callahan and Ms. Naila Britain, Chicago, Illinois
Carroll College, Helena, Montana
Ms. Elizabeth F. Carter, Los Angeles, California
Mr. Tim Cashion, Chicago, Illinois
Chicago Dental Society, Park Ridge, Illinois
Mr. E. Eric Clark and Mrs. Alice H. Clark, Sierra Madre, California
Mr. Steven Anthony Clark and Ms. Janet L. Raymond, Oak Lawn, Illinois
Mr. Courtney B. Conte, Santa Monica, California
Mr. Richard L. Cook, Toluca Lake, California
Mr. and Mrs. David De Bruyn, Seattle, Washington
Dr. George Dunea and Ms. Mary M. Dunea, Chicago, Illinois
Mr. Amon Emanuel, Switzerland
Ms. Rosemary Faulkner, New York, New York
Mr. and Mrs. Paul E. Freehling, Chicago, Illinois
Mr. John R. Gardner and Mrs. Dorothy Hannon Gardner, Winnetka, Illinois
Dr. Gary S. Garofalo, Palos Hills, Illinois
Dr. Victor E. Gould and Dr. Nevenka S. Gould, Wilmette, Illinois
Mr. Frederick Graboske and Mrs. Patricia Graboske, Rockville, Maryland
Mr. Charles W. Graham, Camden, Maine
Mrs. Dorothy H. Greiner, La Jolla, California
Mr. M. Hill Hammock and Mrs. Cheryl Hammock, Chicago, Illinois
Mr. Leo O. Harris and Dr. Cynthia O. Harris, Albuquerque, New Mexico
Mr. John P. Henry and Ms. Jan Isaacs Henry, Colorado Springs, Colorado
Mr. Raad H. Hermes, Chicago, Illinois
Ms. Susan C. Hull, Chicago, Illinois
Mr. Arthur T. Hurley and Ms. Susan L. Hurley, Napa, California
International Business Machines Corporation, Armonk, New York
Mr. and Mrs. George T. Jacobi, Milwaukee, Wisconsin
Dr. Joseph Jarabak and Dr. Rebecca Jarabak, Hinsdale, Illinois
Mr. Dee Morgan Kilpatrick, Chicago, Illinois
Mr. Henry H. Kohl and Mrs. Annie A. Kohl, Media, Pennsylvania
Ms. Abigail Ruskin Krystall, Kenya
Dr. Elisabeth Lassers, Chicago, Illinois
Dr. Leonard Henry Lesko and Mrs. Barbara Switalski Lesko, Seekonk, Massachusetts
Mr. James Lichtenstein, Chicago, Illinois
Mr. Paul S. Linsay and Ms. Roni A. Lipton, Newton, Massachusetts
Mr. Michael Lisle and Mrs. Kathleen Lisle, Chicago, Illinois
Mrs. Glen A. Lloyd, Libertyville, Illinois
Mr. and Mrs. Richard Marcus, Glencoe, Illinois
Mr. S. Edward Marder, Highland Park, Illinois
Dr. John C. Mason Jr., Danville, Illinois
Mr. Terrence D. McMahon and Mr. Daniel W. Bednarz, Chicago, Illinois
Mr. Richard A. Miller, Oak Lawn, Illinois
Mr. and Mrs. Jeffrey E. Miripol, Hockessin, Delaware
Natural History Museum of Los Angeles Co., Los Angeles, California
Mr. Charles R. Nelson, Seattle, Washington
Mr. John P. Nielsen, Lombard, Illinois
The Northern Trust Company, Chicago, Illinois
Mr. and Mrs. Richard C. Notebaert, Chicago, Illinois

$250–$499 (cont.)

Mr. Larry Paragano, Springfield, New Jersey
Mr. Eric Pelander and Dr. Evalyn Gates, Chicago, Illinois
Ms. Katherine E. Rakowsky, Chicago, Illinois
Mr. and Mrs. Gary W. Rexford, Topeka, Kansas
Ms. Diane Ruzevich, Berwyn, Illinois
Mr. Harold Sanders and Mrs. Deloris Sanders, Chicago, Illinois
Mr. Paul Schoessow and Ms. Patricia Cavenee, Lakewood, Colorado
Mr. Zekir Share, Aurora, Illinois
Mr. Michael J. Sobczyk, Des Plaines, Illinois
Dr. John Sobolski and Dr. Zara Khodjasteh, Chicago, Illinois
Mr. Hugo F. Sonnenschein and Mrs. Elizabeth Sonnenschein, Chicago, Illinois
Mr. David Allan Stoudt, Clackamas, Oregon
Dr. Arnold L. Tanis and Mrs. Maxine K. Tanis, Fernandina Beach, Florida
Mr. and Mrs. Walter H. Teninga, Village of Golf, Florida
Mr. Randy Thomas and Ms. Barbara Thomas, Chicago, Illinois
Mr. and Mrs. James M. Trapp, Chicago, Illinois
Mr. David J. Vitale and Ms. Marilyn Fatt Vitale, Chicago, Illinois
Mr. Thomas J. White and Ms. Leslie Scalapino, Oakland, California
Dr. Willard E. White, Riverside, Illinois
Mrs. Barbara Breasted Whitesides, Newton, Massachusetts
Ms. Carrie C. Wilson and Ms. Herminia Wilson, Chicago, Illinois
Dr. Wendall W. Wilson, Chicago, Illinois
Mr. and Mrs. Richard L. Wood, Barrington Hills, Illinois

$100–$249

Mr. D. M. Abadi and Mrs. Mary C. Abadi, Iowa City, Iowa
Lester & Hope Abelson Foundation., Chicago, Illinois
Mrs. Lester S. Abelson, Chicago, Illinois
Mr. and Mrs. Daniel L. Ables, Scottsdale, Arizona
Ms. Judith Akers, Wilmette, Illinois
Mrs. Karen B. Alexander, Geneva, Illinois
Mr. James P. Allen and Mrs. Susan J. Allen, Ridgefield, Connecticut
Dr. Michael Amaral, Powder Springs, Georgia
Mr. Edward Anders and Mrs. Joan Anders, Chicago, Illinois
Mr. Robert Andersen and Ms. Elaine Quinn, Chicago, Illinois
Dr. Thomas Andrews, Hinsdale, Illinois
Mrs. Julie Antelman, Chicago, Illinois
Dr. Robert Arensman and Mrs. Marilyn C. Arensman, Chicago, Illinois
Dr. Claresa Armstrong, Chicago, Illinois
Mr. James Armstrong and Ms. Beverly Armstrong, Watertown, Massachusetts
Dr. Arthur O. Aufderheide, Duluth, Minnesota
Prof. and Mrs. William Baker, Santa Fe, New Mexico
Mr. Paul Barron and Ms. Mary Anton, Chicago, Illinois
Ms. Margaret Bates, Sarasota, Florida
Mrs. Elizabeth Baum, Chicago, Illinois
Mr. Barry Baumgardner, Dunnellon, Florida
Dr. David Bawden and Ms. Jan Bawden, Northfield, Illinois
Mr. and Mrs. Bruce L. Beavis, Chicago, Illinois
Ms. Jane E. Belcher, Chicago, Illinois
Benjamin Foundation, Inc.
Mr. and Mrs. John F. Benjamin, Chicago, Illinois

$100–$249 (cont.)

Mr. Richard Benjamin and Ms. Sally Benjamin, North Augusta, South Carolina
Ms. Katharine L. Bensen, Chicago, Illinois
Mr. George W. Benson and Ms. Ellen C. Benson, Chicago, Illinois
Mr. Robert W. Benson, Chicago, Illinois
Mrs. Edwin A. Bergman, Chicago, Illinois
Mr. Keki R. Bhote and Mrs. Mehroo K. Bhote, Glencoe, Illinois
Mr. Edward McCormick Blair, Lake Bluff, Illinois
Mr. Edward C. Blau, Alexandria, Virginia
Mr. Mervin Block, New York, New York
Mr. Bob Blumling, San Diego, California
Dr. Glenn F. Boas, Chicago, Illinois
Mrs. George V. Bobrinskoy Jr., Chicago, Illinois
Dr. Constance Bonbrest, Chicago, Illinois
Mr. Seymour Bortz and Mrs. Katherine Biddle Austin, Highland Park, Illinois
Mr. James T. Bradbury and Mrs. Louise Bradbury, Knoxville, Tennessee
Mrs. Jerald C. Brauer, Chicago, Illinois
Ms. Catherine Novotny Brehm, Chicago, Illinois
Mr. Jonathan Brookner, Fairfield, Connecticut
Mr. John A. Bross, Chicago, Illinois
Mr. Willard W. Brown Jr., Bucksport, Maine
Ms. Myllicent Buchanan, Chicago, Illinois
Mr. and Mrs. Allan E. Bulley III, Chicago, Illinois
Ms. Christine Cahill, Chicago, Illinois
Mr. and Mrs. Joseph Camarra, Chicago, Illinois
Ms. Jeanny Vorys Canby, Bryn Mawr, Pennsylvania
Mr. Thomas Cassidy, Littleton, Colorado
Miss Mary E. Chase, Flossmoor, Illinois
CIGNA Foundation, Philadelphia, Pennsylvania
Mr. William A. Claire, Washington, D.C.
Mr. Harris H. Clark, Tempe, Arizona
Mr. Robert Clinkert, Aurora, Illinois
Mrs. Lydia G. Cochrane, Chicago, Illinois
Mr. Douglas E. Cohen and Mrs. Carol B. Cohen, Highland Park, Illinois
Mr. Lawrence M. Coleman, New Orleans, Louisiana
Mrs. Zdzislawa Coleman, Chicago, Illinois
Ms. Cynthia Green Colin, New York, New York
Ms. Johna S. Compton, Chancellor, Alabama
Mr. William Cottle and Mrs. Judith Cottle, Winnetka, Illinois
Ms. Marylouise Cowan, Booth Bay Harbor, Maine
Mr. David Crabb and Mrs. Dorothy Crabb, Chicago, Illinois
Mr. Albert V. Crewe and Mrs. Doreen P. Crewe, Dune Acres, Indiana
Dr. Eugene D. Cruz-Uribe and Dr. Kathryn Cruz-Uribe, Flagstaff, Arizona
Mr. Edwin L. Currey Jr., Napa, California
Mr. David Currie and The Honorable Barbara Currie, Chicago, Illinois
Mr. Charles Custer and Ms. Irene Custer, Chicago, Illinois
Mrs. Thelma E. Dahlberg, Franklin Grove, Illinois
Mr. Leo Darwit and Mr. Reid Selseth, Chicago, Illinois
Mr. Merritt J. Davoust† and Mrs. Lynne Rauscher-Davoust, Elmhurst, Illinois
Mr. Walter E. De Lise, Indian Head Park, Illinois
Mr. Kevin M. Dent, Terre Haute, Indiana
Mr. David Detrich, Mattituck, New York
Mr. and Mrs. Nirmal S. Dhesi, Santa Rosa, California
Ms. Mary Dimperio, Washington, D.C.
Mr. Henry S. Dixon and Ms. Linda Giesen, Dixon, Illinois

$100–$249 (cont.)

Mr. J. McGregor Dodds and Ms. Christine Dodds, Grosse Pointe Farms, Michigan
Mr. Jim Douglas and Mrs. Mary Lou Douglas, West LaFayette, Indiana
Dow Corning Corporation, Midland, Michigan
Mr. Justin E. Doyle and Ms. Deborah S. Doyle, Pittsford, New York
Ms. Ellen M. Dran, DeKalb, Illinois
Mr. Pedro Duenas and Mrs. Catherine J. Duenas, Chicago, Illinois
Dr. Patty L. Dunkel, Chicago, Illinois
Mr. Bruce Dunn and Ms. Nancie Dunn, Chicago, Illinois
Mrs. Bettie Dwinell, Chicago, Illinois
Mr. John E. Dyble and Mrs. Patricia A. Dyble, Hawthornwoods, Illinois
Mr. Robert Dyson, Gladwyne, Pennsylvania
Mr. C. David Eeles, Columbus, Ohio
Mr. Lawrence R. Eicher and Mrs. Vicky C. Eicher, Charlottesville, Virginia
Mr. William L. Ekvall and Mrs. Marie A. Ekvall, Evanston, Illinois
Mr. Frederick Elghanayan, New York, New York
Mr. Alex Elson and Ms. Miriam Elson, Chicago, Illinois
Mr. Sidney Epstein and Mrs. Sondra Epstein, Chicago, Illinois
Ms. Ann Esse, Sioux Falls, South Dakota
Dr. Richard H. Evans and Mrs. Roberta G. Evans, Chicago, Illinois
Mr. Barton Faber and Ms. Elizabeth Byrnes, Paradise Valley, Arizona
Mr. Eugene Fama and Ms. Sallyann Fama, Chicago, Illinois
Dr. Valerie Fargo, Midland, Michigan
Mr. Charles J. Fisher, Sioux City, Iowa
Mr. and Mrs. Gerald F. Fitzgerald Jr., Inverness, Illinois
Dr. Michael Flom, Boynton Beach, Florida
Mr. Richard E. Ford, Wabash, Indiana
Ms. Tara Fowler, Chicago, Illinois
Dr. Samuel Ethan Fox and Mrs. Beverly F. Fox, Chicago, Illinois
Mr. and Mrs. Jay Frankel, Chicago, Illinois
Mrs. Eleanor B. Frew, Flossmoor, Illinois
Mr. Thomas F. Frey and Mrs. Barbara D. Frey, Sarasota, Florida
Mr. and Mrs. Stephen Fried, Kingston, Massachusetts
Mr. Charles Barry Friedman and Mrs. Terry Friedman, Chicago, Illinois
Ms. Mirah Gaines, Burr Ridge, Illinois
Mr. Gregory Gajda, Mt. Prospect, Illinois
Miss Mary Virginia Gibson, Middleton, Wisconsin
Mrs. Willard Gidwitz, Highland Park, Illinois
Ms. Nancy Gidwitz, Chicago, Illinois
Mr. Thomas Gillespie, Chicago, Illinois
Mr. Gregory T. Gillette, Chicago, Illinois
Mr. Lyle Gillman, Bloomingdale, Illinois
Rev. Raymond Goehring, Lansing, Michigan
Mr. and Mrs. William H. Gofen, Chicago, Illinois
Mrs. Ethel Frank Goldsmith, Chicago, Illinois
Mr. Eugene Goldwasser and Ms. Deone Giffith Jackman, Chicago, Illinois
Mr. Kenneth and Mrs. Doris Granath, St. John, Indiana
Mr. Anthony F. Granucci, San Francisco, California
Mr. and Mrs. David Gratner, Sulpher Springs, Indiana
Mr. John Greaves and Ms. Patricia McLaughlin, Hinsdale, Illinois
Mrs. Anita Greenberg, Highland Park, Illinois
Dr. Joseph Greene and Mrs. Eileen Caves, Belmont, Massachusetts
Mr. C. O. Griffin and Ms. Gillian Griffin, Newburyport, Massachusetts
Ms. Ellen R. Hall and Ms. Betty Ann Cronin, West Allis, Wisconsin
Mr. Joel L. Handelman and Ms. Sarah R. Wolff, Chicago, Illinois

$100–$249 (cont.)

Dr. Lowell Kent Handy, Des Plaines, Illinois
Commissioner and Mrs. Carl R. Hansen, Mount Prospect, Illinois
Ms. Ednalyn Hansen, Chicago, Illinois
Ms. Katherine Haramundanis, Westford, Massachusetts
Dr. Thomas Harper, Sherman Oaks, California
Mr. Chauncy D. Harris and Mrs. Edith Harris, Chicago, Illinois
Mr. James B. Hartle, Santa Barbara, California
Mr. and Mrs. Richard Harwood, Colorado Springs, Colorado
Mr. Robert Haselkorn and Mrs. Margot Haselkorn, Chicago, Illinois
Ms. Ginny Hayden, Boulder, Colorado
Mr. Thomas E. Hemminger, New Lenox, Illinois
Mr. John A. Herschkorn Jr. and Mrs. Gloria Herschkorn, San Jose, California
Mr. Walter Hess and Ms. Hedda Hess, Chicago, Illinois
Mr. David C. Hilliard and Mrs. Celia Schmid Hilliard, Chicago, Illinois
Prince Abbas Hilmi, Egypt
Mrs. Harold Hines, Winnetka, Illinois
Mrs. Joan L. Hoatson, Hinsdale, Illinois
Mr. and Mrs. Marshall Hoke, Elkins, New Hampshire
Ms. Debbie Holm, Chicago, Illinois
Ms. Jean Hontz, Niceville, Florida
Ms. Catherine Howard, Okanogan, Washington
Mr. Bill Hudson and Mr. Wade Adkisson, New York, New York
Mr. Richard Huff, Oak Park, Illinois
Dr. Kevin S. Hughes, Boston, Massachusetts
Mr. Robert A. Hull, La Porte, Indiana
Mr. Alan Hutchinson, Chicago, Illinois
Dr. Kamal Ibrahim and Dr. Lucy Ibrahim, Oak Brook, Illinois
Ms. Sandra Jacobsohn, Chicago, Illinois
Ms. Lise Jacobson, Evanston, Illinois
Mr. Thomas Jedele and Dr. Nancy J. Skon Jedele, Laurel, Maryland
Mr. Charles E. Jones and Ms. Alexandra Alice O'Brien, Chicago, Illinois
Mr. Richard E. Jones and Ms. Marie Thourson Jones, Wilmette, Illinois
Rev. Prof. Douglas Judisch, Fort Wayne, Indiana
Mr. John Cletus Kaminski and Ms. Maria M. Duran, Chicago, Illinois
Dr. Michael Steven Kaplan, Lexington, Massachusetts
Dr. Richard I. Kaufman and Dr. Louis Kaufman, Chicago, Illinois
Ms. Susan Kezios, Chicago, Illinois
Dr. and Mrs. Raja Khuri, Evanston, Illinois
Ms. Henriette Klawans, Chicago, Illinois
Mr. Gregory Gene Knight, Chicago, Illinois
Mr. William J. Knight and Mrs. Julie F. Knight, South Bend, Indiana
Mr. Michael E. Koen, Chicago, Illinois
Mr. Frank Kohout, Iowa City, Iowa
Ms. Aphrodite Kokolis, Chicago, Illinois
Mr. Bryan Krakauer and Ms. Marie Poppy, Chicago, Illinois
Mr. Bernard L. Krawczyk, Chicago, Illinois
Mrs. Alice Kittell Kuzay, Naperville, Illinois
Mr. and Mrs. William J. Lawlor III, Kenilworth, Illinois
Mr. John Lawrence, Ann Arbor, Michigan
Dr. Mark Lehner, Milton, Massachusetts
Mr. John G. Levi and Mrs. Jill F. Levi, Chicago, Illinois
Mr. Theodore W. Liese and Mrs. Gabrielle M. Liese, Prescott, Arizona
Mr. Robert B. Lifton and Ms. Carol Rosofsky, Chicago, Illinois
Mr. John Michael Lindert, Livermore, California

$100–$249 (cont.)

Mr. and Mrs. David H. Lipsey, McLean, Virginia
Mr. Richard Lo and Ms. Lo Luong Lo, Oak Park, Illinois
Mrs. Nina A. Longley, Park Forest, Illinois
Mr. Juan Lopez and Ms. Carmen Heredia, Chicago, Illinois
Prof. and Mrs. James Lorie, Chicago, Illinois
Mr. Jo Desha Lucas and Ms. Johanna W. Lucas, Chicago, Illinois
Mr. Bruce L. Ludwig, Los Angeles, California
Mr. Philip R. Luhmann and Mrs. Dianne C. Luhmann, Chicago, Illinois
Ms. Mary Sue Lyon, Chicago, Illinois
Mr. Laurance L. MacKallor and Mrs. Margaret E. MacKallor, San Carlos, California
Mr. Daniel R. Malecki, Kensington, California
Ms. Maria Danae Mandis, Chicago, Illinois
Ms. Leah Maneaty, Chicago, Illinois
Ms. Glennda Susan Marsh-Letts, Australia
Ms. Eva C. May, New Rochelle, New York
Mayer, Brown, Rowe & Maw LLP, Chicago, Illinois
Ms. Marilyn McCaman, La Verne, California
Mr. William J. McCluskey, Hinsdale, Illinois
Mr. W. Sloan McCrea, Miami, Florida
Mrs. Marie Therese McDermott, Chicago, Illinois
Mr. Robert B. McDermott and Ms. Sarah P. Jaicks, Chicago, Illinois
Dr. Jane W. Stedman† and Mr. George C. McElroy, Chicago, Illinois
Mr. Michael J. McInerney, Chicago, Illinois
Dr. Ernest E. Mhoon Jr. and Mrs. Deborah Ann Mhoon, Chicago, Illinois
Mr. Charles R. Michael, Woodbridge, Connecticut
Mr. Michael Millar and Ms. Ruth Millar, Cedar Falls, Iowa
Mr. Dean Miller and Ms. Martha Swift, Chicago, Illinois
Mr. Gene Miller, Madison, Wisconsin
Mr. Phillip L. Miller and Mrs. Barbara H. Miller, Oregon, Illinois
Dr. William K. Miller, Duluth, Minnesota
Dr. Morton Millman and Dr. Ann K. Millman, Chicago, Illinois
The Honorable Martha A. Mills, Chicago, Illinois
Mr. Sam Mirkin, Mishawaka, Indiana
Mr. J. Y. Miyamoto, Los Angeles, California
Dr. and Mrs. D. Read Moffett, Chatham, Massachusetts
Mr. Joseph A. Moriarty and Ms. June J. Moriarty, Kingsport, Tennessee
Mr. and Mrs. William L. Morrison, Chicago, Illinois
Mr. Charles H. Mottier, Chicago, Illinois
Prof. Ian Mueller and Prof. Janel Mueller, Chicago, Illinois
Ms. Maureen Mullen, Greenfield, Wisconsin
Mr. Manly W. Mumford and Mrs. Luigi H. Mumford, Chicago, Illinois
Ms. Janet Murphy, Chicago, Illinois
Mr. David E. Muschler and Ms. Ann L. Becker, Chicago, Illinois
Mrs. Margaret Wilson Myers, Blue Hill, Maine
Mrs. Marcia B. Nachtrieb, Joliet, Illinois
Mr. and Mrs. James L. Nagle, Chicago, Illinois
Mrs. F. Esther Naser, Chicago, Illinois
Ms. Mary B. Naunton, Chicago, Illinois
Mr. James R. Neil and Ms. D. Rosanne Barker, Tallahassee, Florida
Dr. William F. Nelson, Martin, Tennessee
Mr. Walter A. Netsch Jr. and Ms. Dawn Clark Netsch, Chicago, Illinois
Mr. and Mrs. Robert M. Newbury, Chicago, Illinois
Mrs. Eleanor K. Nicholson, Evanston, Illinois
Mr. and Mrs. James Nicholson, Pickerington, Ohio

$100–$249 (cont.)

Mr. Dale George Niewoehner, Rugby, North Dakota

Mr. Timothy Michael Nolan and Ms. Mary Ann Nolan, Palos Park, Illinois

Mrs. Beth Noujaim, New York, New York

Mr. Dennis O'Connor, Chicago, Illinois

Ms. Marilynn Oleck, Chicago, Illinois

Ms. Virginia O'Neill, Chicago, Illinois

Mr. Gary A. Oppenhuis and Ms. Mary E. Oppenhuis, Flossmoor, Illinois

Mr. Richard Orsan and Mr. Sen Gan, Chicago, Illinois

Mr. Mark M. Osgood, Burr Ridge, Illinois

Oslin Nation Co., Fort Worth, Texas

Mr. Myras Osman and Ms. Linda Osman, Flossmoor, Illinois

Enrique Ospina, Houston, Texas

Dr. Jacques Ovadia and Mrs. Florence Ovadia, Chicago, Illinois

Mr. John Thomas F. Oxaal and Ms. Marjorie Roitman Oxaal, Woodside, California

Paragano Management Corporation, Morristown, New Jersey

Ms. Marie Parsons, New York, New York

Mr. Thomas G. Patterson and Mrs. Nancy P. Patterson, Chicago, Illinois

Mrs. Denise G. Paul, Chicago, Illinois

Mr. Donald Payne, Chicago, Illinois

Mr. Robert H. Pelletreau and Ms. Pamela Day, Washington, D.C.

PepsiCo Foundation Inc., Purchase, New York

Mr. Norman Perman and Mrs. Lorraine Perman, Chicago, Illinois

Mr. Robert R. Perodeau and Mrs. Evelyn C. Perodeau, Haddonfield, New Jersey

Mr. Thomas T. Peyton, Minneapolis, Minnesota

Phoenix Foundation, Hartford, Connecticut

Ms. Nella Piccolin, Frankfort, Illinois

Mr. James Piojda, Racine, Wisconsin

Dr. Audrius Vaclovas Plioplys, Chicago, Illinois

Mr. and Mrs. Jeffrey Pommerville, Scottsdale, Arizona

Mr. Robert J. Poplar, Kenosha, Wisconsin

Mrs. Elizabeth M. Postell, Chicago, Illinois

Mr. J. M. Prescott and Ms. Semra Prescott, De Kalb, Illinois

Mr. Richard H. Prins and Mrs. Marion L. Prins, Chicago, Illinois

Ms. Sheila W. R. Putzel, Chicago, Illinois

Mr. Francis Quemada, Palo Alto, California

Ms. Susannah Ruth Quern-Pratt, Chicago, Illinois

Mr. Thad D. Rasche and Mrs. Diana Olson Rasche, Oak Park, Illinois

Dr. Charles Dean Ray, Yorktown, Virginia

Mr. David Reese and Dr. Catherine Sease, New Haven, Connecticut

Mr. David E. Reese, Chicago, Illinois

Mr. Alan Reinstein and Ms. Laurie Reinstein, Highland Park, Illinois

Dr. Maxine H. Reneker, Monterey, California

Mr. Charles S. Rhyne and Mrs. Barbara B. Rhyne, Portland, Oregon

Mr. and Mrs. George G. Rinder, Burr Ridge, Illinois

Ms. Agnes Ann Roach, Gurnee, Illinois

Mr. William Hughes Roberts, Las Vegas, Nevada

Mr. Chris Roling, United Kingdom

Mr. Howard J. Romanek, Skokie, Illinois

Prof. Lawrence S. Root and Prof. Margaret Cool Root, Ann Arbor, Michigan

Mrs. Ludwig Rosenberger, Chicago, Illinois

Dr. Janet Caryl Rountree, Tucson, Arizona

Mr. Bertram I. Rowland and Ms. Susan Blake, Hillsborough, California

Dr. David S. Rozenfeld and Mrs. Barbara Weisbaum Rozenfeld, Chicago, Illinois

Dr. Randi Rubovits-Seitz, Washington, D.C.

$100–$249 (cont.)

Dr. James B. Rule, Little Rock, Arkansas
Rule's Antiques and Fine Books, Little Rock, Arkansas
Mr. George Rumney, Bowie, Maryland
Ms. Janice B. Ruppel, Chicago, Illinois
Mrs. Carolyn L. Sachs, Chicago, Illinois
Mr. Bruce Sagan and Ms. Bette Cerf Hill, Chicago, Illinois
Dr. Paul Saltzman and Ms. Bettylu K. Saltzman, Chicago, Illinois
Mr. Hafez Sami and Ms. Sharon Reeves-Sami, Naperville, Illinois
Dr. Bonnie Sampsell, Chapel Hill, North Carolina
Mr. John Sanders and Ms. Peggy Sanders, Chicago, Illinois
Mr. Calvin Sawyier and Dr. Fay Sawyier, Chicago, Illinois
Dr. Lawrence J. Scheff and Mrs. Dorothy Adelle Scheff, Chicago, Illinois
Mr. Rolf Scherman and Ms. Charlotte Scherman, Greenbrae, California
Mr. Frank Schneider and Ms. Karen Schneider, Chicago, Illinois
Mr. and Mrs. Hans Schreiber, Chicago, Illinois
Mr. Theodore N. Scontras, Saco, Maine
Dr. Michael Sha, Carmel, Indiana
Mr. R. Chesla Sharp and Ms. Ruth M. Sharp, Limestone, Tennessee
Mr. Thomas C. Sheffield Jr., Chicago, Illinois
Ms. Deborah Shefner, Chicago, Illinois
Ms. Emma Shelton, Bethesda, Maryland
Ms. Mary Ellen Sheridan, Chicago, Illinois
Mr. Jon Shomer and Mrs. Marilyn Shomer, Phoenix, Arizona
Mr. Henry Showers and Mrs. Patricia A. Showers, Crown Point, Indiana
Ms. Lois Siegel, Chicago, Illinois
Mr. Michael Simon, Cleveland Heights, Ohio
Mr. Michael A. Sisinger and Ms. Judith E. Waggoner, Columbus, Ohio
Mr. and Mrs. Kenneth Small, Irvine, California
Ms. Mary Small, Kensington, California
Ms. Katherine E. Smith, Chicago, Illinois
Ms. Louise Tennent Smith, Columbus, Georgia
Mr. Robert K. Smither, Hinsdale, Illinois
Mr. Lawrence Snider and Mrs. Maxine Snider, Chicago, Illinois
Ms. Patricia A. Soltys, Bandon, Oregon
Sonnenschein Nath & Rosenthal, Chicago, Illinois
Mr. Stephen C. Sperry, Litchfield, Minnesota
Mr. David A. Spetrino, Wilmington, North Carolina
Mr. Fred Stafford and Ms. Barbara Stafford, Chicago, Illinois
Prof. Ruggero P. Stefanini, Oakland, California
Mr. Gil J. Stein and Ms. Elise C. Levin, Evanston, Illinois
Mr. Mayer Stern and Ms. Gloria Stern, Chicago, Illinois
The Honorable and Mrs. Adlai E. Stevenson III, Chicago, Illinois
Mr. and Mrs. Stephen M. Stigler, Chicago, Illinois
Mr. Frederick H. Stitt and Ms. Suzanne B. Stitt, Wilmette, Illinois
Mr. David G. Streets and Ms. W. Elane Streets, Darien, Illinois
Mr. George R. Sundell, Wheaton, Illinois
Mrs. Peggy Lewis Sweesy, Santa Fe, New Mexico
Dr. and Mrs. C. Conover Talbot, Chicago, Illinois
Mrs. John F. Tatum, Oxford, Mississippi
Mr. Justin Tedrowe, Downers Grove, Illinois
Ms. Betsy Teeter, San Francisco, California
Mr. Frederick Teeter and Mrs. Shirley Teeter, Ransomville, New York
Ms. Denise Thomas, Pontiac, Michigan
Mr. Gregory Thomas, Grandview, Texas

$100–$249 (*cont.*)

Miss Kristin Thompson, Madison, Wisconsin
Mr. Dieter Tomczak, Germany
Mr. and Mrs. John Tonkinson, Torrance, California
Mr. Robert L. Toth and Mrs. Rosemary A. Toth, Medina, Ohio
Dr. and Mrs. Nohad A. Toulan, Portland, Oregon
Mr. and Mrs. John E. Townsend, Winnetka, Illinois
Ms. Barbara Trentham, Lake Bluff, Illinois
Miss Janice Trimble, Chicago, Illinois
Mrs. Nancy E. Turchi, Lake Zurich, Illinois
Mrs. Harriet M. Turk, Joliet, Illinois
Dr. Robert Y. Turner, Philadelphia, Pennsylvania
Mr. Edgar J. Uihlein Jr. and Mrs. Lucia Ellis Uihlein, Lake Bluff, Illinois
Mr. Mustafa Ulken and Ms. Tayyibe C. Ulken, Hoffman Estates, Illinois
United Educational & Charitable Fdn. Inc., Elkins, New Hampshire
Ms. Jeannette K. Van Dorn, Wauwatosa, Wisconsin
Ms. Barbara H. VanBaalen, East Lansing, Michigan
Mr. Karl H. Velde Jr., Lake Forest, Illinois
Mr. John Vinci, Chicago, Illinois
Mr. Don Wacker and Ms. Mary W. Wacker, Issaquah, Washington
Mr. and Mrs. James Wagner, Chicago, Illinois
Mr. Thaddeus Walczak and Mrs. Carole J. Lewis, Chesterton, Indiana
Mrs. Marguerite A. Walk, Chicago, Illinois
Mr. John F. Warnock, Mason City, Illinois
Mrs. Elizabeth C. Warren, Glencoe, Illinois
Ms. Marjorie H. Watkins, Winnetka, Illinois
Mr. Russ Thomas Watson and Ms. Mary Katherine Danna, Chicago, Illinois
Mr. Richard F. Watt and Ms. Sherry Goodman Watt, Chicago, Illinois
Mr. Jerry Wegner, Munster, Indiana
Mr. John R. Weiss, Wilmette, Illinois
Mr. Douglas J. Wells, Valparaiso, Indiana
Mr. and Mrs. Edward F. Wente, Chicago, Illinois
Mr. Wayne W. Whalen, Chicago, Illinois
Mr. John J. White III and Mrs. Patricia W. White, Columbus, Ohio
Mrs. Warner A. Wick, Needham, Massachusetts
Ms. Jane M. Wickstrom, La Porte, Indiana
Mr. John L. Wier and Ms. Elizabeth B. Wier, Naperville, Illinois
Mr. Wayne M. Wille and Mrs. Lois J. Wille, Chicago, Illinois
Mr. and Mrs. Robert I. Wilson, Peoria, Illinois
Mrs. George P. Winkelman, Janesville, Wisconsin
Mr. James S. Winn Jr. and Mrs. Bonnie Hicks Winn, Winnetka, Illinois
Mrs. Jack Witkowsky, Chicago, Illinois
Ms. Melanie R. Wojtulewicz, Chicago, Illinois
Rabbi Arnold Jacob Wolf, Chicago, Illinois
Ms. Judith M. Wright, Carson City, Nevada
Mr. Robert M. Wulff, Washington, D.C.
Dr. Sidney H. Yarbrough III and Mrs. Rebecca Yarbrough, Columbus, Georgia
Mr. Robert R. Yohanan and Ms. Joan Yohanaxn, Kenilworth, Illinois
Mr. Quentin Young and Ms. Ruth Young, Chicago, Illinois
Mr. Arnold Zellner and Mrs. Agnes Zellner, Chicago, Illinois

In addition to the gifts listed above, many other people and organizations have supported
the Oriental Institute with their generous contributions.
Thank you for your continued support.

HONORARY AND MEMORIAL GIFTS
HONORARY GIFTS

In Honor of Erl Dordal and Dorothy Powers' Marriage

Mrs. Catherine J. Duenas and Mrs. Terry Friedman, Chicago, Illinois
Mrs. Anita Greenberg, Highland Park, Illinois

In Honor of Albert F. Haas' Birthday

Mr. Paul J. Gerstley, Santa Monica, California

In Honor of Albert F. Haas

Mr. Jay F. Mulberry and Mrs. Alice J. Mulberry, Chicago, Illinois

In Honor of Roger D. Isaacs

Mr. John P. Henry and Ms. Jan Isaacs Henry, Colorado Springs, Colorado

In Honor of Carlotta Maher

Mr. Patrick G. Ryan and Mrs. Shirley Ann Ryan, Winnetka, Illinois

In Honor of O. J. Sopranos

Mr. Karl Velde Jr., Lake Forest, Illinois

MEMORIAL GIFTS

In Memory of William A. Boone

Dow Corning Corporation, Midland, Michigan
Mr. Robert I. Dvorak, Sleepy Hollow, Illinois
Mr. Abner Ganet and Mrs. Janet Ganet, Elmhurst, Illinois
Dr. and Mrs. Herbert A. Lederer, Riverside, Illinois
The Lester Family, Rome, Georgia
Oslin Nation Co., Fort Worth, Texas
Vintage Sportscar Club, Bannockburn, Illinois
Mrs. Elizabeth C. Warren, Glencoe, Illinois
Ms. Marjorie H. Watkins, Winnetka, Illinois

In Memory of Robert and Linda Braidwood

Dr. Miriam Reitz Baer, Chicago, Illinois
Mr. James R. Neil and Ms. D. Rosanne Barker, Tallahassee, Florida
Mr. Tim Cashion, Chicago, Illinois
Mrs. Thelma E. Dahlberg, Franklin Grove, Illinois
Feitler Family Fund, Chicago, Illinois
Mr. Robert Feitler and Mrs. Joan E. Feitler, Chicago, Illinois
Fidelity Investments Charitable Gift Fund, Boston, Massachusetts
Mr. James L. Foorman and Mrs. Margaret E. Foorman, Winnetka, Illinois
Mr. and Mrs. Paul E. Freehling, Chicago, Illinois

In Memory of Robert and Linda Braidwood (*cont.*)

Ms. Roselyn L. Friedman, Chicago, Illinois
Mr. Charles Barry Friedman and Mrs. Terry Friedman, Chicago, Illinois
Mr. and Mrs. William H. Gofen, Chicago, Illinois
Mrs. Gwendolyn Gracie, La Porte, Indiana
Mrs. Dorothy H. Greiner, La Jolla, California
Mr. and Mrs. William Harms, Alsip, Illinois
Mr. Robert A. Hull, La Porte, Indiana
Dr. Richard I. Kaufman and Dr. Louis Kaufman, Chicago, Illinois
Mr. Neil J. King and Ms. Diana Hunt King, Chicago, Illinois
Mrs. Mary C. Lee, San Francisco, California
Mr. Daniel E. Lewis and Mrs. Linda A. Lewis, La Porte, Indiana
Mr. Bradley Lindborg and Mrs. Elizabeth Lindborg, Savannah, Georgia
Mr. and Mrs. Richard Marcus, Glencoe, Illinois
Ms. Jan McDole, Ms. Juli Greenwald, and Dr. E. James Greenwald, Reno, Nevada
Dr. Charlotte M. Otten, Stoughton, Wisconsin
Mr. A. V. Pogaryan and Ms. Chilton Watrous, Turkey
Ms. Jacqueline L. Price, Orland Park, Illinois
Ms. Judith L. Rose, Chicago, Illinois
Ms. Bonnie B. Smith, Bloutstown, Florida
Mr. and Mrs. Walter H. Teninga, Village of Golf, Florida
Mr. Douglas S. Twells and Mrs. Annette L. Twells, St. Louis, Missouri
The Ronald C. Warner Family, Lapeer, Michigan
Mrs. Roderick S. Webster, Winnetka, Illinois
Ms. Jane M. Wickstrom, La Porte, Indiana
Rev. and Mrs. W. William Wimberly II, Champaign, Illinois
Mrs. Jack Witkowsky, Chicago, Illinois

In Memory of Vera Greaves

Manchester Ancient Egypt Society, United Kingdom

In Memory of Georgia Greenspan

Mr. George Bor and Mrs. Darcy Bor, Washington, D.C.
Mr. and Mrs. James Furlong, Washington, D.C.
Ms. Mary Anne Karmes, Kentwood, Michigan

In Memory of Hans G. Güterbock

Mrs. Hans G. Güterbock, Chicago, Illinois
Prof. Lawrence S. Root and Prof. Margaret Cool Root, Ann Arbor, Michigan

In Memory of Libby Hurbanek

Dr. Carol Meyer, Chicago, Illinois

In Memory of Dorothy Iz

Ms. Zeynep Man, Turkey
Mr. A. V. Pogaryan and Ms. Chilton Watrous, Turkey

In Memory of Jake Longley

Mr. James L. Foorman and Mrs. Margaret E. Foorman, Winnetka, Illinois

In Memory of Helaine R. Staver

Mr. Mervin Block, New York, New York

In Memory of Eleanor Ransom Swift

Mr. E. M. Bakwin, Chicago, Illinois
Mr. Leo N. Bradley and Mrs. Patricia Q. Bradley, Golden, Colorado
Mr. and Mrs. Isak V. Gerson, Chicago, Illinois
Mrs. Hans G. Güterbock, Chicago, Illinois
Dr. Richard I. Kaufman and Dr. Louis Kaufman, Chicago, Illinois
Dr. Jacques Ovadia and Mrs. Florence Ovadia, Chicago, Illinois
Mr. Jon Shomer and Mrs. Marilyn Shomer, Phoenix, Arizona

In Memory of Jerry F. Wood

Mr. Anthony Syrett and Ms. Ann S. Syrett, APO, Military - A.E.

MATCHING GIFTS

Abbott Laboratories Fund, Abbott Park, Illinois
American Electric Power Company, Inc., Columbus, Ohio
Armstrong Foundation, Lancaster, Pennsylvania
The Boeing Company, Seattle, Washington
BP Foundation, Inc., Chicago, Illinois
CIGNA Foundation, Philadelphia, Pennsylvania
CNA Foundation, Chicago, Illinois
R. R. Donnelley & Sons Company, Chicago, Illinois
The Dow Chemical Company Foundation, Midland, Michigan
Ernst & Young Foundation, New York, New York
Exxon Mobil Foundation, Irving, Texas
Harris Bank Foundation, Chicago, Illinois
International Business Machines Corporation, Armonk, New York
Johnson Controls Foundation, Milwaukee, Wisconsin
Lucent Technologies, Stuart, Florida
Mayer, Brown, Rowe & Maw LLP, Chicago, Illinois
Merrill Lynch and Co. Foundation, Inc., Princeton, New Jersey
Motorola Foundation, Schaumburg, Illinois
The NCR Foundation, Dayton, Ohio
The Northern Trust Company, Chicago, Illinois
The John Nuveen Company, Chicago, Illinois
PepsiCo Foundation Inc., Purchase, New York
Pfizer Foundation Inc., Princeton, New Jersey
Philip Morris Companies, Inc., New York, New York
Phoenix Foundation, Hartford, Connecticut
SBC Foundation, Princeton, New Jersey
State Farm Companies Foundation, Bloomington, Illinois
Trans Union Corporation, Chicago, Illinois
United Technologies Corporation, Hartford, Connecticut
The Williams Companies, Tulsa, Oklahoma

MEMBERSHIP

Rebecca Laharia

I would like to thank the membership for the warm welcome I have received. It has been a pleasure serving you over the last six months, and I hope that you will continue to see positive changes after the transitions of the last year. As examples, we re-investigated the most efficient way to manage membership renewals, the *News & Notes* newsletter has been receiving incremental make-overs (including the occasional use of full-color images) that will result in a more readable format, the Members Lecture program has been re-invigorated, the office has been reorganized for improved efficiency, and new travel opportunities are being examined.

Last year, the James Henry Breasted Society enjoyed two special events. A dinner and lecture were held for the Breasted Society on December 4, 2002, at the University Club of Chicago. Mark Lehner, Director of the Giza Plateau Mapping Project, presented the results of his recent archaeological discoveries in Giza. On May 1, 2003, the Breasted Society visited The Field Museum to view *Eternal Egypt: Masterworks of Ancient Art from The British Museum*, an exhibit for which the Oriental Institute's Robert K. Ritner served as academic consultant. As always, the Oriental Institute is grateful to the members of the Breasted Society who recognize the necessity for an annual renewable source of unrestricted funds to be used at the Director's discretion for the most pressing needs of the Oriental Institute. A wide range of Oriental Institute activities, from Anatolian archaeology to seed funding for new projects, benefit from the generosity of the Breasted Society.

The March 2003 trip to Egypt, *Oases of the Western Desert*, was cancelled due to the political climate. However, Clemens Reichel, Research Associate, escorted a trip to Atlanta, Georgia, in August 2002. Clemens guided our group through temporary exhibit *Ancient Empires, Syria: Land of Civilization*s at the Fernbank Museum of Natural History, while Peter Lacovara, Curator of Ancient Art at Emory University, gave a tour of their Near Eastern galleries at the Michael C. Carlos Museum.

New travel opportunities are being developed. We have brought back the Egypt destination, *Oases of the Western Desert,* escorted by Robert K. Ritner. Our 2004 destinations also include *Splendors of Western Turkey,* escorted by Gil J. Stein, and a voyage aboard a three-masted sailing ship: *Crossroads of Empires: Cairo to Crete*, with Emily Teeter as the Oriental Institute leader.

In Chicago, W. Raymond Johnson, Director of the Epigraphic Survey, gave a gallery talk on the temporary exhibit *Lost Egypt: Images of a Vanished Past* to the membership on July 10, 2003. Approximately fifty people enjoyed the informal lecture and refreshments. The exhibit features exquisite photographic prints culled from the Epigraphic Survey's archive. Taken in Egypt between 1880 and 1930, they provide an extraordinary impression of the land and people of the Nile Valley as they appeared before the onset of the modern era.

Five Members Lectures were offered last year. On October 30, 2002, Christopher Woods, Assistant Professor of Sumerology at the Oriental Institute, gave a lecture titled "Sumerian Writing: Some Problems Relating to Origin, Nature, and Development." Lawrence E. Stager, Dorot Professor of the Archaeology of Israel at Harvard University, visited the Oriental Institute on November 13 and gave the Members Lecture "Two Phoenician Shipwrecks Off Ashkelon in the Deep Sea." On January 22, 2003, Stephen P. Harvey, Assistant Professor of Egyptian Archaeology at the Oriental Institute, lectured on "Egypt's Last Royal Pyramid: The Monuments of King Ahmose and His Family at Abydos." William Dever, Professor of Near Eastern Archaeology, University of Arizona, gave our April 2 Members Lecture, "Did God Have a Wife? Archaeology and Popular Religion in Ancient Israel." This lecture was co-sponsored by the Archaeological Institute of America (AIA). Our May 7 lecture, also cosponsored by the AIA, was given by Yizhar Hirshfeld, Associate Professor at the Institute of Archaeology at the Hebrew University of Jerusalem, on "Qumran in Context: New Discoveries Along the Dead Sea Shore."

Those of you who were disappointed in the absence of our annual dinner, *Romancing the Past*, may rest assured that it is returning next spring. As of this writing, I am working on finalizing the date for our gala at the Drake Hotel.

Many people have contributed to last year's successes. Tom Urban, Senior Editor in the Publications Office, was instrumental in the publishing of *News & Notes* and this *Annual Report*, sharing his skills at layout and his advice on editing. Carole Krucoff, Head, Museum Education and Public Programming, shared her insight into the community that composes our membership and her extensive knowledge of resources for events and programming. Emily Napolitano, former Membership Coordinator and current Assistant to the Director, Epigraphic Survey, edited the Winter *News & Notes*, continued to maintain the web pages, and shared her familiarity with functions of the Membership Office freely. Faculty members including Robert Ritner, Martha Roth, and Jan Johnson took the time to explain their research so that I could better communicate with our members. Karen Wilson, Museum Director, Chuck Jones, Research Archivist, and John Sanders, Head, Computer Laboratory, have been generous with their time. Nicole Torres, Assistant to the Director, and Matthew Szydagis, work-study student, were essential to the day-to-day running of the office last fall and winter. My thanks, as well, go to the many contributors to *News & Notes* and the *Annual Report*.

Oriental Institute volunteers have been quick to offer their assistance, and I look forward to working with more of you. Last year, Rita Picken and Gabriele Da Silva generously gave of their time. University student Mica Shender, Laboratory School student Levi Smith, and recent Lab School graduate Jo Burgess helped with tasks as varied as making name badges, updating scrapbooks, organizing our bookshelves and binders, and, endlessly, stuffing and stamping envelopes. Thank you for your help.

The Membership Office can be contacted by phone at (773) 702-9513 or by e-mail at oi-membership@uchicago.edu.

HONOR ROLL OF MEMBERS

We are pleased to recognize the members of the Oriental Institute during the period from July 1, 2002 through June 30, 2003. Thank you for your support.

The Membership Honor Roll is arranged in alphabetical order within each membership level and reflects Associate and Breasted Society Membership dues received as of June 30, 2003. Non-Membership gifts and donations of gift memberships are reflected in the Donor Honor Roll.

We have made every effort to verify membership levels and member names. Please contact the Membership Office at (773) 702-9513 if you wish to make changes in your honor roll listing.

James Henry Breasted Society

The James Henry Breasted Society is a special category of membership created to provide a direct, renewable source of unrestricted funds for Oriental Institute projects and for matching money to private and federal grants. Members annually contribute $1,000 or more (Patron) and $2,500 or more (Director's Circle). We thank each of our Breasted Society Members for their ongoing generosity.

Director's Circle

Prof. Robert Z. Aliber and Mrs. Deborah Aliber, Hanover, New Hampshire
Mr. Anthony T. Dean and Mrs. Lawrie C. Dean, Long Grove, Illinois
Mrs. Emily Huggins Fine, San Francisco, California
Dr. Marjorie M. Fisher, Bloomfield Hills, Michigan
Mr. Collier Hands, Lovell, Maine
Mr. Thomas C. Heagy and Mrs. Linda H. Heagy, Chicago, Illinois
Mr. Robert M. Levy and Mrs. Diane Levy, Chicago, Illinois
Mr. Roger R. Nelson and Mrs. Marjorie Nelson, Glenview, Illinois
Ms. Muriel Kallis Newman, Chicago, Illinois
Mrs. Rita T. Picken, Chicago, Illinois
Mr. Patrick Regnery and Mrs. Deborah K. Regnery, Burr Ridge, Illinois
Mr. Robert G. Schloerb and Mrs. Mary W. Schloerb, Chicago, Illinois
Mr. O. J. Sopranos and Mrs. Angeline B. Sopranos, Winnetka, Illinois

Patron

Mrs. James W. Alsdorf, Chicago, Illinois
Mr. Joseph Alvarado and Mrs. Doris A. Alvarado, Munster, Indiana
Mr. Ronald R. Baade and Mrs. Marsha Baade, Winnetka, Illinois
Mr. William M. Backs and Ms. Janet Rizner, Evanston, Illinois
Mr. John Batchelor and Mrs. Suzanne Batchelor, Fernandina Beach, Florida
Ms. Laurie A. Boche, North Saint Paul, Minnesota
Mr. William A. Boone† and Mrs. Florence H. Boone. Glencoe, Illinois
Mr. Cameron Brown and Mrs. Jean McGrew Brown, Lake Forest, Illinois
Mr. Thomas J. Charters and Mrs. Ann J. Charters, New York, New York
Mr. James E. Conway and Ms. Patricia Conway, Flossmoor, Illinois
Ms. Marion E. Cowan, Evanston, Illinois
Mr. Terry D. Diamond and Mrs. Marilyn Diamond, Chicago, Illinois

Patron (*cont.*)

Mr. Matthew W. Dickie and Ms. Elizabeth R. Gebhard, Chicago, Illinois
Ms. Andrea M. Dudek, Orland Park, Illinois
Mr. Robert Feitler and Mrs. Joan E. Feitler, Chicago, Illinois
Mr. James L. Foorman and Mrs. Margaret E. Foorman, Winnetka, Illinois
Dr. Leila M. Foster, Evanston, Illinois
Mr. John W. Fritz II† and Mrs. Marilyn F. Fritz, Kenilworth, Illinois
Mr. Paul E. Goldstein and Mrs. Iris S. Goldstein, Chicago, Illinois
Mr. Robert M. Grant and Mrs. Margaret H. Grant, Chicago, Illinois
Mrs. Joseph N. Grimshaw, Wilmette, Illinois
Mr. I. A. Grodzins and Mrs. Diana L. Grodzins, Chicago, Illinois
Mr. Dietrich M. Gross and Mrs. Erika Gross, Wilmette, Illinois
Dr. Benjamin Gruber and Dr. Petra Maria Blix, Chicago, Illinois
Mr. Lewis S. Gruber and Mrs. Misty S. Gruber, Chicago, Illinois
Ms. Louise Grunwald, New York, New York
Mr. Albert F. Haas and Mrs. Cissy R. Haas, Chicago, Illinois
Mr. Howard G. Haas and Mrs. Carolyn W. Haas, Chicago, Illinois
Mr. Philip Halpern and Mrs. Deborah G. Halpern, Chicago, Illinois
Mr. David P. Harris and Mrs. Judith A. Harris, Lake Forest, Illinois
Mr. Robert A. Helman and Mrs. Janet W. Helman, Chicago, Illinois
Dr. Arthur L. Herbst and Mrs. Lee Herbst, Chicago, Illinois
Dr. Donald H.J. Hermann, Chicago, Illinois
Dr. David C. Hess and Mrs. Betty S. Hess, Downers Grove, Illinois
Mr. Marshall M. Holleb and Mrs. Doris B. Holleb, Chicago, Illinois
Mr. Wayne J. Holman III, Glen Ellyn, Illinois
Mr. Peter P. Homans and Mrs. Celia E. Homans, Chicago, Illinois
Ms. Mariye C. Inouye, New York, New York
Mr. Roger David Isaacs and Mrs. Joyce R. Isaacs, Glencoe, Illinois
Mr. Jonathan Janott, Chicago, Illinois
Mr. Glen A. Khant, Chicago, Illinois
Mr. Neil J. King and Mrs. Diana Hunt King, Chicago, Illinois
Mr. Jack A. Koefoot, Evanston, Illinois
Mr. Richard Kron and Mrs. Deborah A. Bekken, Chicago, Illinois
Mrs. Edward H. Levi†, Chicago, Illinois
Mr. Thomas Lenz and Mrs. Ulla Lenz, Chicago, Illinois
Mr. Daniel A. Lindley, Jr. and Mrs. Lucia Woods Lindley, Evanston, Illinois
Mr. Barry L. MacLean and Mrs. Mary Ann Shirley MacLean, Mettawa, Illinois
Mr. David W. Maher and Mrs. Carlotta Maher, Chicago, Illinois
Mrs. Janina Marks, Chicago, Illinois
Mr. John W. McCarter, Jr. and Mrs. Judith McCarter, Northfield, Illinois
Mr. William Brice McDonald, Chicago, Illinois
Mrs. Barbara Mertz, Frederick, Maryland
Ms. Bobbi Newman, Chicago, Illinois
Mr. David J. Paldan and Mrs. Karen S. Paldan, Scottsdale, Arizona
Mr. Harvey B. Plotnick and Mrs. Elizabeth Plotnick, Chicago, Illinois
Mr. J. Dwight Prade and Ms. Stephanie G. Prade, St. Louis, Missouri
Mr. Don M. Randel and Mrs. Carol E. Randel, Chicago, Illinois
Mr. David K. Ray and Mrs. Crennan M. Ray, Santa Fe, New Mexico
Dr. Miriam Reitz Baer, Chicago, Illinois
Mr. John Fleming Richards and Mrs. Marilyn M. Richards, Wilmette, Illinois
Mr. Robert Ritner and Mrs. Margaret S. Ritner, Houston, Texas
Mr. William J.O. Roberts and Mrs. Ann V. Roberts, Lake Forest, Illinois
Mr. John W. Rowe and Mrs. Jeanne Rowe, Chicago, Illinois
Mrs. Maurice Schwartz, Los Angeles, California

Patron *(cont.)*

Mr. Charles M. Shea and Mrs. Mary G. Shea, Wilmette, Illinois
The Honorable George P. Shultz, Stanford, California
Mr. Michael J. Silverstein and Ms. Geraldine M. Silverstein, Glencoe, Illinois
Mr. John Howell Smith, New York, New York
Mrs. Eleanor Ransom Swift†, Chicago, Illinois
Dr. David M. Terman and Mrs. Mari D. Terman, Wilmette, Illinois
Ms. Karen M. Terras, Sawyer, Michigan
Mrs. Roderick S. Webster, Winnetka, Illinois
Ms. Anna M. White, Terre Haute, Indiana
Ms. Flora Yelda, Chicago, Illinois
Mrs. Jeannette Yelda, Chicago, Illinois
Dr. Sharukin Yelda and Mrs. Elizabeth Yelda, Chicago, Illinois

Sponsoring Members ($500–$999)

Miss Janice V. Bacchi, Encinitas, California
Mr. and Mrs. Robert O. Delaney, Winnetka, Illinois
Dr. Erl Dordal, Chicago, Illinois
Mrs. Ann B. Fallon, Tucson, Arizona
Mr. and Mrs. Robert Dunn Glick, Chicago, Illinois
Mr. Michael L. Keiser and Mrs. Rosalind C. Keiser, Chicago, Illinois
Mr. Stephen Mican, Rockford, Illinois
Mr. Richard M. Morrow and Mrs. Janet Morrow, Glenview, Illinois
Dr. Harlan R. Peterjohn, Bay Village, Ohio
Mr. Charles N. Secchia, Grand Rapids, Michigan
Dr. Clyde Curry Smith and Mrs. Ellen Marie Smith, River Falls, Wisconsin
Ms. Toni Sandor Smith, Chicago, Illinois
Ms. Lowri Sprung, San Pedro, California
Mr. Robert Wagner and Ms. Rose Wagner, Chicago, Illinois
Mr. Charles Mack Wills Jr., East Palatka, Florida

Contributing Members ($250–$499)

Mrs. Mary S. Allan, Chicago, Illinois
Dr. Donald H. Amidei, Park Ridge, Illinois
Dr. and Mrs. Robert M. Ball, Amarillo, Texas
Mrs. Guity Nashat Becker, Chicago, Illinois
Dr. Sidney J. Blair and Ms. LaMoyne C. Blair, Oak Park, Illinois
Ms. Susan Boche, North St. Paul, Minnesota
Ms. Laurie A. Boche, North St. Paul, Minnesota
Mr. Charles N. Callahan and Ms. Naila Britain, Chicago, Illinois
Mr. Bruce P. Burbage, Nokomis, Florida
Ms. Elizabeth F. Carter, Los Angeles, California
Mr. Courtney B. Conte, Santa Monica, California
Dr. George Dunea and Ms. Mary M. Dunea, Chicago, Illinois
Mr. Amon Emanuel, Switzerland
Ms. Rosemary Faulkner, New York, New York
Dr. Gary S. Garofalo, Palos Hills, Illinois
Dr. Victor E. Gould and Dr. Nevenka S. Gould, Wilmette, Illinois

Contributing Members ($250–$499) *(cont.)*

Mr. M. Hill Hammock and Mrs. Cheryl Hammock, Chicago, Illinois
Mr. Leo O. Harris and Dr. Cynthia O. Harris, Albuquerque, New Mexico
Mr. Raad Hermes, Chicago, Illinois
Ms. Susan C. Hull, Chicago, Illinois
Mr. and Mrs. George T. Jacobi, Milwaukee, Wisconsin
Dr. Joseph Jarabak and Dr. Rebecca Jarabak, Hinsdale, Illinois
Dr. John Sobolski and Dr. Zara Khodjasteh, Chicago, Illinois
Mr. Dee Morgan Kilpatrick, Chicago, Illinois
Dr. Elisabeth Lassers, Chicago, Illinois
Mr. Paul S. Linsay and Ms. Roni A. Lipton, Newton, Massachusetts
Mrs. Glen A. Lloyd, Libertyville, Illinois
Mr. S. Edward Marder, Highland Park, Illinois
Mr. Terrence D. McMahon and Mr. Daniel W. Bednarz, Chicago, Illinois
Mr. Richard A. Miller, Oak Lawn, Illinois
Mr. and Mrs. Jeffrey E. Miripol, Hockessin, Delaware
Ms. Vivian B. Morales, Miami, Florida
Mr. Anthony Mourek and Dr. Karole Schafer Mourek, Riverside, Illinois
Ms. Holly J. Mulvey, Evanston, Illinois
Mr. Douglas G. Murray, Santa Barbara, California
Mr. Charles R. Nelson, Seattle, Washington
Mr. and Mrs. Richard C. Notebaert, Chicago, Illinois
Mr. Larry Paragano, Springfield, New Jersey
Mr. Eric Pelander and Dr. Evalyn Gates, Chicago, Illinois
Mr. Steven Anthony Clark and Ms. Janet L. Raymond, Oak Lawn, Illinois
Mr. and Mrs. Gary W. Rexford, Topeka, Kansas
Ms. Diane Ruzevich, Berwyn, Illinois
Mr. Paul Schoessow and Ms. Patricia Cavenee, Lakewood, Colorado
Mr. Zekir Share, Aurora, Illinois
Dr. Henry D. Slosser, Altadena, California
Mr. Michael J. Sobczyk, Des Plaines, Illinois
Mr. David Allan Stoudt, Clackamas, Oregon
Dr. Arnold Tanis and Mrs. Maxine Tanis, Fernandina Beach, Florida
Mr. Joseph Daniel Cain and Ms. Emily Teeter, Chicago, Illinois
Mr. and Mrs. James M. Trapp, Chicago, Illinois
Mr. David J. Vitale and Ms. Marilyn Fatt Vitale, Chicago, Illinois
Mr. Thomas J. White and Ms. Leslie Scalapino, Oakland, California
Dr. Willard E. White, Riverside, Illinois
Ms. Carrie Wilson and Ms. Herminia Wilson, Chicago, Illinois
Dr. Wendall W. Wilson, Chicago, Illinois

Supporting Members ($100–$249)

Mr. D.M. Abadi and Mrs. Mary C. Abadi, Iowa City, Iowa
Mrs. Lester S. Abelson, Chicago, Illinois
Ms. Judith Akers, Wilmette, Illinois
Mrs. Karen B. Alexander, Geneva, Illinois
Mr. James P. Allen and Mrs. Susan J. Allen, Ridgefield, Connecticut
Mr. Edward Anders and Mrs. Joan Anders, Chicago, Illinois
Dr. Thomas Andrews, Hinsdale, Illinois
Dr. Robert Arensman and Mrs. Marilyn C. Arensman, Chicago, Illinois
Dr. Claresa Armstrong, Chicago, Illinois

Supporting Members ($100–$249) (*cont.*)

Mr. James Armstrong and Ms. Beverly Armstrong, Watertown, Massachusetts
Mr. Seymour Bortz and Mrs. Katherine Biddle Austin, Highland Park, Illinois
Mr. Paul Barron and Ms. Mary Anton, Chicago, Illinois
Ms. Margaret Bates, Sarasota, Florida
Mrs. Elizabeth Baum, Chicago, Illinois
Mr. Barry Baumgardner, Dunnellon, Florida
Dr. David Bawden and Ms. Jan Bawden, Northfield, Illinois
Mr. and Mrs. Bruce L. Beavis, Chicago, Illinois
Ms. Jane E. Belcher, Chicago, Illinois
Dr. Barbara Bell, Cambridge, Massachusetts
Mr. and Mrs. John F. Benjamin, Chicago, Illinois
Mr. Richard Benjamin and Ms. Sally Benjamin, North Augusta, South Carolina
Ms. Katharine L. Bensen, Chicago, Illinois
Mr. George W. Benson and Ms. Ellen C. Benson, Chicago, Illinois
Mr. Robert W. Benson, Chicago, Illinois
Mrs. Edwin A. Bergman, Chicago, Illinois
Mr. Keki R. Bhote and Mrs. Mehroo K. Bhote, Glencoe, Illinois
Mr. Edward McCormick Blair, Lake Bluff, Illinois
Mr. Edward C. Blau, Alexandria, Virginia
Mr. Bob Blumling, San Diego, California
Mrs. George V. Bobrinskoy Jr., Chicago, Illinois
Dr. Constance Bonbrest, Chicago, Illinois
Mr. O. John Brahos, Wilmette, Illinois
Mr. Raymond Tindel and Ms. Gretel Braidwood, Chicago, Illinois
Mrs. Jerald C. Brauer, Chicago, Illinois
Ms. Catherine Novotny Brehm, Chicago, Illinois
Mr. Alan R. Brodie, Chicago, Illinois
Mr. John A. Bross, Chicago, Illinois
Ms. Myllicent Buchanan, Chicago, Illinois
Mr. and Mrs. Allan E. Bulley III, Chicago, Illinois
Ms. Christine Cahill, Chicago, Illinois
Mr. and Mrs. Joseph Camarra, Chicago, Illinois
Ms. Jeanny Vorys Canby, Bryn Mawr, Pennsylvannia
Mr. Thomas Cassidy, Littleton, Colorado
Miss Mary E. Chase, Flossmoor, Illinois
Mr. E. Eric Clark and Mrs. Alice H. Clark, Sierra Madre, California
Mr. Robert Clinkert, Aurora, Illinois
Mrs. Lydia G. Cochrane, Chicago, Illinois
Mr. Douglas E. Cohen and Mrs. Carol B. Cohen, Highland Park, Illinois
Mr. Lawrence M. Coleman, New Orleans, Louisiana
Mrs. Zdzislawa Coleman, Chicago, Illinois
Ms. Cynthia Green Colin, New York, New York
Ms. Johna S. Compton, Chancellor, Alabama
Mr. William Cottle and Mrs. Judith Cottle, Winnetka, Illinois
Mr. David Crabb and Mrs. Dorothy Crabb, Chicago, Illinois
Mr. Albert V. Crewe and Mrs. Doreen P. Crewe, Dune Acres, Indiana
Dr. Eugene D. Cruz-Uribe and Dr. Kathryn Cruz-Uribe, Flagstaff, Arizona
Mr. Edwin L. Currey Jr., Napa, California
Mr. Charles Custer and Ms. Irene Custer, Chicago, Illinois
Mr. Russ Thomas Watson and Ms. Mary Katherine Danna, Chicago, Illinois
Mr. Leo Darwit and Mr. Reid Selseth, Chicago, Illinois
Mr. Merritt J. Davoust† and Mrs. Lynne Rauscher-Davoust, Elmhurst, Illinois
Mr. Walter E. De Lise, Indian Head Park, Illinois

Supporting Members ($100–$249) *(cont.)*

Mr. Kevin M. Dent, Terre Haute, Indiana

Mr. Irving L. Diamond and Ms. Dorothy J. Speidel, Wilmette, Illinois

Ms. Mary Dimperio, Washington, D.C.

Mr. Henry S. Dixon and Ms. Linda Giesen, Dixon, Illinois

Mr. J. McGregor Dodds and Ms. Christine Dodds, Grosse Pointe Farms, Michigan

Mr. Jim Douglas and Mrs. Mary Lou Douglas, West LaFayette, Indiana

Ms. Ellen M. Dran, DeKalb, Illinois

Ms. Andrea M. Dudek, Orland Park, Illinois

Mr. Bruce Dunn and Ms. Nancie Dunn, Chicago, Illinois

Mrs. Bettie Dwinell, Chicago, Illinois

Mr. John E. Dyble and Mrs. Patricia A. Dyble, Hawthornwoods, Illinois

Mr. Robert Dyson, Gladwyne, Pennsylvannia

Mr. C. David Eeles, Columbus, Ohio

Mr. Lawrence R. Eicher and Mrs. Vicky C. Eicher, Charlottesville, Virginia

Mr. William L. Ekvall and Mrs. Marie A. Ekvall, Evanston, Illinois

Mr. Frederick Elghanayan, New York, New York

Mr. Alex Elson and Ms. Miriam Elson, Chicago, Illinois

Mr. Sidney Epstein and Mrs. Sondra Epstein, Chicago, Illinois

Ms. Ann Esse, Sioux Falls, South Dakota

Dr. Richard H. Evans and Mrs. Roberta G. Evans, Chicago, Illinois

Mr. Eugene Fama and Ms. Sallyann Fama, Chicago, Illinois

Dr. Valerie Fargo, Midland, Michigan

Mr. Charles J. Fisher, Sioux City, Iowa

Mr. and Mrs. Gerald F. Fitzgerald Jr., Inverness, Illinois

Dr. Michael Flom, Boynton Beach, Florida

Mr. Richard E. Ford, Wabash, Indiana

Ms. Tara Fowler, Chicago, Illinois

Dr. Samuel Ethan Fox and Mrs. Beverly F. Fox, Chicago, Illinois

Mr. and Mrs. Paul E. Freehling, Chicago, Illinois

Ms. Eleanor B. Frew, Flossmoor, Illinois

Mr. Thomas F. Frey and Mrs. Barbara D. Frey, Sarasota, Florida

Mr. and Mrs. Stephen Fried, Kingston, Massachusetts

Mr. Charles Barry Friedman and Mrs. Terry Friedman, Chicago, Illinois

Ms. Mirah Gaines, Burr Ridge, Illinois

Mr. Gregory Gajda, Mt. Prospect, Illinois

Mr. and Mrs. Isak V. Gerson, Chicago, Illinois

Miss Mary Virginia Gibson, Middleton, Wisconsin

Mrs. Willard Gidwitz, Highland Park, Illinois

Ms. Nancy Gidwitz, Chicago, Illinois

Mr. Thomas Gillespie, Chicago, Illinois

Mr. Gregory T. Gillette, Chicago, Illinois

Mr. Lyle Gillman, Bloomingdale, Illinois

Ms. Ann Goddard, St. Louis, Missouri

Mr. and Mrs. William H. Gofen, Chicago, Illinois

Mrs. Ethel Frank Goldsmith, Chicago, Illinois

Mr. Frederick Graboske and Mrs. Patricia Graboske, Rockville, Maryland

Mr. and Mrs. Robert Graham, River Forest, Illinois

Mr. Kenneth and Mrs. Doris Granath, St. John, Indiana

Mr. Anthony F. Granucci, San Francisco, California

Ms. Melati Granucci, San Francisco, California

Mr. and Mrs. David Gratner, Sulpher Springs, Indiana

Mr. John Greaves and Ms. Patricia McLaughlin, Hinsdale, Illinois

Dr. Joseph Greene and Mrs. Eileen Caves, Belmont, Massachusetts

Supporting Members ($100–$249) *(cont.)*

Mr. C.O. Griffin and Ms. Gillian Griffin, Newburyport, Massachusetts
Mr. and Mrs. Richard C. Haines, Atlanta, Georgia
Ms. Ellen R. Hall and Ms. Betty Ann Cronin, West Allis, Wisconsin
Mr. Joel L. Handelman and Ms. Sarah R. Wolff, Chicago, Illinois
Dr. Lowell Kent Handy, Des Plaines, Illinois
Commissioner and Mrs. Carl R. Hansen, Mount Prospect, Illinois
Ms. Ednalyn Hansen, Chicago, Illinois
Ms. Katherine Haramundanis, Westford, Massachusetts
Dr. Thomas Harper, Sherman Oaks, California
Mr. Chauncy D. Harris and Mrs. Edith Harris, Chicago, Illinois
Mr. James B. Hartle, Santa Barbara, California
Mr. Robert Haselkorn and Mrs. Margot Haselkorn, Chicago, Illinois
Mr. Thomas E. Hemminger, New Lenox, Illinois
Mr. Juan Lopez and Ms. Carmen Heredia, Chicago, Illinois
Mr. John A. Herschkorn Jr. and Mrs. Gloria Herschkorn, San Jose, California
Mr. Walter Hess and Ms. Hedda Hess, Chicago, Illinois
Mr. Bruce Sagan and Ms. Bette Cerf Hill, Chicago, Illinois
Mr. David C. Hilliard and Mrs. Celia Schmid Hilliard, Chicago, Illinois
Mrs. Harold Hines, Winnetka, Illinois
Mrs. Joan L. Hoatson, Hinsdale, Illinois
Ms. Debbie Holm, Chicago, Illinois
Ms. Jean Hontz, Niceville, Florida
Ms. Catherine Howard, Okanogan, Washington
Mr. Bill Hudson and Mr. Wade Adkisson, New York, New York
Mr. Richard Huff, Oak Park, Illinois
Dr. Kevin S. Hughes, Boston, Massachusetts
Mr. Arthur T. Hurley, Napa, California
Mr. Alan Hutchinson, Chicago, Illinois
Dr. Kamal Ibrahim and Dr. Lucy Ibrahim, Oak Brook, Illinois
Ms. Lise Jacobson, Evanston, Illinois
Mr. Thomas Jedele and Dr. Nancy J. Skon Jedele, Laurel, Maryland
Dr. Donald Whitcomb and Dr. Janet H. Johnson, Chicago, Illinois
Rev. Prof. Douglas Judisch, Fort Wayne, Indiana
Mr. John Cletus Kaminski and Ms. Maria M. Duran, Chicago, Illinois
Dr. Michael Steven Kaplan, Lexington, Massachusetts
Ms. Susan Kezios, Chicago, Illinois
Mrs. Marjorie H. Buchanan Kiewit, Chestnut Hill, Massachusetts
Mr. H. David Kirby and Mrs. Faye Taylor Kirby, West Linn, Oregon
Mr. William J. Knight and Mrs. Julie F. Knight, South Bend, Indiana
Mr. Michael E. Koen, Chicago, Illinois
Mr. Henry H. Kohl and Mrs. Annie A. Kohl, Media, Pennsylvania
Mr. Frank Kohout, Iowa City, Iowa
Ms. Aphrodite Kokolis, Chicago, Illinois
Mr. Bryan Krakauer and Ms. Marie Poppy, Chicago, Illinois
Mr. Bernard L. Krawczyk, Chicago, Illinois
Mr. and Mrs. William J. Lawlor III, Kenilworth, Illinois
Mr. John Lawrence, Ann Arbor, Michigan
Dr. Mark Lehner, Milton, Massachusetts
Dr. Leonard Henry Lesko and Mrs. Barbara Switalski, Seekonk, Massachusetts
Mr. John G. Levi and Mrs. Jill F. Levi, Chicago, Illinois
Mr. Thaddeus Walczak and Mrs. Carole J. Lewis, Chesterton, Indiana
Mr. Theodore W. Liese and Mrs. Gabrielle M. Liese, Prescott, Arizona
Mr. Robert B. Lifton and Ms. Carol Rosofsky, Chicago, Illinois

Supporting Members ($100–$249) (*cont.*)

Mr. John Michael Lindert, Livermore, California

Mr. Richard Lo and Ms. Lo Luong Lo, Oak Park, Illinois

Mrs. Nina A. Longley, Park Forest, Illinois

Prof. and Mrs. James Lorie, Chicago, Illinois

Mr. Bruce L. Ludwig, Los Angeles, California

Mr. Philip R. Luhmann and Mrs. Dianne C. Luhmann, Chicago, Illinois

Ms. Mary Sue Lyon, Chicago, Illinois

Mr. Laurance L. MacKallor and Mrs. Margaret E. MacKallor, San Carlos, California

Mr. Daniel R. Malecki, Kensington, California

Ms. Maria Danae Mandis, Chicago, Illinois

Ms. Leah Maneaty, Chicago, Illinois

Mr. and Mrs. Richard Marcus, Glencoe, Illinois

Ms. Glennda Susan Marsh-Letts, Australia

Dr. John Mason, Danville, Illinois

Ms. Marilyn McCaman, La Verne, California

Mr. William J. McCluskey, Hinsdale, Illinois

Mr. W. Sloan McCrea, Miami, Florida

Mrs. Marie Therese McDermott, Chicago, Illinois

Mr. Robert B. McDermott and Ms. Sarah P. Jaicks, Chicago, Illinois

Mr. George C. McElroy and Dr. Jane W. Stedman†, Chicago, Illinois

Mr. Michael J. McInerney, Chicago, Illinois

Dr. Ernest E. Mhoon Jr. and Mrs. Deborah Ann Mhoon, Chicago, Illinois

Mr. Charles R. Michael, Woodbridge, Connecticut

Mr. Michael Millar and Ms. Ruth Millar, Cedar Falls, Iowa

Mr. Gene Miller, Madison, Wisconsin

Mr. Phillip L. Miller and Mrs. Barbara H. Miller, Oregon, Illinois

Dr. William K. Miller, Duluth, Minnesota

Dr. Morton Millman and Dr. Ann K. Millman, Chicago, Illinois

The Honorable Martha A. Mills, Chicago, Illinois

Mr. Sam Mirkin, Mishawaka, Indiana

Mr. J. Y. Miyamoto, Los Angeles, California

Mr. Joseph A. Moriarty and Ms. June J. Moriarty, Kingsport, Tennessee

Mr. and Mrs. William L. Morrison, Chicago, Illinois

Mr. Charles H. Mottier, Chicago, Illinois

Prof. Ian Mueller and Prof. Janel Mueller, Chicago, Illinois

Ms. Maureen Mullen, Greenfield, Wisconsin

Mr. Manly W. Mumford and Mrs. Luigi H. Mumford, Chicago, Illinois

Ms. Janet Murphy, Chicago, Illinois

Mr. David E. Muschler and Ms. Ann L. Becker, Chicago, Illinois

Mrs. Marcia B. Nachtrieb, Joliet, Illinois

Mr. and Mrs. James L. Nagle, Chicago, Illinois

Ms. Mary B. Naunton, Chicago, Illinois

Dr. William F. Nelson, Martin, Tennessee

Mr. Walter A. Netsch Jr. and Ms. Dawn Clark Netsch, Chicago, Illinois

Mr. and Mrs. Robert M. Newbury, Chicago, Illinois

Mrs. Eleanor K. Nicholson, Evanston, Illinois

Mr. and Mrs. James Nicholson, Pickerington, Ohio

Mr. John P. Nielsen, Lombard, Illinois

Mr. Dale George Niewoehner, Rugby, North Dakota

Mr. Timothy Michael Nolan and Ms. Mary Ann Nolan, Palos Park, Illinois

Mr. Charles E. Jones and Ms. Alexandra Alice O'Brien, Chicago, Illinois

Mr. Dennis O'Connor, Chicago, Illinois

Ms. Marilynn Oleck, Chicago, Illinois

Supporting Members ($100–$249) *(cont.)*

Ms. Virginia O'Neill, Chicago, Illinois

Mr. Gary A. Oppenhuis and Ms. Mary E. Oppenhuis, Flossmoor, Illinois

Mr. Richard Orsan and Mr. Sen Gan, Chicago, Illinois

Mr. Mark M. Osgood, Burr Ridge, Illinois

Mr. Myras Osman and Ms. Linda Osman, Flossmoor, Illinois

Mr. John Thomas F. Oxaal and Ms. Marjorie Roitman Oxaal, Woodside, California

Ms. Marie Parsons, New York, New York

Mrs. Denise G. Paul, Chicago, Illinois

Mr. Donald Payne, Chicago, Illinois

Mr. Norman Perman and Mrs. Lorraine Perman, Chicago, Illinois

Mr. Robert R. Perodeau and Mrs. Evelyn C. Perodeau, Haddonfield, New Jersey

Ms. Nella Piccolin, Frankfort, Illinois

Mr. James Piojda, Racine, Wisconsin

Dr. Audrius Vaclovas Plioplys, Chicago, Illinois

Mr. Robert J. Poplar, Kenosha, Wisconsin

Mrs. Elizabeth M. Postell, Chicago, Illinois

Mr. J.M. Prescott and Ms. Semra Prescott, De Kalb, Illinois

Mr. Richard H. Prins and Mrs. Marion L. Prins, Chicago, Illinois

Mr. Francis Quemada, Palo Alto, California

Mrs. Arthur Quern, Wilmette, Illinois

Mr. Robert Andersen and Ms. Elaine Quinn, Chicago, Illinois

Ms. Katherine E. Rakowsky, Chicago, Illinois

Mr. Thad D. Rasche and Mrs. Diana Olson Rasche, Oak Park, Illinois

Dr. Charles Dean Ray, Yorktown, Virginia

Mr. David Reese and Dr. Catherine Sease, New Haven, Connecticut

Mr. David E. Reese, Chicago, Illinois

Mr. Alan Reinstein and Ms. Laurie Reinstein, Highland Park, Illinois

Mr. and Mrs. George G. Rinder, Burr Ridge, Illinois

Ms. Agnes Ann Roach, Gurnee, Illinois

Mr. William Hughes Roberts, Las Vegas, Nevada

Mr. Howard J. Romanek, Skokie, Illinois

Prof. Lawrence S. Root and Prof. Margaret Cool Root, Ann Arbor, Michigan

Mrs. Ludwig Rosenberger, Chicago, Illinois

Dr. David S. Rozenfeld and Mrs. Barbara Weisbaum Rozenfeld, Chicago, Illinois

Dr. Randi Rubovits-Seitz, Washington, D.C.

Mr. George Rumney, Bowie, Maryland

Mr. and Mrs. F. Garland Russell Jr., Columbia, Missouri

Mrs. Carolyn L. Sachs, Chicago, Illinois

Dr. Paul Saltzman and Ms. Bettylu K. Saltzman, Chicago, Illinois

Mr. Hafez Sami and Ms. Sharon Reeves-Sami, Naperville, Illinois

Dr. Bonnie Sampsell, Chapel Hill, North Carolina

Mr. Harold Sanders and Ms. Deloris Sanders, Chicago, Illinois

Mr. John Sanders and Ms. Peggy Sanders, Chicago, Illinois

Mr. Calvin Sawyier and Dr. Fay Sawyier, Chicago, Illinois

Dr. Lawrence J. Scheff and Mrs. Dorothy Adelle Scheff, Chicago, Illinois

Mr. Rolf Scherman and Ms. Charlotte Scherman, Greenbrae, California

Mr. Frank Schneider and Ms. Karen Schneider, Chicago, Illinois

Mr. and Mrs. Hans Schreiber, Chicago, Illinois

Dr. Michael Sha, Carmel, Indiana

Mr. R. Chesla Sharp and Ms. Ruth M. Sharp, Limestone, Tennessee

Mr. Thomas C. Sheffield Jr., Chicago, Illinois

Ms. Deborah Shefner, Chicago, Illinois

Ms. Emma Shelton, Bethesda, Maryland

Supporting Members ($100–$249) *(cont.)*

Ms. Mary Ellen Sheridan, Chicago, Illinois

Mr. Henry Showers and Mrs. Patricia A. Showers, Crown Point, Indiana

Mr. Michael A. Sisinger and Ms. Judith E. Waggoner, Columbus, Ohio

Ms. Mary Small, Kensington, California

Ms. Katherine E. Smith, Chicago, Illinois

Mr. Robert K. Smither, Hinsdale, Illinois

Mr. Lawrence Snider and Mrs. Maxine Snider, Chicago, Illinois

Ms. Patricia A. Soltys, Bandon, Oregon

Mr. Stephen C. Sperry, Litchfield, Minnesota

Mr. Fred Stafford and Ms. Barbara Stafford, Chicago, Illinois

Prof. Ruggero P. Stefanini, Oakland, California

Mr. Mayer Stern and Ms. Gloria Stern, Chicago, Illinois

The Honorable and Mrs. Adlai E. Stevenson III, Chicago, Illinois

Mr. and Mrs. Stephen M. Stigler, Chicago, Illinois

Mr. Frederick H. Stitt and Ms. Suzanne B. Stitt, Wilmette, Illinois

Dr. Francis H. Straus and Mrs. Lorna P. Straus, Chicago, Illinois

Mr. David G. Streets and Ms. W. Elane Streets, Darien, Illinois

Ms. Linda Stringer, Garland, Texas

Mrs. Peggy Lewis Sweesy, Santa Fe, New Mexico

Dr. and Mrs. C. Conover Talbot, Chicago, Illinois

Mr. Justin Tedrowe, Downers Grove, Illinois

Mr. Frederick Teeter and Mrs. Shirley Teeter, Ransomville, New York

Ms. Denise Thomas, Pontiac, Michigan

Mr. Randy Thomas and Ms. Barbara Thomas, Chicago, Illinois

Miss Kristin Thompson, Madison, Wisconsin

Mr. Dieter Tomczak, Germany

Mr. and Mrs. John Tonkinson, Torrance, California

Mr. Robert L. Toth and Mrs. Rosemary A. Toth, Medina, Ohio

Mr. and Mrs. John E. Townsend, Winnetka, Illinois

Miss Janice Trimble, Chicago, Illinois

Mrs. Nancy E. Turchi, Lake Zurich, Illinois

Mrs. Harriet M. Turk, Joliet, Illinois

Mr. Edgar J. Uihlein Jr. and Mrs. Lucia Ellis Uihlein, Lake Bluff, Illinois

Mr. Mustafa Ulken and Ms. Tayyibe C. Ulken, Hoffman Estates, Illinois

Mr. Karl H. Velde Jr., Lake Forest, Illinois

Mr. John Vinci, Chicago, Illinois

Mr. Don Wacker and Ms. Mary W. Wacker, Issaquah, Washington

Mr. and Mrs. James Wagner, Chicago, Illinois

Mrs. Marguerite A. Walk, Chicago, Illinois

Mr. John F. Warnock, Mason City, Illinois

Mr. A.V. Pogaryan and Ms. Chilton Watrous, Turkey

Mr. Jerry Wegner, Munster, Indiana

Mr. John R. Weiss, Wilmette, Illinois

Mr. Douglas J. Wells, Valparaiso, Indiana

Mr. and Mrs. Edward F. Wente, Chicago, Illinois

Mr. Wayne W. Whalen, Chicago, Illinois

Mr. John J. White III and Mrs. Patricia W. White, Columbus, Ohio

Mrs. Barbara Breasted Whitesides, Newton, Massachusetts

Mrs. Warner A. Wick, Needham, Massachusetts

Mr. John L. Wier and Ms. Elizabeth B. Wier, Naperville, Illinois

Mr. Wayne M. Wille and Mrs. Lois J. Wille, Chicago, Illinois

Mr. James S. Winn Jr. and Mrs. Bonnie Hicks Winn, Winnetka, Illinois

Ms. Melanie R. Wojtulewicz, Chicago, Illinois

Supporting Members ($100–$249) *(cont.)*

Rabbi Arnold Jacob Wolf, Chicago, Illinois
Ms. Judith M. Wright, Carson City, Nevada
Mr. Robert M. Wulff, Washington, D.C.
Dr. Sidney H. Yarbrough III and Mrs. Rebecca Yarbrough, Columbus, Georgia
Mr. Robert R. Yohanan and Ms. Joan Yohanan, Kenilworth, Illinois
Mr. Quentin Young and Ms. Ruth Young, Chicago, Illinois
Mr. Arnold Zellner and Mrs. Agnes Zellner, Chicago, Illinois

The Oriental Institute also acknowledges the generosity of our many Sustaining, Annual, Senior, University of Chicago Faculty and Staff, National Associate, and Student Members. Thank you for your continued support.

GIFT MEMBERSHIP DONORS

The following people gave memberships appearing above. Gift membership donations also appear in the total gift of the donor listed in the Donor Honor Roll.

Ms. Laurie A. Boche, North Saint Paul, Minnesotta
Mr. and Mrs. E. Eric Clark, Sierra Madra, California
Mr. and Mrs. James L. Foorman, Winnetka, Illinois
Mr. Anthony F. Granucci, San Francisco, California
Ms. Susannah Ruth Quern-Pratt, Chicago, Illinois

MATCHING GIFTS

The following companies matched memberships appearing above.

Abbott Laboratories Fund, Abbott Park, Illinois
American Electric Power Company, Inc., Columbus, Ohio
The Boeing Company, Seattle, Washington
CNA Foundation, Chicago, Illinois
R. R. Donnelley & Sons Company, Chicago, Illinois
The Dow Chemical Company Foundation, Midland, Michigan
Ernst & Young Foundation, New York, New York
Harris Bank Foundation, Chicago, Illinois
Johnson Controls Foundation, Milwaukee, Wisconsin
Motorola Foundation, Schaumburg, Illinoismakes paldan breasted
The NCR Foundation, Dayton, Ohio
SBC Foundation, Princeton, New Jersey
Trans Union Corporation, Chicago, Illinois
United Technologies Corporation, Hartford, Connecticut

VISITING COMMITTEE TO THE ORIENTAL INSTITUTE

Thomas C. Heagy, Chair

Deborah Aliber	Daniel A. Lindley, Jr.
Mrs. James W. Alsdorf	Lucia Woods Lindley
Gretel Braidwood	Carlotta Maher
Alan R. Brodie	Janina Marks
Jean McGrew Brown	John W. McCarter, Jr.
Marion Cowan	Roger Nelson
Anthony T. Dean	Muriel Kallis Newman
Lawrie C. Dean	Rita T. Picken
Matthew Dickie	Crennan M. Ray
Emily Huggins Fine	Patrick Regnery
Dr. Marjorie M. Fisher	William J. O. Roberts
Margaret E. Foorman	Barbara W. Rollhaus
Paul E. Goldstein	John W. Rowe
Margaret H. Grant	Alice E. Rubash
Mary L. Gray	Norman J. Rubash
Mary J. Grimshaw	Robert G. Schloerb
Diana L. Grodzins	Lois M. Schwartz
Albert F. Haas*	Mary G. Shea
Howard G. Haas	Professor W. Kelly Simpson
Deborah Halpern	O. J. Sopranos
Janet W. Helman	Mrs. Gustavus F. Swift†
Arthur L. Herbst, M.D.	Arnold L. Tanis, M.D.
Donald H. J. Hermann	Mari Terman
Doris B. Holleb	Gerald L. Vincent
Marshall M. Holleb	Marjorie K. Webster
Neil J. King	Sharukin Yelda, M.D.

* Denotes Life Member

† Denotes Deceased

FACULTY AND STAFF OF THE ORIENTAL INSTITUTE
July 1, 2002–June 30, 2003

EMERITUS FACULTY

Lanny Bell, Associate Professor Emeritus of Egyptology

Robert J. Braidwood†, Professor Emeritus, Prehistoric Archaeology

John A. Brinkman, Charles H. Swift Distinguished Service Professor Emeritus of Mesopotamian History,
j-brinkman@uchicago.edu, 702-9545

Miguel Civil, Professor Emeritus of Sumerology,
m-civil@uchicago.edu, 702-9542

Harry A. Hoffner, Jr., John A. Wilson Distinguished Service Professor Emeritus of Hittitology & Editor of Chicago Hittite Dictionary Project,
h-hoffner@uchicago.edu, 702-9527

Erica Reiner, John A. Wilson Distinguished Service Professor Emeritus of Assyriology,
e-reiner@uchicago.edu, 702-9550

William M. Sumner, Professor Emeritus, Archaeology,
sumner.1@osu.edu

Edward F. Wente, Professor Emeritus of Egyptology,
e-wente@uchicago.edu, 702-9539

FACULTY

Robert D. Biggs, Professor of Assyriology & Editor of Journal of Near Eastern Studies,
r-biggs@uchicago.edu, 702-9540

Fred M. Donner, Professor of Islamic History,
f-donner@uchicago.edu, 702-9544

Peter F. Dorman, Associate Professor of Egyptology & Chairman of the Department of Near Eastern Languages and Civilizations,
p-dorman@uchicago.edu, 702-9533

Walter T. Farber, Professor of Assyriology,
w-farber@uchicago.edu, 702-9546

McGuire Gibson, Professor of Mesopotamian Archaeology,
m-gibson@uchicago.edu, 702-9525

Norman Golb, Ludwig Rosenberger Professor in Jewish History and Civilization,
n-golb@uchicago.edu, 702-9526

Gene B. Gragg, Professor of Near Eastern Languages,
g-gragg@uchicago.edu, 702-9511

FACULTY (*cont.*)

Stephen P. Harvey, Assistant Professor of Egyptian Archaeology (from 1/1/03),
spharvey@uchicago.edu, 834-9761

Janet H. Johnson, Professor of Egyptology & Editor of Chicago Demotic Dictionary Project,
j-johnson@uchicago.edu, 702-9530

Walter E. Kaegi, Professor of Byzantine-Islamic Studies,
kwal@midway.uchicago.edu, 702-8346, 702-8397

Dennis G. Pardee, Professor of Northwest Semitic Philology,
d-pardee@uchicago.edu, 702-9541

Robert K. Ritner, Associate Professor of Egyptology,
r-ritner@uchicago.edu, 702-9547

Martha T. Roth, Professor of Assyriology & Editor-in-Charge of Chicago Assyrian Dictionary Project,
m-roth@uchicago.edu, 702-9551

David Schloen, Assistant Professor of Syro-Palestinian Archaeology,
d-schloen@uchicago.edu, 702-1382

Gil J. Stein, Professor of Near Eastern Languages and Civilizations & Director of the Oriental Institute,
gstein@uchicago.edu, 702-4098

Matthew W. Stolper, John A. Wilson Professor of Assyriology,
m-stolper@uchicago.edu, 702-9553

Theo van den Hout, Professor of Hittitology & Editor of Chicago Hittite Dictionary Project,
tvdhout@uchicago.edu, 834-4688, 702-9527

Christopher Woods, Assistant Professor of Sumerology,
woods@uchicago.edu, 834-8560

K. Aslıhan Yener, Associate Professor of Archaeology,
a-yener@uchicago.edu, 702-0568

RESEARCH ASSOCIATES

Abbas Alizadeh, Senior Research Associate, Chogha Mish Project,
a-alizadeh@uchicago.edu, 702-9531

Richard H. Beal, Senior Research Associate, Chicago Hittite Dictionary Project,
r-beal@uchicago.edu, 702-3644

Linda Braidwood†, Research Associate (Prehistoric Project)

Timothy J. Collins, Research Associate, Chicago Assyrian Dictionary Project (until 8/31/02)

Stuart Creason, Research Associate, Syriac Archives Project,
s-creason@uchicago.edu, 834-8348

Gertrud Farber, Research Associate, Sumerian Lexicon Project,
g-farber@uchicago.edu, 702-9548

RESEARCH ASSOCIATES (*cont.*)

Thomas A. Holland, Research Associate, Tell es-Sweyhat Project & Managing Editor, Publications Office,
  t-holland@uchicago.edu, 702-1240

W. Raymond Johnson, Research Associate (Associate Professor) & Field Director, Epigraphic Survey,
  wr-johnson@uchicago.edu, 834-4355

Charles E. Jones, Research Associate & Research Archivist and Bibliographer
  ce-jones@uchicago.edu, 702-9537

Fumi Karahashi, Visiting Instructor, Sumerian (until 9/23/02)

Mark Lehner, Research Associate, Giza Plateau Mapping Project,
  MarkLehner@aol.com

Carol Meyer, Research Associate, Bir Umm Fawakhir Project,
  c-meyer@uchicago.edu

Alice Mouton, Research Associate, Chicago Hittite Dictionary Project (as of 1/1/03),
  alicemouton@hotmail.com, 702-9527

Jennie Myers, Research Associate, Chicago Assyrian Dictionary Project,
  jmyers1@uchicago.edu, 834-9887

Clemens Reichel, Research Associate, Diyala Project,
  cdreiche@midway.uchicago.edu, 702-1352

John Sanders, Senior Research Associate & Head, Computer Laboratory,
  jc-sanders@uchicago.edu, 702-0989

Oğuz Soysal, Senior Research Associate, Chicago Hittite Dictionary Project,
  o-soysal@uchicago.edu, 702-3644

Emily Teeter, Research Associate & Curator, Egyptian and Nubian Antiquities,
  e-teeter@uchicago.edu, 702-1062

Joan Westenholz, Visiting Scholar, Chicago Assyrian Dictionary Project
  702-9543

Donald Whitcomb, Research Associate (Associate Professor), Islamic and Medieval Archaeology,
  d-whitcomb@uchicago.edu, 702-9530

Magnus Widell, Research Associate, Modeling Ancient Settlements System Project,
  widell@uchicago.edu, 702-1407

Tony J. Wilkinson, Research Associate (Associate Professor), Regional and Environmental Archaeology,
  t-wilkinson@uchicago.edu, 702-9552

Karen L. Wilson, Research Associate & Museum Director,
  k-wilson@uchicago.edu, 702-9520

STAFF

Eleanor Barbanes, Project Manager and Assistant Curator for Reinstallation, Museum (until 9/26/02)

Denise Browning, Manager, Suq, d-browning1@uchicago.edu, 702-9509

Steven Camp, Associate Director, Finance and Administration (from 6/14/03), shcamp@uchicago.edu, 702-1404

Tim Cashion, Director of Development (until 10/4/02)

Laura D'Alessandro, Head, Conservation Laboratory, Museum, l-dalessandro@uchicago.edu, 702-9519

Margaret DeJong, Artist, Epigraphic Survey, 702-9524

Evelien Dewulf, Administrative Assistant for Reinstallation (from 2/19/03), dewulf@babylon-orinst.uchicago.edu, 834-8950

Simrit Dhesi, Financial Manager (until 1/19/03)

Christina DiCerbo, Artist, Epigraphic Survey, 702-9524

Markus Dohner, Museum Installation Coordinator, mdohner@uchicago.edu, 702-9516

Debora Donato, Director of Development (from 1/6/03), ddonato@uchicago.edu, 834-9775

Catherine Dueñas, Volunteer Services Coordinator, cduenas@babylon-orinst.uchicago.edu, 702-1845

Wendy Ennes, Teacher Services and Family Projects Coordinator, Museum Education, wennes@uchicago.edu, 834-7606

Terry Friedman, Volunteer Services Coordinator, et-friedman@uchicago.edu, 702-1845

Jean Grant, Photographer, Museum, jm-grant@uchicago.edu, 702-9517

Lamia Hadidy, Conservator, Epigraphic Survey (from 11/1/02 until 3/03), 702-9524

Lotfi Hassan, Conservator, Epigraphic Survey, 702-9524

Harold Hays, Epigrapher, Epigraphic Survey, h-hays@uchicago.edu, 702-9524

Thomas A. Holland, Managing Editor, Publications Office & Research Associate, t-holland@uchicago.edu, 702-1240

STAFF (*cont.*)

Carla Hosein, Financial Manager,
cchosein@uchicago.edu, 834-9886

Helen Jacquet, Egyptologist Consultant, Epigraphic Survey,
702-9524

Jean Jacquet, Architect Consultant, Epigraphic Survey,
702-9524

Charles E. Jones, Research Archivist and Bibliographer & Research Associate,
ce-jones@uchicago.edu, 702-9537

Hiroko Kariya, Conservator, Epigraphic Survey,
702-9524

Jen Kimpton, Librarian and Epigrapher, Epigraphic Survey (from 12/6/02),
702-9524

Yarko Kobylecky, Photographer, Epigraphic Survey,
702-9524

Maria Krasinski, Education Programs Assistant, Museum Education and Public Programming,
mck@babylon-orinst.uchicago.edu, 702-9507

Carole Krucoff, Head, Public and Museum Education,
c-krucoff@uchicago.edu, 702-1845

Rebecca Laharia, Membership Director (from 1/2/03),
rlaharia@uchicago.edu, 702-9513

John Larson, Museum Archivist,
ja-larson@uchicago.edu, 702-9924

Susan Lezon, Photo Archivist and Photographer, Epigraphic Survey,
702-9524

Erik Lindahl, Gallery Preparator, Museum,
lindahl@uchicago.edu, 702-9516

Jill Carlotta Maher, Assistant to the Director of the Epigraphic Survey,
702-9524

J. Brett McClain, Epigrapher, Epigraphic Survey,
jbmcclai@uchicago.edu, 702-9524

Linda McLarnan, Manuscript Editor, Chicago Assyrian Dictionary Project,
l-mclarnan@uchicago.edu, 702-9543

Kathy Mineck, Research Project Professional, Chicago Hittite Dictionary Project,
kmineck@uchicago.edu, 702-9527

Vanessa Muros, Assistant Conservator, Conservation Laboratory, Museum,
muros@babylon-orinst.uchicago.edu, 702-9519

STAFF (*cont.*)

Marlin Nassim, Accountant, Epigraphic Survey,
    702-9524

Emily Napolitano, Assistant to the Director, Epigraphic Survey,
    e-napolitano@uchicago.edu, 702-9524

Susan Osgood, Artist, Epigraphic Survey,
    702-9524

Safinaz Ouri, Financial Manager, Epigraphic Survey,
    702-9524

Florence Ovadia, Suq Assistant,
    702-9510

Vicki Parry, Contract Conservator, Conservation Laboratory (until 9/22/02)

Conor Power, Structural Engineer, Epigraphic Survey,
    702-9524

Henri Riad, Egyptian Egyptologist Consultant, Epigraphic Survey,
    702-9524

James Riley, Engineer and Conservation Assistant, Epigraphic Survey,
    702-9524

Dany Roy, Stonecutter, Epigraphic Survey,
    702-9524

John Sanders, Head, Computer Laboratory & Senior Research Associate,
    jc-sanders@uchicago.edu, 702-0989

William Schenck, Artist, Epigraphic Survey (until 5/15/03)

Margaret Schröeder, Security Supervisor, Museum,
    m-schroeder@uchicago.edu, 702-9522

Joe Scott, Preparator, Museum (until 4/27/03)

Edythe Seltzer, Typist, Chicago Assyrian Dictionary Project,
    702-9543

Randy Shonkwiler, Epigrapher, Epigraphic Survey,
    702-9524

Elinor Smith, Photo Archives Assistant, Epigraphic Survey,
    702-9524

William Stafford, Mount Maker, Museum,
    702-9516

John Stewart, Conservator, Epigraphic Survey,
    702-9524

Emily Teeter, Curator, Egyptian and Nubian Antiquities & Research Associate,
    e-teeter@uchicago.edu, 702-1062

STAFF (*cont.*)

Raymond Tindel, Registrar and Senior Curator, Museum,
    r-tindel@uchicago.edu, 702-9518

Nicole I. Torres, Assistant to the Director,
    nitorres@midway.uchicago.edu, 834-8098

Thomas Urban, Senior Editor, Publications,
    t-urban@uchicago.edu, 702-5967

Paula von Bechtolsheim, Managing Editor, Journal of Near Eastern Studies,
    702-9592

Elliott Weiss, Assistant Preparator, Museum (until 12/2/02)

Karen L. Wilson, Museum Director & Research Associate,
    k-wilson@uchicago.edu, 702-9520

Alison Whyte, Assistant Conservator, Conservation Laboratory, Museum,
    aawhyte@uchicago.edu, 702-9519

† Denotes Deceased

———————————

INFORMATION

The Oriental Institute
1155 East 58th Street
Chicago, Illinois 60637

Museum gallery hours:
Tuesday through Saturday 10:00 am–4:00 pm
Wednesday 10:00 am–8:30 pm
Sunday 12:00 noon–4:00 pm

Telephone Numbers (Area Code 773) and Electronic Addresses

Administrative Office, oi-admin@uchicago.edu, 702-9514
Archaeology Laboratory, 702-1407
Associate Director's Office for Finance and Administration, 702-1404
Assyrian Dictionary Project, 702-9543
Computer Laboratory, 702-9538
Conservation Laboratory, 702-9519
Department of Near Eastern Languages and Civilizations, 702-9512
Demotic Dictionary Project, 702-9528
Development Office, 834-9775
Director's Office, 834-8098
Epigraphic Survey, 702-9524
Facsimile, 702-9853
Hittite Dictionary Project, 702-9527
Journal of Near Eastern Studies, 702-9592
Membership Office, oi-membership@uchicago.edu, 702-9513
Museum Archives, 702-9520
Museum Education and Public Programs, adult-ed@orinst.uchicago.edu, 702-9507
Museum Information, 702-9520
Museum Office, oi-museum@uchicago.edu, 702-9520
Museum Registration, 702-9518
Publications Editorial Office, 702-1240
Research Archives, oi-library@uchicago.edu, 702-9537
Security, 702-9522
Suq Gift and Book Shop, 702-9510
Suq Office, 702-9509
Volunteer Guides, 702-1845

World Wide Web Address

http://www-oi.uchicago.edu
